MANTRA
TANTRA
YANTRA

Ways of Worshipping; Inner Growth;
Attainment of Celestial Power

Prof. Shrikant Prasoon

HINDOOLOGY
BOOKS

Published by

HINDOOLOGY
BOOKS

An imprint of

Pustak Mahal®

Administrative office and sale centre
J-3/16 , Daryaganj, New Delhi-110002
☎ 23276539, 23272783, 23272784 • *Fax:* 011-23260518
E-mail: info@pustakmahal.com • *Website:* www.pustakmahal.com

Branches
Bengaluru: ☎ 080-22234025 • *Telefax:* 080-22240209
E-mail: pustak@airtelmail.in • pustak@sancharnet.in
Mumbai: ☎ 022-22010941 • 022-22053387
E-mail: rapidex@bom5.vsnl.net.in
Patna: ☎ 0612-3294193 • *Telefax:* 0612-2302719
E-mail: rapidexptn@rediffmail.com

© **Hindoology Books**
ISBN 978-81-223-1455-7

Edition 2013

Printed at : AR Emm International, Delhi

Dedication

Mantra, Tantra and Yantra

is dedicated to

all the worshippers of

Shiva-Shakti; Shiva or Shakti; Shiva and Shakti

And to

my neighbour

Shri Rama Nath Gupta;

And to two known practitioners

Shri Vidya Kant Dubey

and

Pandey Ashok Kumar Rakesh

–Prof. Prasoon

Contents

Preface

When I felt that my sojourn in Delhi was over and was returning home, Shri Rama Avatar Gupta, the Chairman of M/s. Pustak Mahal, gave me his solemn assurance that he would remain in contact and keep on giving assignments for writing books. Before I was able to complete the previous assignments, I got his call and he assigned me another work of my choice: a book on **Mantra, Tantra** and **Yantra**. I have been working on these devotional ways and related things for decades. I collected my notes and diaries and the resultant work is before you: *Mantra, Tantra and Yantra.*

Shivā is the integral power of Brahma and Shiva is the manifest form of Brahma. Both Shiva and Shivā are one and inseparable. There is no distinction between them other than the fact that one is the male and the other is female. To worship one is to worship the other. Most people worship both but some worship Shiva and others Shivā. The worship of both is the same. This is the theory behind creation. Power is inherent in the object and the object contains power. Throughout the cosmos, whatever is male in nature is Shiva and whatever is female, is Bhagawati Umā. The praise of one is the praise of the other.

This book, *Mantra, Tantra and Yantra,* presents these three different ways of worshipping and the philosophy and psychology behind the worshipping of the manifest form of Shiva and Shivā. Shiva and Shivā pervade all and are projected through each living and non-living entity. *The whole Brahmānd contains sounds like Mantras and functions as Tantra or Yantra.* In other words, the total universe is based on Mantra, Tantra and Yantra; and inseparable from them. It is beauty behind worshipping; the aesthetic sense; scientific function and general and spiritual philosophy behind them. As we are unable to grasp the mystery behind the creation, in the same way we are unable to understand these three ways:

Mantra; Tantra and Yantra. That may be our weakness but these three represent the value and power of Sound; System and Machines. *Our body, like the universe and other bodies has divine sound akin to life; it is itself a mysterious machine and works on a designed system.* All the different systems of the body are one system; as all the systems of the cosmos are one system.

Separate worshipping or combined worshipping, whatever the case may be, they are worshipped in all the three ways: Mantra; Tantra and Yantra; and all the three ways are actually one thing; oneway, and inseparable. The worshipping through the three ways mentioned above are to show one's respect and gratitude to the Creator; for inner growth; for acquisition of immense power; for Union with the Soul, Self or Revelation of Truth; for celestial pleasure and finally, for Moksha, Salvation.

The book **Mantra, Tantra, Yantra** is complete and gives comprehensive details of both the theoretical and practical aspects, and will provide insight into each aspect of these three differently named but similar or one worshipping. It will definitely prove helpful to general readers; researchers; learned devotees; practitioners, Pandits; Sādhakas; Sādhus; Yagis and Tāntriks; and for that young generation who knows nothing about them and has no inkling of the enormous power they generate and give. It is a handbook for revelation and inner growth for all.

Only ā has been taken from Scriptural Transliteration for long 'a' sound, which is otherwise impossible to write in the Roman script. Rest is as written in government papers, magazines, newspapers and general books. It will help readers to read the Mantrās and Shlokas quoted in it and also the names of numerous persons and books.

Sarve Shubhe!

Prof. Shrikant Prasoon
Solomon Complex, Motihari 845 401
Email: shrikantprasoon@yahoo.co.in
Web: www. shrikantprasoon.com
Mobile: 09430994377

Obeisance and Prayers

Sahasra-chandra-pratimo-dayāluh-lakshmi-mukha-
avalokan-lola-netrah;
Dasha-avatāraih paritah pareeto nri-kesari mangalam-tanotu.

Glowing like numerous groups of moon and is kind; who possesses impatient eyes for intently looking at the face of Lakshmi; and who is surrounded by ten incarnations; that Bhagwān Nrisingh may shower blessings on us.

Sarve varnātmakā mantrāste cha shaktyāt-ātmakāh priye;
Shaktih-tu mātrikā gyeyā sā cha gyeyā shivātmikā.

She is the mātrik varnas of the Mnatras and dear and closer and replica of Shakti. She is known as Mātrikā Shakti. She is Shiva-Shakti, the inseparable loving part of Shiva.

Yāma viditvā akhilam vandham nirmathyā khilavatramanā;
Yogi yāti param sthānam sā mām pātu Saraswati.

When one comes to know Bhagawati Saraswati then a Yogi breaks all the fetters and gets absolute command. That Bhagawati may save me!

Sarva mangala mangalye shive sarvārtha sādhike,
Sharanye trayambake gauri nārāyani namostute.

O Nārāyani! You are auspicious and keep everything auspicious! You are Shivā that fulfills every wish! You are Gauri with three eyes and take care of those that seek shelter! I salute Thee!

Yā Devi sarva bhooteshu Shaktirupena sansthitā
Namastasyai namastasyai namastasyai namo namah.

(O Goddess! That pervades all as energy! I salute Thee thrice.)

Kāla rātri brahma stutām vaishanawim skandamātaram,
Saraswatim aditim daksha duhitaram namāmah pāwanām shivām.

We salute the Shiva Shakti, Vaishanavi Shakti and Brahma Shakti, Mother of Gods Aditi and Sati, the daughter of Daksha that control the Time.

Pustaka-abhikarām vāme dakshe-aksha-var-dhārinim;
Shuklām trinnayanām ādyām bālām shri tripurām shraye.

One who has a book in the left hand and the right hand is raised to shower endless blessings; is the youthful Shri Tripurā Devi who is white in colour and has three eyes.

Tāntrik Prayer

Namāmi tvām mahādevim mahābhaya vināshinim;
Mahā-durga prashaneem mahā-kārunya-rupinim.

I salute and pray to Mahādevi who destroys all deadly fears; who pacifies dangers of extreme types and who is the idol of immense compassion.

Namostute: Salutations to Kāla Rātri

Ādhārbhute chādheye dhritirupe dhurandhare,
Dhruve dhruvapade dheere jagadhātri namostute. (1)

आधारभूते चाधेये धृतिरूपे धुरन्धरे ।
ध्रुवं ध्रुवपदे धीरे जगद्धात्रि नमोऽस्तु ते ॥1॥

Shavākāre shaktirupe shaktisye shaktivigrahe,
Shāktya-āchār-priye devi jagadhātri namostute. (2)

शवाकारे शक्तिरूपे शक्तिस्ये शक्तिविग्रहे ।
शाक्त्य-आचार-प्रिये देवि जगद्धात्रि नमोऽस्तु ते॥2॥

Jayade jagadānande jagadeka prapujite,
Jai sarva gate durge jagadhātri namostute. (3)

जय-दे जगत्-आनन्दे जगत्-एक प्रपूजिते ।
जय-सर्वगते दुर्गे जगद्धात्रि नमोऽस्तु ते॥3॥

Paramānu swarupe cha dvainuka ādiswarupini,
Sthula ati sukshma rupena jagadhātri namostute. (4)

परमाणु स्वरूपे च द्वयणुक आदि स्वरूपिणि ।
स्थूल अति सूक्ष्म रूपेण जगद्धात्रि नमोऽस्तु ते॥4॥

Sukshma-ati-sukshma-rupe cha prāna-apāna-ādirupini,
Bhāva abhāva swarupe cha jagadhātri namostute. (5)

सूक्ष्म-अति-सूक्ष्म-रूपे च प्राण-अपान-आदि-रूपिणि।
भाव अभाव स्वरूपे च जगद्धात्रि नमोऽस्तु ते॥5॥

Kālādi rupe kāleshe kāla akāla vibhedini,
Sarva swarupe sarvagye jagadhātri namostute. (6)

कालादि रूपे कालेशे कालाकाल विभेदिणि।
सर्व स्वरूपे सर्वज्ञे जगद्धात्रि नमोऽस्तु ते॥6॥

Mahā vighne mahā utsāhe mahāmāye baraprade,
Prapanch asāre sādhwishe jagadhātri namostute. (7)

महा-विघ्ने महोत्साहे महामाये वर प्रदे।
प्रपंच असारे साध्वीशे जगद्धात्रि नमोऽस्तु ते॥7॥

Agamye jagatām ādye māheshwari varāngane,
Ashesha rupa rupasye jagadhātri namostute. (8)

अगम्ये जगतां आद्ये माहेश्वरि वरांगने।
अशेश रूप रूपस्ये जगद्धात्रि नमोऽस्तु ते॥8॥

Dwi saptakoti mantrānām shakti rupe sanātani,
Sarva shakti swarupe cha jagadhātri namostute. (9)

द्वि सप्त कोटि मंत्राणां शक्तिरूपे सनातनि।
सर्वशक्ति स्वरूपे च जगद्धात्रि नमोऽस्तु ते॥9॥

Teerthayagya tapodān yoga sāre jagan mayi,
Twameva sarva sarvasye jagadhātri namostute. (10)

तीर्थ-यज्ञ तपो-दान योग सारे जगन्मयि।
त्वमेव सर्व सर्वस्ये जगद्धात्रि नमोऽस्तु ते॥10॥

Dayā rupe dayā drishte dayādre dukh mochani
Sarva apattārike durge jagadhātri namostute. (11)

दया-रूपे दया-दृष्टे दयाद्रे दुःख-मोचनि।
सर्व-अपत्तारिके दुर्गे जगद्धात्रि नमोऽस्तु ते॥11॥

Agamya-dhām adhāmasye mahā yoshish-hritpure,
Ameya-bhāva-kutasye jagadhātri namostute. (12)

अगम्य-धाम अधामस्ये महा-योगीश-हृत्पुरे।
अमेय-भाव-कूटस्ये जगद्धात्रि नमोऽस्तु ते॥12॥

Yah pathet strotametattu poojānte sādhaka uttamah,
Sarva pāpād vinirmuktah poojā phalam awāmuyāt. (13)

यः पठेत् स्तोत्रं एतत्तु पूजान्ते साधक उत्तमः।
सर्व पापाद् विनिर्मुक्तः पूजा फलं अवामुयात्॥13॥

Tantrokta Devisuktam (तन्त्रोक्त देवीसुक्तम्)

Namo devyai mahādevyai shivāyai satatam namah.
Namah prakrityai bhadrāyai niyatāh pranatāh sma tām. (1)

नमो देव्यै महादेव्यै शिवायै सततं नमः।
नमः प्रकृत्यै भद्रायै नियताः प्रणताः स्म ताम्॥1॥

Rodrāyai namo nityāyai gouryai dhātrayai namo namah,
Jyotsanāyai chendu-rupinyai sukhāyai satatam namah. (2)

रौद्रायै नमो नित्यायै गौर्यै धात्र्यै नमो नमः।
ज्योत्स्नायै च इन्दु-रूपिण्यै सुखायै सततं नमः॥2॥

Kalyānyai pranatām vriddhyai siddhyai kurmo namo namah,
Nairityai bhubhritām lakshmyai shavārnyai te namo namah. (3)

कल्याण्यै प्रणतां वृद्ध्यै सिद्ध्यै कुर्मो नमो नमः।
नैर्ऋत्यै भूभृतां लक्ष्म्यै शार्वाण्यै ते नमो नमः॥3॥

Durgāyai durga-pārāyai sārāyai sarva kārinyai,
Khyātyai tathaiva krishnāyai dhoomrāyai satatam namah. (4)

दुर्गायै दुर्ग-पारायै सारायै सर्व-कारिण्यै।
ख्यात्यै तथैव कृष्णायै धूम्रायै सततं नमः॥4॥

Ati-soumya-ati-roudryai natāstasyai namo namah,
Namo jagat-pratishthāyai devyai krityai namo namah. (5)

अति-सौम्य-अति-रौद्रायै नतास्तस्यै नमो नमः।
नमो जगत्-प्रतिष्ठायै देव्यै कृत्यै नमो नमः॥5॥

Yā devi sarvabhuteshu vishnum āyeti shabditā,
Namastasyai Namastasyai Namastasyai Namo Namah. (6)

या देवी सर्व-भूतेषु विष्णुं आयेति शब्दिता।
नमस्तस्यै नमस्तस्यै नमस्तस्यै नमो नमः ॥6॥

Yā devi sarvabhuteshu chetanetya abhidhiyate,
Namastasyai Namastasyai Namastasyai Namo Namah. (7)

या देवी सर्वभूतेषु चेतनेत्य-अभिधीयत।
नमस्तस्यै नमस्तस्यै नमस्तस्यै नमो नमः ॥7॥

Yā devi sarvabhuteshu buddhi-rupena samsthitā,
Namastasyai Namastasyai Namastasyai Namo Namah. (8)

या देवी सर्वभूतेषु बुद्धि-रूपेण संस्थिता।
नमस्तस्यै नमस्तस्यै नमस्तस्यै नमो नमः ॥8॥

Yā devi sarvabhuteshu nidrā-rupena samsthitā,
Namastasyai Namastasyai Namastasyai Namo Namah. (9)

या देवी सर्वभूतेषु निद्रा रूपेण संस्थिता।
नमस्तस्यै नमस्तस्यै नमस्तस्यै नमो नमः ॥9॥

Yā devi sarvabhuteshu kshuddhā rupena samsthitā,
Namastasyai Namastasyai Namastasyai Namo Namah. (10)

या देवी सर्वभूतेषु क्षुधा-रूपेण संस्थिता।
नमस्तस्यै नमस्तस्यै नमस्तस्यै नमो नमः ॥10॥

Yā devi sarvabhuteshu chhāyā rupena samsthitā,
Namastasyai Namastasyai Namastasyai Namo Namah. (11)

या देवी सर्वभूतेषु छाया-रूपेण संस्थिता।
नमस्तस्यै नमस्तस्यै नमस्तस्यै नमो नमः ॥11॥

Yā devi sarvabhuteshu shakti rupena samsthitā,
Namastasyai Namastasyai Namastasyai Namo Namah. (12)

या देवी सर्वभूतेषु शक्ति-रूपेण संस्थिता।
नमस्तस्यै नमस्तस्यै नमस्तस्यै नमो नमः ॥12॥

Yā devi sarvabhuteshu trishnā-rupena samsthitā,
Namastasyai Namastasyai Namastasyai Namo Namah. (13)

या देवी सर्वभूतेषु तृष्णा-रूपेण संस्थिता।
नमस्तस्यै नमस्तस्यै नमस्तस्यै नमो नम: ॥13॥

Yā devi sarvabhuteshu kshānti-rupena samsthitā,
Namastasyai Namastasyai Namastasyai Namo Namah. (14)

या देवी सर्वभूतेषु क्षान्ति-रूपेण संस्थिता।
नमस्तस्यै नमस्तस्यै नमस्तस्यै नमो नम: ॥14॥

Yā devi sarvabhuteshu jāti-rupena samsthitā,
Namastasyai Namastasyai Namastasyai Namo Namah. (15)

या देवी सर्वभूतेषु जाति-रूपेण संस्थिता।
नमस्तस्यै नमस्तस्यै नमस्तस्यै नमो नम: ॥15॥

Yā devi sarvabhuteshu lajjā-rupena samsthitā,
Namastasyai Namastasyai Namastasyai Namo Namah. (16)

या देवी सर्वभूतेषु लज्जा-रूपेण संस्थिता।
नमस्तस्यै नमस्तस्यै नमस्तस्यै नमो नम: ॥16॥

Yā devi sarvabhuteshu shānti-rupena samsthitā,
Namastasyai Namastasyai Namastasyai Namo Namah. (17)

या देवी सर्वभूतेषु शान्ति-रूपेण संस्थिता।
नमस्तस्यै नमस्तस्यै नमस्तस्यै नमो नम: ॥17॥

Yā devi sarvabhuteshu shraddhā-rupena samsthitā,
Namastasyai Namastasyai Namastasyai Namo Namah. (18)

या देवी सर्वभूतेषु श्रद्धा-रूपेण संस्थिता।
नमस्तस्यै नमस्तस्यै नमस्तस्यै नमो नम: ॥18॥

Yā devi sarvabhuteshu kānti-rupena samsthitā,
Namastasyai Namastasyai Namastasyai Namo Namah. (19)

या देवी सर्वभूतेषु कांति-रूपेण संस्थिता।
नमस्तस्यै नमस्तस्यै नमस्तस्यै नमो नम: ॥19॥

Yā devi sarvabhuteshu lakshmi-rupena samsthitā,
Namastasyai Namastasyai Namastasyai Namo Namah. (20)

या देवी सर्वभूतेषु लक्ष्मी-रूपेण संस्थिता।
नमस्तस्यै नमस्तस्यै नमस्तस्यै नमो नमः ॥20॥

Yā devi sarvabhuteshu vritti-rupena samsthitā,
Namastasyai Namastasyai Namastasyai Namo Namah. (21)

या देवी सर्वभूतेषु वृत्ति-रूपेण संस्थिता।
नमस्तस्यै नमस्तस्यै नमस्तस्यै नमो नमः ॥21॥

Yā devi sarvabhuteshu smriti-rupena samsthitā,
Namastasyai Namastasyai Namastasyai Namo Namah. (22)

या देवी सर्वभूतेषु स्मृति-रूपेण संस्थिता।
नमस्तस्यै नमस्तस्यै नमस्तस्यै नमो नमः ॥22॥

Yā devi sarvabhuteshu dayā-rupena samsthitā,
Namastasyai Namastasyai Namastasyai Namo Namah. (23)

या देवी सर्वभूतेषु दया-रूपेण संस्थिता।
नमस्तस्यै नमस्तस्यै नमस्तस्यै नमो नमः ॥23॥

Yā devi sarvabhuteshu tushti-rupena samsthitā,
Namastasyai Namastasyai Namastasyai Namo Namah. (24)

या देवी सर्वभूतेषु तुष्टि-रूपेण संस्थिता।
नमस्तस्यै नमस्तस्यै नमस्तस्यै नमो नमः ॥24॥

Yā devi sarvabhuteshu mātri-rupena samsthitā,
Namastasyai Namastasyai Namastasyai Namo Namah. (25)

या देवी सर्वभूतेषु मातृ-रूपेण संस्थिता।
नमस्तस्यै नमस्तस्यै नमस्तस्यै नमो नमः ॥25॥

Yā devi sarvabhuteshu bhrānti-rupena samsthitā,
Namastasyai Namastasyai Namastasyai Namo Namah. (26)

या देवी सर्वभूतेषु भ्रान्ति-रूपेण संस्थिता।
नमस्तस्यै नमस्तस्यै नमस्तस्यै नमो नमः ॥26॥

Indriyānām adhishthātri bhutānām cha akhileshu yā,
Bhuteshu satatam tasyai vyāpti devyai namo namah. (27)

इन्द्रियाणां-अधिष्ठात्री भूतानां च अखिलेशु या।
भूतेषु-सततं तस्यै व्याप्ति देव्यै नमो नमः ॥27॥

Chiti rupena yā kritsnam-yetad vyāpya sthitā jagat,
Namastasyai Namastasyai Namastasyai Namo Namah. (28)

चिति रूपेण या कृत्स्नमेतद् व्याप्य स्थिता जगत्।
नमस्तस्यै नमस्तस्यै नमस्तस्यै नमो नमः ॥28॥

The above given **'Devi Suktam'** forms the major part of the 5th Chapter of 'Durgā Saptashati'. Obviously, many epithets have been used for 'Devi Mā' and the salutations **'namo namah'** and **'namastasyai'** have been repeated for more than hundred times, i.e. both the salutations have been profusely used to lay stress on the emotional outburst of the hymn, praise and the feelings associated with the instant relief that the Devatās and the devotees got (for that matter, they still get). Moreover, it also expresses the exuberant emotions of the seeker that discovers true 'self', identity with the sought and success in realizing the Supreme Entity. During that rare excitement the sense of surrender, prostration and salutation rule the mind and hence, the repetitions. (The same thing is true to the repetition of *'rupam dehi jayam dehi yasho dehi dvisho jahi'*, where the seeker eagerly and repeatedly asks to shower the boons.)

By repeating the same salutation the seeker gets an opportunity to see, feel, absorb and imbibe the present better and needs not to concentrate hard on 'ideas and words'. The present is overwhelmingly meaningful (and eventful too) that other poetical and extraneous matters lose significance. The repetition of names and adjectives is an outcome of the knowledge that all the forms of the Goddess are one and and there is no difference in their manifest and unmanifest forms. Different looking incidents have also merged into one and the fact is established inside the seeker that all of them are the deeds of the same Supreme Power. He is relieved from the selfish burden of 'I' and 'mine'; his mind has expanded to such an extent that he perceives all the forms to be one. He has perceived the Mahā Māyā's illusive play, Her empirical and transcendental aspects and 'the worlds of plurality' that she creates and pervades. That is one important reason that the devotee salutes Her again and again. He thrice repeats 'namastasyai' before finally uttering the closing salutation 'namo namah'; and it occurs in every alternate line with increasing emphasis. Every time it seems to touch the climax, and each next utterance gives the same feeling. 'Chaturthi singular vibhakti' heightens the effect. It is chanted with longer breaths. Often the seeker gets little time to breath in. It is a real outburst of extreme nature expressed with a torrent-like vehemence. The names: Prakriti, Bhadrā, Jagadambā, Roudrā, Nityā, Gauri, Dhātri, Jyotsanā, Chandrarupini, Sukha Swarupā, Vriddhi, Siddhi, Lakshmi, Sharvāni Durgā, Khyāti and many more get so easily mixed that the difference is never felt or the person chanting it never gets an opportunity to think about the names. It is the surrender and salutation that matters.

In its under current flow, it establishes another fact that it is almost impossible to describe Her manifested forms. The names are enough. The details are totally missing. It is enough to know that She is the 'extreme happiness', who removes the sorrows, as She is both 'Pranatārati' and 'Sharvāni'. As 'Kalyāni' she cures from diseases, ensures prosperity and liberates in its true sense. She is everything, does everything and gives everything: both mundane and transcendental.

'Devi Suktam' a hymn of rare beauty that invokes the Mother Supreme is known as 'Aparājita Stotram', the hymn to the unvanquished and the hymn that endows the worshipper with indefatigable powers.

Mantras in Spiritual Quadruplets

Aum 1.

Mantras are coded sound meant for divine spirit;
Unbelievable and unexpected power they exhibit;
Mantras move with the speed of sound in space:
In and away from gravitational forces with grit.

Aum 2.

Mantra is the inner message to be communicated;
To the supernatural forces which are to it related;
When heard and accepted by the deity/ spirit divine:
Are reciprocated fast with actions result-oriented.

Aum 3.

Mantras are powerful means of worshipping and devotion;
Silently prayed inside deeply or made pompous exhibition;
Mantras can be used in different ways for different gains:
For construction, demolition, restoration or total annihilation.

Aum 4.

As symbolic sound for deities based on Varna formation;
They're common in Tantra procedure and Yantra ovation;
The prayers that fulfill desires; give success to one and all:
For they are chanted thousands of times with resolution.

Aum 5.

There are infinite number of Mantras for every occasion;
Classified and sanctified for resurrection and divine vision;
Deities can be approached through righteous deeds, means:
Select for own Ishta Devatā from suitable group or division

SECTION I

Ways for Inner Growth and Power

- ➢ Mantra, Tantra and Yantra for Brahma
- ➢ Mantra and Yantra in Tantra
- ➢ Mantra on Yantra

Mantra, Tantra and Yantra for Brahma

The pious sound that gives meditative power, control and concentration, and saves is called Mantra: *Mananāt trāyat iti Mantrah*. It is the Dharma, religion or duty of Mantra to save those who think deeply and recite Mantras with concentration: *Manan trāna dharmāno mantrāh*.

The name and form given to or possessed by a being binds them to worldly affairs. The beings are ignorant because of that form, name and natural resources and riches. They don't know that they have neither the body nor the life nor the riches or worldly things. It is the fallacy that they feel they are an individual and that the God has created everything for their use and utilization. It is because of their ignorance. While the fact is that they are a part of the creator who created everything and entered them: *tad srishtvā tadanu-prāvishat*. That Omnipresent; Omnipotent and Omniscient resides in our body not only for pleasure but also for protecting everything and everyone. We don't need arms and weapons for protection but faith and moral character. That is why He is in us: *manushya-deham āshritya chhanāste parmeshwarāh*.

We must know that we are not one but all: *ātmavat sarva bhuteshu*; others are like them and they are Brahma, the creator: *aham brahmāsmi*. They have not been created to endlessly exploit resources but to save them for all else; for pleasure as Brahma is the form of pleasure: *ānandam brahmano roopam*. Brahma was alone and he multiplied: *eko-aham bahu-syām*. We all must praise Him for what He has done; must pray to Him and must be satisfied with what He gives. They don't have to take anything by force or manipulate things for their benefit. This knowledge changes one into an abstract idea, *bhāva roop*a; one accepts subtle nature and acquire inner consciousness. The power that makes one realize it, is Mantra and the effort to realize it is called Mantra Yoga. It is based on sound which pervades the whole creation: *nādamaya sansriti*. This is the knowledge which one gets through penance, chanting of Mantra and sustaining on the bare minimum.

This subtle and divine knowledge is present only in India. The whole world opposes it because of excessive indulgence in luxury and luxurious life and physical pleasures. The organs, including the sense organs are not for excessive indulgence but for creation, for growing better, cultured and refined. One growing with Mantra, becomes refined, cultured, sublime, powerful and divine.

In India, only Brahma is worshipped in all its manifest and unmanifest forms. Because of Him and along with Him, the Eternal Energy as Brahma-rupini is also worshipped. Brahma is projected through Shiva and his other part Shivā. Whenever and whoever is worshipped, generally speaking only Shiva and Shivā are worshipped. Brahmā, Vishnu and their Brāhmni Shakti and Vaishnavi Shakti are the same.

Shiva holds the objective world. So, He is experienced as separate from the self but does not have a separate existence. The manifest world is the Shakti of Shiva: integral and inseparable as in Shiva so in all living beings, and also in the non-living beings. The ignorant conclude that the world is separate from his shakti and energy, claiming that his energy is the separate formal cause of the objective world. whereas, It is not.

The objective world comprised of numerous matters and objects, cognition and subjects, is nothing more than the expansion of the Shakti of Shiva. It is not separate from Shiva's energy. He holds Shakti and hence, is Shaktimān. He also holds the objective world that is the outer projection of His Shakti, the Eternal Mother.

Shivā is *Trigunātmikā*, has all the three traits: *Sāttavika*, pure and divine; *Rājasi*, royal and luxurious and *Tāmasika*, impure and demonic. Since She is all: **sarva swarupā sarveshā sarva ādhārā parātparā**; hence She is both auspicious and inauspicious; pain and pleasure; curse and beatitude, good and bad: **sarva mangal** and **amangalā**. She is prayed to and worshipped:

> *Sarva mangal-amangaleshu shive sarvārth sādhike;*
> *Sharaneye tryambakam gauri nārāyani namostute.*

Mantra, Tantra and Yantra are different ways of worshipping Brahma for what? For our own self; our own life; our own existence, survival and sustenance. The Mantras are the power and use of our knowledge and wisdom; the Tantra contains the procedures and systems that are there and that we follow or must follow, and the Yantras are the equipments and machines that we use for our benefit; and that nature uses in almost everything including our body and all the other bodies: living or non-living. The classification into living and non-living are our classifications, for Brahma; for the Creator; for Shiva and Shivā; all are their creations and a part of the complete Brahmānd. Karma-Kānd is different but it gives insight into them; we derive the meaning and learn different uses.

Sādhanā aur Prārthanā

Separate worshipping or combined worshipping, whatever the case may be, they are worshipped in all the three ways: Mantra; Tantra and Yantra.

Worshipping through the three ways mentioned are to show one's respect and gratitude to the creator and creatrix; for inner growth; for acquisition of immense power; for union with the soul or revelation of truth; for celestial pleasure and finally, for moksha, salvation.

It is claimed and believed that the Yantras were created from the devastating Tāndava Dance by Shiva. That Tāndava Dance is not the ordinary dance of a dancer; it is the eternal dance by the creator who is the sum total of the three qualities and states and pervades all. So, when He dances, each atom of everything starts moving and the danger of total destruction looms large over the creation, as the earth and other planets and celestial bodies start moving in a different way, breaking the cosmic order. It is that Tāndava dance which fixes all creation at its place or displaces or replaces them: one, some or all.

Three Ways of Worshiping

Linguistically, the three words *Mantram, Tantram* and *Yantram* are related to the ancient Indian tradition of worshipping, as well as phonologically. *Mantram* denotes the chant, or "knowledge". *Tantram* denotes philosophy, or ritual actions. *Yantram* denotes the means by which a human is expected to worship and work.

The whole of the body is Yantra; its different functions are Tantra and the sound or life element is Mantra.

Since, the Mantras are the life element, hence the Mantras are perfect. The process of absorbing them is Tantra, and Yantra helps in controlling the organs and their functions by controlling and concentrating the Mind. They give attainments separately and also through their combined effect. It is a wonder that each one is complete in itself and each one takes or gives something to the other two.

According to Tantra, "being-consciousness-bliss" or *Satchidānanda* has the power of both self-evolution and self-involution. *Prakriti* or "reality" evolves into a multiplicity of creatures and things, yet at the same time always remains pure consciousness, pure being and pure bliss. In this process of evolution, *Māyā*, illusion veils reality and separates it into opposites, such as conscious and unconscious, pleasant and unpleasant, and so forth. If not recognized as illusion, these opposing determining conditions bind, limit and fetter, *pāsha* the individual, *jiva*.

Generally speaking, the Hindu God and Goddess Shiva and Shakti are perceived as separate and distinct. However, in Tantra, even in the process of creation, Reality remains pure consciousness, pure being and pure bliss, and Tantra denies neither the act nor the fact of this process. In fact, Tantra affirms that both the world process itself, and the individual *jiva* are themselves real. In this respect, Tantra distinguishes itself both from pure dualism and from the qualified non-dualism of Vedānta.

Creation, or the "outgoing current," is only half of the functioning of *Māyā*. Involution, or the "return current," takes the *jiva* back towards the source, or the root of reality, revealing the infinite. Tantra is understood to teach the method of changing the "outgoing current" into the "return current", transforming the fetters created by *Māyā* into that which "releases" or "liberates". This view underscores two maxims of Tantra: "One must rise by that by which one falls," and "the very poison that kills becomes the elixir of life when used by the wise."

One and Distinct

All the three, Mantra, Tantra and Yantra are weapons in the hands of devotees and seekers, and most effective ones. Weapons can be easily misused. So, it should be given to only wise, righteous persons of moral character.

In their respective results, they are similar but differ in their processes. Even Mantras are different. Vedic Mantras are for growth, purification, refinement, prosperity, satisfaction and health for all as the fundamental theory of the Vedas is *'Sarve bhavantu sukhinah'*; all should be happy. But in Tāntric Mantras, the selfish end and aim of the seeker is prominent. They have some darker purpose. They aim at individual gain and there is nothing as yet in modern science to save the life giving and life saving element for the living beings and the posterity. All are vying to gain the complete treasures of nature before they depart from the world. They don't want to save anything for the great grandsons of their great grandsons.

Tantra and the modern science don't suit Indian mind. That is the reason that Tantra could not penetrate Indian society and remained far away from it like the Yantras which were not for the common folk. Tāntriks failed to get the respect and support of the society. They were kept aloof and remained aloof.

Yantra works as the Mantra dictates. It is the handling of the Yantra, machines and weapons that is important. In the name of peace, if weapons for mass destruction are used to kill the living beings then the purpose of safety vanishes.

☆☆☆

2

Mantra and Yantra in Tantra

Creation envisages both Purush and Prakriti; Shiva and Shakti; Surya and Dharati. When it is the Sun at the centre, it is Nigam Shāstra, the Vedas and when it is Prithivi at the centre, then it is Āgam Shāstra which has come out of the Nigam and so it is Āgam. The Vedas have come out of the breathing of the Brahma, the Creator and hence need no proof. They are proofs in themselves and proofs of all else: *Vedāh Pramānam*. The Āgam Granthas have come out of the breathing of Shiva so they need no proof. They are proofs unto themselves: *Āgamāh Pramānam*. Tantra represents Āgam. The meaning of Āgam is very clear: That which shows the ways of physical and spiritual welfare; mundane and divine ways and means is called Āgam: *Āgachchhati buddhim ārohati yasmād abhyudaya nihshreyasa upāyah sa āgamah*. The word Tantra is a substitute for Āgam:

> *Tanoti vipulān arthān tattva-mantra samāshritān;*
> *Trānam cha kurute punsām tena tantram iti smritam.*

तनोति विपुलान् अर्थान् तत्त्वमन्त्र समाश्रितान्।
त्राणं च कुरुते पुंसां तेन तन्त्रं इति स्मृतम्॥

That which analyses and explains fully, the whole process and systems of *Sādhanā-prakriyā*, the ways of meditative procedures; and makes the meaning clear; removes all sorts of human fears; is called the Tantra Shāstra and Tantra Prayoga. In this sense, the whole of the immense Tantra Literature is based on the procedures of Mantra Yoga.

Vedānta lays down the philosophical principle that only the living being is the Brahma and none else: *jivo brahmaiva nā-parah*.

In the same way, the Āgam Tantras enunciate the philosophical principle-like dictum that pleasure is form of Brahma: *ānandam brahmano roopam*. In Nigam, He is Brahma and in Tantra, He is Shiva; in Nigam it is *Aham Brahmāsmi* and in Āgam it is *Shivoaham*: He is in the body of all beings: Gita 9:11:

> *Avajānanti mām mudhām mānushim tanum-āshritam;*
> *Param bhāvam-jānanto mama bhuta-maheshwaram.*

> अवजानन्ति मां मूढ़ां मानुषीं तनुमाश्रितम्।
> परं भावमजानन्तो मम भूतमहेश्वरम्॥

After creating the beings and reducing their Omnipotent and Omniscient qualities to the bare minimum, Shiva and Shakti, pervade all and play in all and play with all. It is their play only, *leelā-mātra*; through illusion, Māyā. They reduce their power and enter the beings with negligible wisdom and profound ignorance, forcing the being to realize the real entity and grow to that extent to become divine and powerful. Because of the negligible wisdom, the jiva feels the pain and suffering; diseases and illness; misery and agony; poverty and weakness; lack of attachment and affection; lack of material need and physical pleasure; and lack of almost everything. The jiva forgets the power and knowledge within. We learn and get as if it was present inside; we ignore and get nothing. That is the reason that the gods and rishis taught us different ways and means to know oneself; to realize the Soul and Brahma within; the Kunadlini Shakti within; the nectar that we possess and finally to change into Brahma which is termed as union with the Self or Brahma. This is the mystery behind it.

Interrelationship

As given in the Kulārnava Tantra, it is clear beyond all doubt that Mantra, Tantra and Yantra are interrelated. They are not independent. When there are different Nyāsa and Karma Kānda in Mantra which are more prominent in Tantra; when there is vehement use of Mantras in the Tantra and when all the Yantras contain Mantras, and different rituals and rights are performed in getting mastery over the Yantras, then the three cannot be independent. So, neither the Tantra nor Yantra can exist without Mantra.

Mantras in Tantra

The whole of Tantra literature is full of Mantras for everything. The following are a few examples of the dominance of Mantras in Tantra.

In the Kulārnava Tantra Sixth Ullās chapter, the Mantras for the purification of elements are given but with the condition that this Mantra should be chanted after:

Brahma Kalā worship with **Hansa Mantra**;

Vishnu Kalā worship with **Prata Vishnu Mantra**;

Rudra Kalā's worship with **Tryambakam Mantra** and **Tad Vishnuh Mantra**;

Sadāshiva Kalā worship with **Vishnuh-yoni Mantra**;

Pratham prakrite hansah pratad-vishnuh-anantaram;
Trayambakatantu tritiyam syāh-cha-chaturthah-tat-padādika.
Vishnu-yonim kalpayatu panchamah kalpanā-manuh;
Chatuh navati mantrātma-devatā bhāva-siddhidā. 6:47, 48

Only after the Japa of these five Mantras, the first element can be invited:

Mantra jāpashcha samprokt ātma-stavah-cha panchbhih;
Atra te panch samproktā mantrāste kula-nāyike. 6:49

मन्त्र जापश्च सम्प्रोक्त आत्म-स्तव च पंचभिः।
अत्र ते पञ्च सम्प्रोक्त मन्त्रास्ते कुल नायिके॥

Then it gives 35 lettered Amriteshi Mantra:

aing plung sraung jung sah amrite amrit-udabhave amriteshwari amrit-varshini amrit srāvaya swāhā.

ऐं प्लुंड् स्रौंड् जुं सः अमृते अमृत उद्भवे अमृतेश्वरी अमृतवर्षिणी अमृत स्रावय स्वाहा॥

Then it gives 47 lettered Dipāni Mantra:

aing vad vad vāg-vādini aing kling klinne kledani kledaya mahā-moksham kuru kuru kling hansauh moksham kuru kuru hansauh syāhouh.

ऐं वद् वद् वाग्वादिनी ऐं क्लीं क्लीन्ने क्लेदनि क्लेदय महामोक्षकुरु कुरु क्लीं हंसौ मोक्षं कुरु कुरु हंसौ स्याहौः॥

Then, Devi *āvāhan,* invocation Mantra is also given:

Mahā-padma-vanāntah-sthe kāranānd-vigrahe
Sarva-bhuta-hite mātah-yehiyegi parameshwari.
Deveshi bhakti-sulabhe sarva-āvarana-sanyukte
Yāvatvāmpoojayām-iha tāvattvam susthirā bhava. 6:69,70

This Tantra makes it clear that the Unity of Devatā, Mantra and Yantra must be maintained which shows its interdependence and the importance of Mantra and Yantra in Tantra. It says: O Shāmbhavi! Any worship performed without the knowledge of mutual pervasiveness of Devatā, Mantra and Yantra, becomes fruitless.

Devasya mantra-rupasya mantra-vyāptim-ajānatām;
Kritārth-anādikam sarva-vyartham bhavati Shāmbhavi. 6:84

देवस्य मन्त्ररूपस्य मन्त्र व्याप्तिं अजानताम्।
कृतार्थ-अनादिकं सर्व-व्यर्थ भवति शाम्भवि॥

✿ ✿ ✿

3

Mantra on Yantra

Mantras are remembered and chanted for attainment with numerous objectives in mind and even for abstract power without lust and attachment. Mantra in Tantra is one way to remember and meditate on and attain near perfection in life, and Mantra on Yantras is another way with the same objective, making it visual for the practitioner. It also projects scientific form of the Yantras, the machines. It shows the power and practical use of the Mantra.

Mantras Dominate

In every way of worshipping, Mantra Anushthān; or Yantra Poojan or Tāntrik Sādhanā; whether birth or marriage or death; whether victorious, happy or fallen low; Mantras dominate everywhere. It is universal power of the Mantras and the acceptance by one and all since time immemorial. Despite numerous upheavals; invasion; remorseless killing of pundits and burning of rare books, Mantras have retained their place from the grassroots to the helm. It is because of their inherent and latent sublime, supernatural and divine power and effectiveness.

Penance Needed

Mantras are such things that connect one to universal or cosmic power and therefore demand a lot of control over self, penance and time for their *jāgriti*, awakening, so that they become effective. The common folk can't afford to spend that much time and perform such tough penance. Naturally, people turn towards the Siddhas to obtain their help. Only a few determined seekers fulfill all the requirements and get attainment. Taking advantage of this, some other persons falsely claim supernatural attainment and mislead those faithful who seek their help. **One simple test of true Siddhas is that they neither need nor accept money.**

Once, a cheat, a rogue went to another country; and with the help of his friend spread the rumour that he is a great Siddha. He wouldn't take money from anyone and played many tricks to establish his impersonated identity. People from far off lands came to get relief which he willingly offered and took no money. The fruits and other things offered along with salutation were enough for them to survive. The trick worked and they were expecting windfall.

It happened as they had planned and expected. The king of the land came with his family and ministers. He offered a lot of gold and jewels which the rogue refused to take. The king's contingent was impressed.

Next day, the king again came with costlier offers and the same thing happened. The friend of the rogue was eager to accept that immense wealth but the rogue assured him that they will get many times more than that.

The third day, the king again came and offered his daughter in marriage and half of his kingdom as dowry. The rogue had not expected such a windfall. He thought and thought and took a decision.

He requested the king to employ his friend and refused to marry his only daughter and also the wealth that was to come as dowry. The king returned with his family. The friend was angry. They would have become master of a kingdom.

The rogue said: I'm not a Siddha but a rogue yet I'm getting respect and wealth from all the people. Imagine what I can get when I'm a real Siddha. I shall go for penance.'

He took his kamandal, water pot and went towards the forest.

In fact, it is the penance that is the test of many qualities.

✿✿✿

SECTION II

Mantra: Broader and Cosmic Vision

- ➢ Ocean of Mantras
- ➢ Nāda Brahma: Shabda Brahma
- ➢ Different Mantras
- ➢ Collected Mantras and Important Aspects
- ➢ Mantras for Different Gods and Purposes
- ➢ All Gāyatri Mantras
- ➢ Chanting and Repetition of Mantras
- ➢ Limbs of Mantras
- ➢ Indrajāla Mantras
- ➢ Sounds Equivalent to Mantra in other Religions
- ➢ Mantras Give Faith, Hope and Confidence
- ➢ Need of Mantras

4

Ocean of Mantras

Mantra Sristi, creation of Mantras or creation by Mantras began when Vāni appeared as *Pashyanti; Madhyamā* and *Baikhari*. Before that, there were no Mantras. It is no wonder that the collection of only Tāntrik Mantras has been named 'Mantra Mahodadhi', the ocean of Mantras.

In the broader sense, whatever we utter from the inner core of our being for the existence, sustenance and growth of life, is Mantra. In that sense, only the intention becomes the meaning of the Mantra. It makes no difference whether we understand or know the meaning of that word or combination of words or not. Although, the Rishis have repeatedly asked the Sādhaks to concentrate on the meaning of the Mantra while in meditation. Then there is always an apparent or hidden meaning in each Mantra. But since each sound is meaningful so, the Mantras can't be meaningless. What the Rishis, Seers and Saints have observed, felt and expressed come from such deep recesses of the heart or their being; and the distance from them to us is so vast that we are never able to get closer to the Mantras. We are dependent on the learned men of the recent centuries for the meaning which eludes us because neither they nor we have that sort of revelation. We lack concentration, purity, dedication and spiritual depth.

Although, a Mantra can be of one syllable; one word or many syllables and many words or even of many sentences; yet we don't recite or chant them. We have virtually no knowledge of the science, art and technique of chanting of Mantras; neither that of the pronunciation nor of the Mudras and nyāsa. We are groping in the dark; and in ignorance declare that the Mantras give nothing.

We are the men who neither know Mantras nor have memorized them; neither we meditate on them nor chant them. It is our fault.

There is another matter also. During the one thousand years of slavery, from Prithivirāj Chauhan to Mahātmā Gandhi, we drifted far away from our culture; tradition; shāstras; Mantras; Yantras; and the samskārs. etc. We don't know the real meaning and reason behind those things. So, now we have numerous questions and least or no answers at all or we are not satisfied with the scanty material answers to sublime, human and spiritual words and activities. We have to get reconnected to our past to know both the secret and mystical meaning and its apparent and worldly significance. Under such circumstances, we are unable to realize, feel and know the immense power of the Mantras and of many other great things from our past. We must search our inner self for realization and revelation, and follow our pure conscience for the survival, sustenance and growth of all living beings as the earth is the only known planet with life on it.

The epic poet, Mahākavi Dandi has eulogized Mantras by saying that if there was no light in the form of word and sound then all the three worlds would have been under complete darkness:

Idam-andham tamah kritsnam jāyeta bhuwanah trayam;
Yadi shabd-ālayam-jyotih samsārā na deepyate.

इदं अन्धं तमः कृत्स्नं जायेत भुवनः त्रयम्।
यदि शब्दालयमज्योतिः संसारा न दीप्यते॥

Mantras Defined

Mantras are the pious placement of sacred and powerful sound, *Nāda* through *Varnas* that cleanses and purifies, and brings one closer to the Gods, humanity, divinity and perfection. A Mantra contains a string of syllables, set on a pattern and meter. That gives it rhythm. The sacred combination of rhythm and sound make Mantras. Mantras give the most essential and most needed four qualities: control, balance, hope and faith.

That is the reason why Mantras are defined as special arrangement of Varnas. Why that special arrangement? This will be discussed in detail in the subheading **Varnas**.

It is better to see the definition given in Parātra-anshikā:

Manan trān dharmānām sarvesām-yeva vāchya-vāchakādi;
Roopa varna bhatār-kāvyānām mantrānām.

मनन् त्राण धर्माणां सर्वेषां येनवाच्य वाचकादि।
रूपवर्ण भतारकाव्यनां मन्त्रणाम्॥

Whatever sound that can be arranged in a rythmical sequence, they are all Mantras. Varnas possesses energy or are in the form of energy rather in the form of concentrated energy, so, when they are given a sequence they become a store of power, a power house. The Mantras turn into Shaktimān, one who is energy incarnate. That way, many power-houses become one and emit tremendous power. Since, they combine many and different powers they become indomitable. It is spiritual and divine power that has the ability to reveal the truth when meditated upon and chanted.

The word Mantra can be divided in two: *mana* (*mānas*) that means mind; and *tya* or *tra, tāranā*, sanctify, save; that means free or three. Mantras are something that put the *Trideva*, the Trinity: Brahmā, Vishnu, Mahesh, in the heart. A Mantra is something that frees one from negative thought as well as from the worldly bindings. Mantras increase awareness and abilities to know and identify with the Infinite. Mahārth Manjari: 54 mentions:

Mananmayi nija vibhave nija-sankosh-mayi trān-mayi;
Kawalita-vishwa-vikalapa-anubhutih kāpi mantra shabdārthah.

मननमयिनिज विभवे निज-संकोषमयि त्राणमयि।
कवलित-विश्व-विकल्पानुभूति: कापि मन्त्र शब्दार्थ: ॥

Manan trān dharmāno mantra, repeats the same idea that by meditation and chanting Mantras are fully charged and are filled with spiritual and divine power. It generates light and moves with the speed of both light and sound in different directions. Since it is charged power, it never dies. Some years back, modern scientists tried to catch the sound pervading the atmosphere. They succeeded in catching sound but there was no way available to pin point whose sound that was. The effort continues to this day.

Since their presence is not denied; rather, accepted by all, Mantras were classified as inner and outer and disciples were asked to turn the mind from outside to inside to absorb the cosmic power. That is the reason that the Mantras are not constrained by time, space and physical obstructions.

When the Mantras are *chitta-yukta*, inherent in the mind, they are inner and when they are *dhvani-yukta*, bound in sound, they are outer. Naturally, Vigyān Bhairava lays stress on chanting the Mantras silently then to make sound or, *ghosha*. Both are the accepted ways: lound and silent chanting of Mantras.

The world is divided into distinct form: one which is acceptable and the other which accepts. For success, apparent or secret connection between the two is essential. Sound is the only way towards such connectivity. It is a matter of time when the correct or desired frequency is automatically reached through many repetitions of the same Mantra as the sound regularly comes back and goes forth. After aquiring its desired frequency when it bounces back it enriches the Sādhak hundreds or thousands of times.

In the modern age, the natural frequencies have been disturbed by the loud sound of aircraft; nuclear and other blasts and numerous vehicles. Mantras are not working with previous sweetness and subtlety. The vibration of the Mantra sound and its direction is disturbed because of multiple and varied sounds. Thus, the live and subtle power and brightness is not working properly. Moreover, the modern human beings hardly practice the real pronunciation of the Mantras. As a result, the sound that they make is never proper and withers out easily.

We can safely say that whichever word that leads one to the Brahma, the absolute one is a Mantra. It is the final goal of Mantras and chanting of Mantras.

Mantras According to Tantras

By meditation, *manan*, on the luminous deity who is the form of Truth, it saves, *trāyate*, from all fears, therefore, it is called Mantra.

> *Mananā-tattva-rupasya devasya-amit-tejasah;*
> *Trāyate sarva-bhaya tastasmān-mantra iti-riti.*

Kulārnava Tantra 17:54

मनना तत्वरूपस्य देवस्य अमित तेजसः ।
त्रायते सर्वभय तस्तस्मान् मन्त्र इतिऋति ॥

Soul and Life Element in Mantras

Every element and everything concrete or subtle in the cosmos has Shiva, Shakti and Anu. In absence of any one of the above, a thing can't be imagined, can't aquire visible or invisible form and won't move and work. These three are primary and essential. They are integral parts and can't be separated.

Shiva is Nirānand, without pleasure and Shakti is Sānand, with pleasure, so they become one and are inseparable. Both Shiva and Anu work with or through Shakti, which has numerous forms. They form the soul or life element in everything: least or immense; rough or sublime. Mantras too possess them and hence are soulful and living. Because of both Shiva and Shakti the Mantras have the power to give both *Bhoga* and *Moksha*: physical pleasure and salvation.

Mantras: Shlokas: Stotras: Stuties

Mantras are different from Shlokas, Stotras and Stuties. Unlike them, Mantras are not prayers or eulogy and they don't describe the same figure in different words. Moreover, they can be sung while Mantras can only be chanted. Singing of Mantras is prohibited. Shlokas contain subject matter and may be descriptive or may have some teachings. Stuties and Stotras are basically prayers but Mantras are different. They are clusters of powerful sounds for generating more power. The others can be changed, and it will not make any difference to them but Mantras can't be changed, not even a single sound can switch places or substituted or omitted. That is real difference.

Some Stuties and Stotras also take the form of Mantras because of the subtle inner power that they possess or the words being designedly arranged or the powerful sound that they make; as for example: Devi Sukt or Tāndava Stotra by Rāvana or Shivāstaka by Tulasidās and many Stuties by Shankarāchārya.

Mantra Meditation

Manan trāna dharmāno Mantrā: Mantras are rhythmical arrangement of words for meditation. The sound of the Mantras should be meditated upon. The meditation alone generates sublime power through the Mantras. The words and sound are energized during meditation.

Mantras have both physical and subtle body. Mantras are powerful only because they are pure and can't be mitigated. If changed or wrongly pronounced they will not work as they fail to remain Mantras. In both the forms, Mantras work as a medium; a very powerful medium because of their unhindered and ungauged speed.

Through Mantra meditation, one gets both outer consciousness which helps in performing worldly deeds and inner consciousness which gives spiritual growth and advantages for performing supernatural deeds.

Only through meditation we can understand Mantras and activate their inert power and perform extraordinary deeds and finally obtain the cherished union with the supreme creator. It is very clear: that which cannot be understood otherwise, will be understood just by repeating the Mantra time and again; and that which cannot be seen, will be seen just by concentrating on the Mantra time and again. Mantra chanting and repetition is an ancient Indian meditation technique.

Mantra Repetition

Mantra repetition simply means repeating a sentence or group of words that have a phonetic significance in its true rhythmical way.

Mantra is intrinsically related to sound. Mantra is sound, and sound is reverberating in everything in this universe. When water flows, the gurgling sound it makes is also a mantra. When wind blows through the trees, the rustling sound it produces is also a mantra. Within human beings, there is a self-born, indestructible sound, the AUM sound which repeats itself constantly, along with our breathing and this sound is also a mantra.

Sound has enormous power. In fact, it has the power to create an entire universe. It is written that God originally manifested as sound.

According to ancient Indian belief, in the beginning there was sound, *sphot*, which reverberated as *AUM* and from that sound everything came into existence.

The West also follows this belief. It has been repeated with a changed accent in New Testament 1:1-2:

In the beginning was the Word, and the Word was with God, and the Word was God.

Even modern scientists are beginning to recognize as our ancient sages did, that there exists a vibration which reverberates ceaselessly throughout the cosmos.

When letters and syllables come together, they form words. Both our spiritual and mundane life are possible only because of words; without language, we cannot carry out any of our activities. Each word, we use, has its own power and produces its own reaction. A mantra is no ordinary combination of letters and syllables, but a living force. The name of God is not different from God. Mantra has been called the sound body of God: It is God in the form of sound, or Nāda Brahma.

In **Bhagavad Gita** Shri Krishna says,

"Among rituals, I am the ritual of mantra repetition."

By this he means that while other techniques are means of attaining Him, mantra is His very being. That is why it is so easy to experience God by repeating the mantra. Mantra meditation is the repetition of a group of words which create sound vibrations that awake the love of God in hearts and mind, gives faith and hope; and concentration on it clarifies the meaning.

Gender differentiation of Mantras: Classifications of Mantras

Mantras are classified in two ways and five broad groups:

Mantrāh purush-devāh syuh-vidyā stri-devatā priye;
Mantrāh punso humph-dantāh prāne charati dakshine;
Prabudhyante-agni-jāyāntā vidyāh stri devatā priye,
Vāme prāne prabudhyante namo-antāh syuh-napunsakāh;
Nādi-dvya-gate prāne sarve bodham prayāti cha.

Kulārnava Tantra 16: 40, 41

मन्त्रः पुरुषः देवाः स्युः विद्या स्त्री देवता प्रिये।
मन्त्राः पुंसो हुंफदन्ताः प्राणे चरति दक्षिणे॥
प्रबुध्यन्ते अग्नि जायन्ता विद्याः स्त्री देवता प्रिये।
नाडी द्वय गते प्राणे सर्वे बोधं प्रयाति च॥

Pun-stri-napunsak-ātmano mantrāh sarve samiritāh;
Mantrāh pun-devatāh gyeyā vidyā stri devatā smritā.

Mantra Mahodadhi 24/92

पुं स्त्री नपुंसक आत्मनोमन्त्राः सर्वे समीरितः।
मन्त्राः पुं देवताः ज्ञेया विद्या स्त्री देवता स्मृता॥

There are three genders of Mantras: Masculine, Feminine and Neuter. Even Mahāvidyās, Shri Vidyā etc. are also divided in these groups.

(1) **Male**: Mantras that end in *Hung, Futta,* are masculine. These Mantras are chanted for aquiring power.

Thus, it is clear that Mantras of Devatās are masculine. When these Mantras are chanted, the Prāna Vāyu moves through the right nostril, *Idā*.

(2) **Female**: Mantras that end in *Swāhā*, and are chanted to get rid of diseases, be free from problems and to get peace are feminine. In other words, the Mantras of Vidyās are feminine. When these Mantras are chanted, the Prāna Vāyu moves through the left nostril, *Pingalā*.

(3) **Neuter,** Impotent: Mantras that end in *Namah*, and are chanted for wealth, prosperity, knowledge and fame are neuter. When these Mantras are chanted, the Prāna Vāyu moves through both the nostrils.

(4) *Saguna*: Mantras that are directed to the Gods (*Ishta Devatā*) with qualities are called Saguna, for example:

Aum gang ganapataye namah!; Aum shri sarasatvai namah!; Aum shri laxamai namah!

ॐ गं गणपतये नमः, ॐ श्री सरस्वत्यै नमः, ॐ श्री लक्ष्म्यै नमः।

(5) *Nirguna*: Mantras that have no *Ishta Devatā,* any presiding deity are Nirguna. They are directed to gods without qualities.

Other Divisions of Mantras

Mantras are divided in different sets. According to Nityā-tantra one Varna mantras are called '*Pinda*'; two varna mantras are called '*Kartari*'; from three to nine varna mantras are called '*Beeja*'; from ten to twenty varna mantras are called '*Mantra*'; mantras with more than twenty varnas are called '*Mala Mantras*':

Mantrā ekāksharāh pindāh kartayoh dvya-aksharā matāh;
Varna-trayam samārambhya navārnāvidhi-beejakāh.
Tato dashārnām ārambhya yāvad-vinshati mantrakāh;
Atah urdhvam gatā mālāh-tāsu bhedo na vidyate.

मंत्रा: एकाक्षरा: पिण्डा: कर्तयो: द्वय-अक्षरा: मता:
वर्ण त्रयं समारभ्य नवार्णाविधि बीजका:।
ततो दर्शानां आरभ्य यावद् विंशति मन्त्रका:
अत: ऊर्ध्वं गता माला: तासु भेदो न विद्यते॥

These Mantras are *Mitra, Shatru, Sādhya, Siddha, Susidha* for the seekers. Therefore, the Mantras should be selected according to their character and need as they are based on Varnas and possess Shiva: *Mantrāh varnātmikāh sarve sarve varnāh shivātmikāh.*

मन्त्रा: वर्णात्मिका सर्वे सर्वे वर्णा: शिवात्मिका:॥

Tāntrik Mantras

There are four types of Mantras in Tantra. These are: Siddha; Sādhya; Susiddha and Ari. These are again divided in four subcategories each. Among them, Siddha Mantras are considered to be Bāndhava or family members; Sādhya Mantras are Sevaks, servers; Susiddha Mantras are Poshaks, those who nurse; but Ari Mantras are Ghātak, enemies and fatal.

Besides the masculine, feminine and neuter gender the Mantras in Tantra Shāstra are also classified in different ways:

1. *Saumya Mantras* are used in rituals for pacification. The letters of such Mantras are full of amrit tattva or nectar. These Mantras end in Swāhā.

2. *Āgneya Mantras* are used in cruel rituals.

3. *Phat Mantras* are used in the rituals for prosperity.

4. *Vashat Mantras* are used in captivating rituals.

5. *Hung Phat Mantras* are used in the rituals for causing death.

6. *Namah Mantras* are used in immobilization rituals.

Shāntike manavah saumyābhi-tendava-amrit-aksharā;
Swāhā-antā syuh-viyat-prāyāshcha-agneyāh krur-karmasu.
Phat cha pushto vashat vashye hung-phat yeva-cha mārane;
Stambhane cha namah proktam swāhā shāntika-paushtike.

Kulārnava Tantra 16: 42, 43

शान्तिके मनवः सौम्याभि तेन्दव अमृतअक्षराः ।
स्वाहा अन्ता स्युः वियत्प्रायश्च आग्नेयः क्रूर कर्मसु ॥
फट् च पुष्टो वषट् वश्ये हुं फट् येव च मारणे ।
स्तम्भने च नमः प्राक्तं स्वाहा शान्तिक पौष्टिके ॥

Mantras Produce Results

Mantras are a string of syllables, set on a meter and chanted in a set way to produce results. The Mantras and their sound conceal and the chanting projects an image of the deity they represent. When chanted, Mantras produce the image and affect the mind, the organs and the milieu and bring immediate changes. The effects of Mantras are numerous that depend on the place, person, mood, intention and intensity of effort.

Mantras work in different psychological and mysterious ways and serve different known and unknown purpose — including specific purposes. Mantras work both as a *Kawacha* sheath, protection, and as *Trishula* or Trident to remove and clear the negative thoughts and destroy the bad effect. It protects from attacks and destroys the attackers. The brevity in sound gives it a sublime richness and divine thickness that immediatedly charges the atmosphere and changes the mood of the listener. It works in such an effective way and with urgency that the effect is felt immediately. Whatever is working in the mind is immediately shifted and replaced by positive thoughts and positive enrgy. Neutral and negative energies are subdued.

Eventually, the *Sādhak* or seeker is transported easily and often at will to super-conscious state as Mantras never create negative ideas and immediately subdue anger, hatred, jealousy, fear, ego, attachment and lust.

Chanting Mantra

Mantras are never uttered or spoken. Mantras are always recited or chanted, and should be recited or chanted. The spacing between the specific sounds is as important and effective as the sound and the complete Mantra itself. One must keep it in mind that through wrong accent and pronunciation or shifting of sound, the Mantra loses either *Mantra Pāth* or *Mantra Jāpa* fails. It must be rhythmic, *layātmak*. The Varnas or the words sound must be pronounced correctly. It means that the sound must be created clearly.

Effects of Mantras

The moment a Mantra is remembered and/or recited there is a sudden change in the heart, mind, attitude and thought. In those that have practiced Mantras, the remembrance and/or recitation changes him/her into a thoughtless state: calm, cool and *Sanyat*.

The moment one thinks of a Mantra, it appears from nowhere, from deep slumber, from the subconscious mind. It is recited and the sound enters the conscious and subconscious mind as for example: *Aum hreeng cleeng shreenga*. Recite them with open eyes, with eyes closed, with body 'still' or with hands moving in rhythm. Everytime, the effect will be different. The sound is transmitted and absorbed simultaneously. The transmitted sound scatters around and the absorption collects, thickens and strengthens the energy flowing around waywardly.

When a Mantra is chanted we envisage the deity or deities and feel the presence of the deity as well as a sort of divinity and sublimity, as if a safety ring has been created around. The moment a Mantra is chanted and repeated the atmosphere, the surrounding up to the reach of the sound gets surchared and comes under a magic spell: becomes *abhimantrita*.

The greatest thing about a Mantra is that it affects the listeners as much as it affects the one who is reciting or chanting. The Mantras require specific intonation of specific syllables. They must be correctly recited to yield results. If Mantras are incorrectly recited, it is unlikely to yield desired result. Hence, one must obtain the

Mantra from an able preceptor. There is one very important thing. One has to anoint one's head with the soil or dust of the place where one has completed the *Mantra-Jāpa*, otherwise the outcome will be usurped by Indra.

Mantra Sādhanā

Mantra *Sādhanā* is ideally done in isolation, solitude's, where the practitioner feels safe at a clean and dry place, when one has taken a bath and completed the ablutions, either in early or late hours of morning but definitely two hours after taking any meal. Whether it is being performed with or without specific goal, Mantra Sādhanā should not be publicized. Loose talk and unwanted publicity distract one's mind, and the comments of other persons vibrate in the ears and mind. The pure and mature seeker acquires the power to create secret privacy at any public gathering or crowded or desired or undesired place and milieu. Nothing special is needed for him as he himself has turned into something special and divine. They are among those few persons that heal a wound with their touch and change a person or scenario with their words. They get and possess both *Sādhutā* and *Sātviktā*.

With the Mantras one can enrich one's inner self and inner consciousness as much as one desires and works in the right direction with dedication, purity, concentration and earnestness.

Punishment: Atonement

Many things are to be done before starting Mantra Sādhanā. This has been prescribed by the scriptures. Even atonement has been prescribed for lapses in following the dictates. Therefore, one must follow the rules and do away with excesses. Atonements is not difficult as the number of repetition of the Mantras are enhanced. The atonement is to raise one or a few rosary of either hundred japas or thousand japas.

Nityakarma

From rising early in the morning till one falls asleep there are many routine-works prescribed by scriptures or dictated by the Guru.

One has to follow them. There are so many rules and Mantras in this and also the following subheadings that it can't be understood and followed or even pronounced correctly without the help of an able guru.

Naimitika Karma

There are some fixed days like Pancha Parvas: Krishnāshtami; Krishna-chaturdashi; Amāvasyā; Purnimā and Sankrānti, when some fixed duties are to be performed. One cannot succeed without fulfilling them.

Kāmya Karma

Works which are performed for the fulfillment of some definite wish are called Kāmya Karma. Hoama should be performed separately for each wish. Though, the wishes are readily fulfilled but it is always better not to venture into such things as a very simple mistake can reverse the result.

Nishkāma Upāsanā

The Sādhanā must be without any attachment, allurement, affection or expectation. It is the best Sādhanā and always advised by scriptures including the Gita.

Worshipping Mantra Tattva

The following five are counted as Mantra Tattva. One must bow to them and then start chanting after completing other rituals.

   i. Rishi   ii. Devatā   iii. Chhanda
   iv. Beeja   v. Shakti

There is yet another element 'Kilak' which balances a Mantra.

Viniyoga

The guidance regarding the net result of a Mantra is called viniyoga. After worshipping the elements of the Mantras given above, viniyoga is performed.

Nyāsa

Nyāsa is an act of purifing each letter and each part of one's body which is called Anga-nyāsa; that of elements called rishyādi nyāsa; and many other things. The very divisions of Nyāsa will be a solid proof of how complete, complicated and difficult is the nyāsa, The following are some of the Nyāsas:

i.	Varna Nyāsa	ii.	Anga Nyāsa
iii.	Rishyādi Nyāsa	iv.	Jagad-Vashikarana
v.	Sammohan Nyāsa	vi.	Samhār Nyāsa
vii.	Beeja Nyāsa	viii.	Vāga Devatā Nyāsa
ix.	Srishti Nyāsa	x.	Panchāvritti Nyāsa
xi.	Ganesh Mātrikā Nyāsa	xii.	Grah Mātrikā Nyāsa
xiii.	Nakshatra Mātrikā Nyāsa	xiv.	Yogini Mātrikā Nyāsa
xv.	Rāshi Mātrikā Nyāsa	xvi.	Peetha Mātrikā Nyāsa

Mudrā

After each Nyāsa appropriate Mudrās are exhibited. The following are some of the Mudrās:

i.	Vashya Mudrā	ii.	Unmāda Mudrā
iii.	Mahā-ankusha Mudrā	iv.	Mahā Yoni Mudrā
v.	Sankshobha Mudrā	vi.	Drāvini Mudrā
vii.	Ākarshini Mudrā	viii.	Khechari Mudrā
ix.	Beeja Mudrā	x.	Matasya Mudrā
xi.	Ashtra Mudrā	xii.	Kavacha Mudrā
xiii.	Dhenu Mudrā	xiv.	Sannirodha Mudrā
xv.	Musala Mudrā	xvi.	Chakra Mudrā
xvii.	Mahā Mudrā	xviii.	Yoni Mudrā
xviv.	Sathāpanā Mudrā	xx.	Sannidhān Mudrā
xxi.	Samukhikaran Mudrā	xxii.	Sakalikarana Mudrā
xxiii.	Avagunthan Mudrā	xxiv.	Amritikarana Mudrā
xxv.	Paramikarana Mudrā		

Bhuta Shuddhi

Bhuta Suddhi means thinking of all the five gross elements – space; water; air; earth and heat to be at different places. First, Sankalpa is taken with the following Mantra:

Aum adyetyādi deva-poojād-adhikār-siddhye bhutah-suddhyād aham karishye.

ॐ अद्येतादि-देव पूजादधिकार सिद्धये भूतः-शुद्धयादहं करिष्ये।

Then, think of that there is the prithvi mandal from the feet to thighs and chant the mantra:

Aum hrāng bragmane prithvidyādi-pataye nibriti kalātmane hung phat swāhā;

Jala mandal from thighs to navel and chant the mantra: *Aum hring vishnave jalādhi-pataye pratishthā kalātmane hung phat swāhā;*

of agni mandal from navel to heart and chant the mantra: *Aum hrung rudrāya tejo-adhipataye vidyā kalātmane hung phat swāhā;*

of vāyu mandal from heart to brows and chant the mantra: *Aum hang idjā nāth vāyu-adhipataye shānti kalātmane hung phat swāhā;*

and then think of ākāsha mandal from brows to brahma-ranghra and chant the mantra: *Aum haung sadā shivāya ākāsha adhipataye shanty-ateeta kalātmane hung phat swāhā.* With that, surrender your ego to the Brahma.

Psychological Effect of Mantras

There is nothing instant and physical about the Mantras. Mantras take time both in completion of the needed number of chantings and also in showing the effect as so many things determine the net result. Even getting vile and immoral ideas during chanting will spoil everything. The rules are to be followed honestly, sincerely and meticulously. The things needed are difficult to collect nowadays; and the process, though plain, yet is so tough that one can hardly remember the sequence and follow it correctly. Even the experts miss this or that action and do it when it comes to mind. This too will affect the net result. It is also very difficult to get an able preceptor. Moreover, there is so much of sound pollution; dearth of peaceful places and restlessness that it is almost impossible for a modern man, to complete the Mantra Anushthāna and fulfill the resolve, Sankalpa.

When one is determined to follow all the rituals correctly; but fails because of lack of knowledge then depression sets in and porvades the mind.

Once the faith and confidence is lost it is very tough to regain it. This is so because modern man wants results immediately. A lot of wealth is desired by one and all. No one is ready to work hard and live a plain life. It is luxury that forces them to go for luxury. It is because of reckless destruction of natural wealth and life giving and life saving elements that living and survival is becoming tougher everyday.

If one is pure at heart; does not think of doing harm to others and never performs immoral deeds then at leisure hours, one can chant the Mantras silently and with cool mind. This will help in many ways, give strength and make fearless. The gods will be pleased. One may not get all that one longs for but one would definitely get everything that is needed for a good, healthy, peaceful and happy life. That is the real effect of the mantras.

Of course, all these things are very difficult, particularly to do away with the easily available facilities and the lust or jealousy, but one has to do something chosen for oneself; otherwise, human life will be completely a waste. The Bhāgawat Mahāpurāna 3:23:56 declares that those who have been religious and have not spent enough time to perform religious deeds; one who is not detached or one who has not served the creator, is dead though alive:

Neha yat-karma dharmāya na virāgāya kalpate;
Na teertha-pāda sevāye jivan-api mrito hi sah.

नेह यत्कर्म धर्माय न विरागाय कल्पते ।
न तीर्थ-पाद्सेवाये जीवनपि मृतो हि सः ॥

Get set and praise Brahma by chanting mantras and obtain illumined light and mind.

Sarve Subhe!

❁ ❁ ❁

Nāda Brahma: Shabda Brahma

Mantras represent Nāda Brahma, the Absolute God in the form of sound, Vāni, word. The meaning from words is as inseparable as Shiva and Shakti. It is the life, *spandan* or *sphot*.

Nāda and Bindu, Sound and Point, are positions or forms of Shakti. Bindu is her condensed form and nāda is the most expanded form. Modern science has worked on this theory that the Bindu expanded within split second to become nād, the universe based on the ancient-most Indian theory of sphot at the time of creation. Imperceptible or loud, sound is bound to occur whenever there is expansion. Expansion was essential at the time of creation for dimension. Naturally, the Space was created first and with the space Time and Sound was created.

In creation, it is always from Bindu to Brahmānd; from a spot to whole; from a tiny seed to a large tree. The creation is based on the theory of seed. Sound changes into Varnas, Varnas into words, sentences, paragraphs and finally into complete oral and written expression. This is the theory behind single syllable Mantras to complete Suktas; from Varna to Mantra and Mahāmantra. It is known as *Vāgārtha Pratipataye*.

Both Nāda and Bindu are Mātrikā Shakti. Tamoguna, darkness, dominates Bindu, Rajoguna (light) dominates nāda and Sattoguna, neutral power, is the knowledge of its correct use. Hence, Shakti is all: Vidyā, Avidyā, Parā, Aparā, Jagat, Brahman, Jagat Prakāshikā and Vināshikā and Ātma Prakāshikā and Vināshikā.

Through the worship and rhythmical chanting Mantras are activated. This act rejuvenates the *Jeeva-bhuta-avyaya shakti* without which the Mantras won't work:

Mantranā jiva bhutā tu yā smritā shaktiravyayā;
Tayā heenā varārohe nishphalā sharadbhra-vat.

मन्त्रणा जीव भूता तु या स्मृता शक्तिरव्यया ।
तया हीना वरारोहे निष्फला शरदभ्रवत् ॥

This jeeva-bhuta avyaya shakti is in each living creature: either least or immense or in between. Human beings possess it more than other creatures. This power gives life and consciousness. Man has greater power and therefore far superior consciousness and conscience. This power endows us with the ability to distinguish things, events, sounds, qualities. We grasp the meaning and by increasing this power can see behind the appearance. If the process is followed and Mantras or sound is chanted rhythmically, then one can get fully absorbed in the cosmic power or Brahma or Shakti:

Mantro-api-antah-gupta bhāshanātamak parmārsha-satatven;
Manantrān dharmāpar-tattva prāptya-upāyah parameshātmaiva.

मन्त्रोऽप्यन्तः गुप्तभाषणात्मक परमार्शसतत्वेन ।
मननत्राण धर्मापर तत्त्व प्राप्त्य उपाय परमेशात्मैव ॥

The fundamental base of the purposeful use, *kāmya prayoga*, of the Mantras is creative and vocal. To be vocal is essential when one has some purpose behind chanting the Mantras but if it is for attainment of light or union then it should be silently chanted from the navel as far as practicable. In other words, at the primary stage or in the beginning, the Mantras should be chanted loudly or making sound loud enough so that a few could hear or the guru could hear and make amend or pass instructions as and when needed. Vocal chanting will help in concentration, memorizing and in correcting pronunciation particularly the accent.

At later stage, when one is adept enough in the chanting of different Mantras and when most of the Mantras are stored in the memory ready to come to the lips then one can start *Mānsik Pāth*, silent chanting.

Varnas: Syllables

All the Varnas have come from the Shakti peethas, one from each of them and are power, full of energy. They represent vowel or consonantal sound. They possess Nāda Brahma as they are concentrated form of energy and take more power when they form a word. Take for example G as in gagan, gahan, gaman, gaha, grāha, gati, gatimān, etc. As a word, they denote power and activity in the form of Shabda Brahma. When they form a Mantra, they absorb and retain immense power in the form of Nāda Brahma. Naturally, the Mantras are indomitable. When activated correctly, they empower the Sādhak with that immense power and make him indomitable.

All the Varnas from A to Ksha are called Mātrikā or Mātrikā Varnas, which means related to mother. All the Mantras have been created with them and hence, possess the power of the Creator- -Mother. They are all, *shaktimaya*. All the Mantras are 'Shiva Shakti Swaroopa':

> *Sarve varnanātmakā mantrāste cha shaktyātmakāh priye;*
> *Shaktih astur-mātrikā gyeyā sā cha gyeyā shivātmikā.*

सर्वे वर्णनात्मका मन्त्रास्ते च शक्तयात्मका: प्रिये।
शक्ति: अस्तुर्मात्रिका ज्ञेया सा च ज्ञेया शिवात्मका॥

Mantras possess immense power which can't even be imagined. It's strength can't be determined and declared: *Mantrānām –achintya shaktitā*, claims Parashurām Kalpa Shutra. It is clarified thus: *achintyo hi mani-mantra-aushadhi-prabhāva*: the effect of jewel, celestial word and medicine. Brahma has created all with chitti-shakti, the power of the mind and with the Mantras:

vāgeva vishvā bhuvanāni jagye.

वागेव विश्वा भुवनानि जज्ञे ।

Mātrātmaka words are called Shabda Brahma because the whole creation is based on the thirty six elements which are based on the Mātrikā Varnas. The movements, activities and working of the creation are also based on 'word' and hence, the power of word is accepted as the greatest power.

Bhagawān Shiva, out of compassion for the creation; created the Mantras so that all the wishes are fulfilled if they are chanted according to the instructions provided by the scriptures.

In order to know and understand the power of the Varnas and the Mantras constituted from the Varnas one must know what sort of power and other constituent they possess. The following charts will make everything clear:

Varnas in Hindi	Roman equivalent	Description with Hindi Words	Effect
अ	A	*Ashtabhujā; Sweta Vana; Chaturmukha; Kurma-vāhan;*	*Mrityu Beeja*
आ	Ā	*Sweta Varna; Kamalāsan; Pāsha-hasta; Hasti-vāhan*	*Ākarshan*
इ	E	*Peeta Varna; Parashu-dhāri; Kachhap-vāhan*	*Pushti Beeja*
ई	Ee	*Sweta Varna; Mauktika-yukta; Hansa-vāhan*	*Bala Dāyaka*
उ; ऊ	U; U:	*Krishna Varna; Gadādhāri; Kāk-vāhan*	*Uchchātan*
ऋ; ॠ	Rī; Rī	*Rakta Varna; Pāsha-dhāri; Ushtra-vāhan*	*Purush Vasha*
लृ; लॄ	Lrī; Lrīī	*Pushpa Varna; Hār Bhushan; Chakra-wāk-vāhan*	*Loka Vasha*
ए	Ye	*Shyāma Varna; Hār-bhushan; Chakra-wāk Vāhan*	*Rāja Vasha*

ऐ	Ai	*Nav-pushpa Varna; Vajra-dhāri; Dvip-vāhan*	*Pashu Vasha*
ओ	O	*Peeta Varna; Sarva-gata; Vrishabh-vāhan*	*Visha Beeja*
औ	Ou	*Kānchan Varna; Pāsha-dhāri; Vyāghra-vāhan*	*Ganapati*
अं	Ang	*Kumkum Varna; Rakt-bhushan; Ripu-nāshak;*	*Māran Beeja*
अ:	Ah	*Dvibhuja; Khar-vāhan*	*Āsuri Beeja*
क	Ka	*Kumkum Varna; Vajra-dhāri; Gaja-vāhan*	*Handra Beeja*
ख	Kha	*Krishna Varna; Tomar-dhāri; Mesha-vāhan*	*Stambhan*
ग	Ga	*Arun Varna; Ankush-dhāri; Sarpa-vāhan*	*Vashikaran*
घ	Gha	*Krishna Varna; Gadādhāri;*	*Mrityu Nāsha*
ड.	Anga	*Krishna Varna; Kāka-vāhan*	*Brahma Beeja*
च	Cha	*Sweta Varna; Kapadikā-bhushan; Chaturbhuja*	*Mohan Beeja*
छ	Chha	*Sweta Varna; Chatur-bāhu*	*Kshobhan Beeja*
ज; झ	Ja; Jha	*Krishna Varna; Dvi-bhuja; Kāk-vāhan*	*Chandra Beeja*
ञ	Yan	*Dwibhuja; Kroach-vāhan*	*Garuda Beeja*
ट	Ta	*Ujjawal Varna; Dwibhuja; Kāk-vāhan*	*Kuber Beeja*
ठ	Tha	*Sweta Varna; Asgta-bāhu; Kamalāsan*	*Asur Beeja*
ड	Da	*Jwalat Varna; Dasha-vāhu; Vyāghra Vāhan; Vistrit Deha*	*Ashta Beeja*
ढ	Dha	*Kumkum Varna; Chatur-vāhu; Swa-alankrit*	*Tama Beeja*

ण	Ńa	*Peeta Varna; Vhatur-vāhu; Vrisha-āvahan*	*Garuda Beeja*
त	Ta	*Shad-bhuja; Mahisha-vāhan*	*Durgā Beeja*
थ	Tha	*Chatur-vāhu; Singha-vāhan*	*Surya Beeja*
द	Da	*Dvi-bhuja; Kāk-vāhan*	*Jvar Nāsak Beeja*
ध	Dha	*Vinsha-bhuja; Vak-vāhan*	*Varun Beeja*
न	Na	*Sweta Varna; Tryabhuja; Singha Vāhan*	*Vishnu Beeja*
प	Pa	*Aruna Varna; Dvibhuja; Hans Vāhan*	*Brahma Beeja*
फ	Pha	*Trihasta; Trimukha; Vyāghra Vāhan*	*Bhadra Kāli*
ब	Ba	*Chaturbhuja; Visha-yukta*	*Rudra Beeja*
भ	Bha	*Dhumra Varna; Chatur Mukha; Mriga Vāhan*	*Vāyu Beeja*
म	Ma	*Chaturja; Mesha Vāhan*	*Agni Beeja*
य	Ya	*Keshar Varna; Chaturbhuja; Gaja Vāhan*	*Indra Beeja*
र	Ra	*Sweta Varna; Dvibhuja; Nakra Vāhan*	*Varun Beeja*
ल	La	*Dvi Varna; Hema-vat; Kamalāsan;*	*Laxmi Beeja*
व	Va/ Wa	*Krishna Varna; Dvibhuja*	*Surya Beeja*
श	Sha	*Sweta Varna; Dvibhuja; Hans Vāhan*	*Vāni Beeja*
ष	Sha	*Sweta Varna; Tribāhu*	*Ākāsha Beeja*
स	Sa	*Dasha Bāhu; Mani Prabhā*	*Prithvi Beeja*
ह	Ha	*Krishna Varna; Dvibhuja*	*Hansa Beeja*
क्ष	Ksha	*Sweta Varna; Dvibhuja; Hans Vāhan*	*Vidyā Beeja*
ज्ञ	Gya/ Jna	*Krishna Varna; Tribāhu*	*Amrit Beeja*

Varnas, Devatās and their Shakti Counterparts

Varna in Hindi	Varna in Roman	Rudra Rupa	Shakti Rupa	Vishnu Rupa	Vaishanavi Rupa
अ	A	Shri Kantha	Purnodari	Keshava	Kirti
आ	Ā	Anant	Virajā	Nārāyan	Kānti
इ	E	Sukshma	Shāmali	Mādhav	Tushti
ई	Ee	Trimurti	Lolākshi	Govind	Pushti
उ;	U;	Amareshwar	Vartulākshi	Vishnu	Dhriti
ऊ	U:	Ardhish	Deerghaghoshā	Madhusudan	Kshānti
ऋ;	Rĭ;	Bhāva Murti	Sudirghmukhi	Trivikram	Kriyā
ॠ	Rĭĭ	Tithi	Gomukhi	Vāman	Dayā
लृ;	Lrĭ;	Sthānu	Deerghajihvā	Shridhar	Medhā
लृ ॎ	Lrĭĭ	Har	Kundodari	Hrishikesh	Harshā
ए	Ye	Jhintish	Urdhvakeshi	Padma-nābha	Shradhā
ऐ	Ai	Bhautika	Vikritmukhi	Dāmodar	Lajjā
ओ	O	Sadyojāt	Jwālāmukhi	Vāsudeva	Lakshmi
औ	Ou	Anugraheshwar	Ulkāmukhi	Sankarshan	Sarswati
अं	Ang	Akrur	Shri Mukhi	Pradyumna	preeti
अः	Ah	Mahāsen	Vidyāmukhi	Aniruddha	Rati
क	Ka	Krodhish	Saraswati	Chakri	Jayā
ख	Kha	Chandesh	Gauri	Gadi	Durgā
ग	Ga	Panchāntak	Trailkya-vidyā	Shārangi	Prabhā
घ	Gha	Shivottam	Mantra Shakti	Khadagi	Satyā
ङ.	Anga	Ek-rudra	Ātma Shakti	Shankhi	Chandā
च	Cha	Kurma	Bhuta-mātā	Hali	Vāni
छ	Chha	Ek Netra	Lambodari	Mushali	Vilāsini
ज;	Ja;	Chaturānan	Lambodari	Shooli	Virajā
झ	Jha	Ajesh	Drāvini	Pāshi	Vijayā
ञ	Yan	Sharba	Nāgari	Ankushi	Vishwā
ट	Ta	Someshwar	Baikhari	Mukunda	Vittadā
ठ	Tha	Lāngali	Manjari	Nandaj	Sutadā
ड	Da	Dāruka	Rupini	Nandi	Smriti
ढ	Dha	Ardhanārishwar	Virani	Nara	Riddhi
ण	Ńa	Umākānt	Kotari	Narakjita	Samriddhi
त	Ta	Āshādhi	Putanā	Hari	Shuddhi

थ	Tha	Dandi	Bhadrakāli	Krishna	Bhukti
द	Da	Adri	Yogini	Satya	Mukti
ध	Dha	Meena	Shankhini	Sātvat	Mati
न	Na	Mesha	Garjini	Shauri	Kshamā
प	Pa	Lohit	Kāla Rātri	Shura	Ramā
फ	Pha	Shikhi	Kubjini	Janārdan	Umā
ब	Ba	Chhagalanda	Kapardini	Bhudhar	Kledani
भ	Bha	Dvirand	Mahā-vajra	Vishwa-murti	Klinnā
म	Ma	Mahākāla	Jayā	Vaikuntha	Vasudā
य	Ya	Kapāli	Sumukheswari	Purushottam	Vasudhā
र	Ra	Bhjagesha	Revati	Bali	Parā
ल	La	Pināki	Mādhavi	Balānuja	Parāyanā
व	Va/ Wa	Khadgish	Vāruni	Bāla	Sukshamā
श	Sha	Vak	Vāyavi	Vrishaghna	Sandhyā
ष	Sha	Bhrigu	Sahajā	Singh	Prabhā
स	Sa	Shweta	Vidārini	Vrisha	Pragyā
ह	Ha	Nakuli	Lakshmi	Vārāha	Nishā
ल	La	Shiva	Vyāpini	Vimal	Amoghā
क्ष	Ksha	Samvartaka	Māyā	Nrisingh	Vidyutā

Nāda: Sound in Mantra

Mantra or Tantra, it depends finally on the Nād, sound. Earth, Moon and Sun make the three worlds, loka but 'Dyāvāprithvi' denote only the two important loka: Surya Loka and Prithvi Loka. Both have heat and hence are Agnimaya. The Fire of the earth is dominated by Gāyatri and the Fire of the Sun is dominated by Sāvitri. Both are called Vāk or Word or Sound. The earth has Anushtupa Vāk and the Sun has Brihati. The Anushtupa Vāk creates the consonants and consonantal sound while Brihati creates vowel sounds and letters. Vowels are immortal but the consonants are mortal. It is the vowel sound that gives immortality to consonantal sounds by giving them a meaning and meaningful place. It means that in the absence of the Sun, Brihati or Sāvitri the earth, the sound and heat cannot exist.

The vowel form of the Sun is called Veda trayee or Traividyā. The concept is clear. The Disc of the Sun is Rig Veda, the circle of the rays is Sāma Veda, and the heat is Yajur Veda. It is the secret behind the prayer:

Trayi mayāya trigunātmane namah.

त्रयी मयाय त्रिगुणात्मने नमः ।

The Vedas came out of the mouth of Brahman so the Rishis called it Nigam. The knowledge of the earth has come out of the Sun, so it is called Āgam. Both Nigam and Āgam describe the Cosmos, the Universe but with a difference. Nigam treats the Sun at the center of the Cosmos while Āgam treats the earth at the center. The Sun at the center of the Solar system is also the gift of the most ancient thinkers of India. So, the Sun is called the father and the earth is called the mother. Both are essential for life on the earth:

Dyauh pitah prithivi mātah.

द्यौः पिताः पृथ्वी मातः ।

In this way, the concept of Veda Purush and Āgam Vidyā originated. In this way, the Sun is Rudra, Shiva and the earth is Shakti, Prakriti. The whole Universe is in the form of Shiva-Shakti. The Universe and life can't be imagined without Shiva-Shakti: *umāsahitah tattvah.* उमासहितः तत्त्वः ।

It may be known by many names but it is in the whole universe as Soma: *Tvamā tatantoh wā antariksham.* त्वमाततन्तोः वा अन्तरिक्षम् it is the Prakriti or the Purush. Without absorbing Shakti it is impossible to know the Brahma.

As Āgam has come out of Nigam, all the principles of Āgam are based on the principles of Nigam. For the followers of Nigam it is *saisā trayi vidyā* सैषा त्रयी विद्या and for the followers of Āgam it is *vidyāsi sa bhagawati*, विद्यासि सा भगवती and Shakti Tattva is called Mahāvidyā. It is Akshar Brahma that knows all, does all and pervades all: knowing-power is *mana*, doing-power is *prāna* and the power to express is *vāk*. They form the part of five *Koshas*.

Akshar Tattva and Parātpar

The Akshar Brahma neither does nor is attached, and yet is powerful and active. Akshar possesses Sat, Chitta and Ānand. Only akshar is active and hence akshar is also popular as Chetanā or consciousness.

The creation depends on **pratishthā**, insertion, placement, Brahma Tattva, **jyoti**, light, Indra Tattva and **yagya**, anna, feeding, Vishnu, Agni and Soma Tattva: *yagyo wai Vishnu.* The power that takes anna, digests it and converts it into energy is called Vishnu. When active inside the womb Indra is known as Fire, and when active inside the womb Vishnu is Soma. The creation is the combined effort of *nām, rupa* and *karma.*

One dynamic *akshar tattva,* in the form of *gati smuchchya,* Brahma, *Shuddha gati,* Indra, *Shuddha agati,* Vishnu, *sthiti garvitā gati,* Agni and *sthiti garvitā agati,* Soma, becomes Fire. One *akshar* with dynamic connectivity becomes Panchākshar. As words are created with *a, i, u, ri,* and *lri,* five *akshars,* in the same way, meaning is also derived from the same five *akshars.* The sequence of the creation of *akshar* and derivation of meaning are the same. *Shabd,* word and *Artha,* meaning, are deeply related.

The inter-mixing or connectivity of Agni and Soma is called yagya. Yagya should not be translated as 'sacrifice'. The word 'sacrifice' misleads all. Among the Panchākshar Brahma, Vishnu and Indra or Rudra or Shiva are mysteriously hidden inside, and only Agni and Soma constitute the form. So, the manifested world is called *'Agnisomātmakam'*.

With the five akshars five *Vikārs* originate, called *Viswashrishta.* From the vikārs *'pancha jana'* are created. When they are inter-mixed then *'panchikrit prāna'* originate. Then the akshar Brahma enters: *tat srishtvā tadevānu prāvishat.* तत्सृस्ट्वा तदेवानु प्रविशत् They are collectively called *'Shodashi Prajāpati'*.

What is popular in *Mantra Samhitās* as **Kāla**, is called **Parātpar** in the Upanishads. The creatures appear or are born like ripples or bubbles and disappear or re-mingle into water, the source. There is tranquility and it is completely pacified within while there is incessant movement on the surface as currents, ripples and bubbles. Seven Lokas, fourteen Bhuta Sarga and infinite number of cycles have come out of that Shiva-Shakti that creates a central illusory force called 'Māyā'. It has the desire, *'eko aham bahu syām'*. एकोऽहं बहुस्याम्।

From that desire comes out *pancha jana* and *puranjan*. There are two elements called *yat* and *ju*. *Yat* is dynamic and is called Prāna or Vāyu. *Ju* is static and is called Vāk or Ākāsh. With their union or amalgamation *āpah* or water was first created that has two elements called *Bhrigu* and *Angirā*. Modern scientists call it oxygen and hydrogen.

The following charts will make it clear.

The Phases of the Absolute Brahman (Shodashi Prajāpati)

S. N.	Absolute Brahman (1)	Avyaya (5)	Akshar (5)	Ātma Akshar(5)
1.	One	Ānand	Amrit Brahmā	Mrit Brahmā
2.	*Viswāteeta*	Vigyān	Amrit Vishnu	Mrit Vishnu
3.	*Parātpar*	Mana	Amrit Indra	Mrit Indra
4.	(One Absolute	Prāna	Amrit Agni	Mrit Agni
5.	God beyond the universe.)	Vāk	Amrit Soma	Mrit Soma

The Phases of the Creation Vishwam: Universe

S. N.	Viswasrishta	Panchjana	Purnjan	Pura
1.	Shuddha Prāna	Panchikrit Prāna	Veda	Swayambhu
2.	Shuddha Āpa	Panchikrit Āpa	Loka	Parameshthi
3.	Shuddha Vāk	Panchikrit Vāk	Prajā	Surya
4.	Shuddha Annāda	Panchikrit Annāda	Bhuta	Prithivi
5.	Suddha Anna	Panchikrit Anna	Pashu	Chandramā

The knowledge as Shodashi Prajāpati, in the above shown sixteen forms, gets condensed and in the compact form becomes Veda, Brahman and Vidyā like the light that shows three colours: Green, Blue and Red. These three dominate the Universe. Shabda Brahma is Veda Tattva, Vishaya Brahma is Brahma Tattva and Samskār Brahma is Vidyā Tattva. What we learn from words, sentences and books is Veda Tattva, what we learn by seeing with the eyes is Brahma Tattva and what we derive, as a conclusion from our knowledge or Shabda and Vishaya, is Samskār, special and deeper knowledge. All are the same. The difference is shown by the dominance of one or the other. All the knowledge of the world or universe is Mahāvidyā. It is known as Virāt Vidyā in the Nigam and as Mahāvidyā in Āgam.

Vidyā, knowledge, the creation of Varnas and Varnamālā, alphabet has played the greatest role in the development of human civilization. Hence, each Varna was treated as Shakti, power, and they have the power. Each Varna or letter is power. In India, Varnas are treated as sacred and divine.

Reasoning says, the history shows and it is a genuine possibility that ancient Rishis who meditated at different Shakti Peethas came up with the creation of different letters. That letter is associated with that Peetha.

The Forms and Phases of Shakti

It is a wonder that the Rishis knew so much about energy and power and its functioning. Both the broad and subtle divisions give so much insight into the physical, mental, moral, social and personal energy on the one hand and the energy of nature, plants, trees, animals, birds, insects on the other and to balance them all, and to complete the triangle.

They had great knowledge of creative energy, Energy that helps in sustaining life and the destructive energy. Modern scientists are at a loss in deciding about it and are busy spending wealth, time and ability to create destructive energy. Often, it is felt that they are unable to distinguish the creative and essential power from destructive and negative.

Under the circumstances, it is very difficult to stop them, as they have cast a spell on world leaders and rich and influential persons under the garb of different fears. Hence, it is all the more difficult to dissuade men and women from desire, lust and related vices, and to make them change their ways and follow the rule of simple and plain living. It is now almost impossible to save life-saving elements, atmosphere, ecology, life and the earth.

The ancient Rishis knew them with their visionary powers and long and deep study. They saved everything with their character, knowledge, wisdom, controlled use and devotion and by asking people to worship and imbibe all such forms of sacred, essential and eternal energy. It is both interesting and illuminating to try to know what they knew and to understand the subtleties of scientific divisions of Shakti.

There are two forms of Shakti: **Unmani**, Inactive and **Samani**, Active. She is always in two forms. As Unmni or Inactive, She resides in Brahma or Shiva and as Samani, active, she pervades the universe in Kalā or Phases or different forms and sub-forms. At most of the places sixteen Kalā, Phases of Shakti has been mentioned, at some places 17 but the fact is that with Her Kalā, forms and sub-forms Shakti takes numerous forms. When in possession of all the sixteen Kalās, she is called '*Purna Kalā Murti*' when divided or with lesser number of Kalā she is called '*Ansha Kalā Murti*', and the sub-forms are called '*Anshānsh Murti*'. What we term as Kalā is visible only in the illusory creation or the manifest world. What we perceive as power in space or other celestial bodies is the form of Samani Shakti.

The phases of Shakti can be perceived as different activities, *Bibhuti* of Shakti. In that form She separates herself from the Brahma, gets filled up with 'Asmi' and appears as 'Aham'. It is the condensed power of the infinity or Eternal Energy. Such condensation is seen in six forms called: Māyā, Kāla, Niyati, Rāga, Vidyā and Kalā.

10.	Krodha shānti	*Aum shānte prashānte sarva krodho-upashamani swāhā.*	To pacify anger; face should be washed with the *abhimantrit* water with this mantra
11.	Loka Vashikaran	*Aum namah sarva-loka-vashang-kurāya kuru kuru swāhā.*	Bind at the top of arm the root of Punarnavā in Pusha Nakshatra
12.	Agni-stambhan	*Aum namo agni-rupāya mam sharire stambhanam kuru kuru swāhā.*	For safety from fire
13.	Shatru-stambhan	*Aum namah kāla rātri trishul-dhārini mam shatu-sainya-stambhan kuru kuru wāhā.*	To prevent the actions by enemy.
14.	Nidrā-stambhan	*Aum namo bhagawate rudrāya nidrām stambhaya stambhaya thah thah thah.*	To control sleep
15.	Mukti Mantra	*Krishna*	For salvation
16.	Dashākshar Mantra	*Gopi-jana-ballabhāya swāhā.*	To know all worldly affairs.
17.	Ashtādash Mantra	*Kling krishnāya govindāya gopi-jana-ballabhāya swāhā.*	For freedom from *jivan chakra.*
18.	Peeth Mantra	*Aum namo bhagawate sarva-bhuta-ātmane vāsucevāya sarvātma sanyog yoga padma peeth ātmane namah.*	For union with Vāsudeva.
19.	Mantra Rāja	*Aum Shring Hring Kling Krisnāya Swāhā.*	For material wealth and salvation.
20.	Brahma Mantra	*Aum sachidekam Brahma.*	For all the four *purushasārth.*
21.	Ārādhan Mantra	*Aum amg sachidekam Brahma hring sachidekam Brahma shring sachidekam Brahma.*	For truth and knowledge.
22.	Brahma Gāyatri	*Aum parmeshwarāya vid-mahe para-tattvāya dhee-mahi. Tanno Brahma Prachodayāt.*	For inner purification at the time of meditation.

23.	Ādyā Mantra	*Hring hring kring parmeshwari swāhā.*	For wisdom.
24.	Arghya Mantra	*Aum hring hans ghrini surya idam arghyam tubhyam swāhā.*	To strengthen heat.
25.	Kāli Gāyatri Mantra	*Aum Ādāyāyavai vidmahe parmaeshwaryai dhee-mahi. Tannah kāli prachodayāt.*	For getting rid of sins.
26.	Pashu-pāsh Gāyatri	*Aum Pashu-pāshāya vidmahe vishwa karmane dhee-mahi. Tanno jivah prachodayāt.*	For freedom from the eight fetters of life.
27.	Agni Prajjwalan	*Aum chitta-pingal han hand ah dah pach pach sarvagyāā-gyāpaya swāhā.*	For fire and heat energy.

Some important things to know about Mantras

15 Devatās of Mantras

Rudra	*Mangal*	*Garuda*	*Gandharva*	*Yaksha*
Raksha	*Bhujanga*	*Keelar*	*Pishācha*	*Bhuta*
Daitya	*Indra*	*Siddha*	*Vidyādhar*	*Asura*

Number of Varnas	Name of Mantra	Used in
1	Kartari	*Mantrachheda*
2	Suchi	*Bheda*
3	Mudagar	*Bhanjan*
4	Musala	*Shoshan*
5	Krure	*Bandhan*
6	Shrinkhal	*Bandhan*
7	Kukacha	*Chhedan*
8	Shoola	*Ghāta Karma*
9	Vajra	*Stambhan*

10	Shānti	*Bandhan*
11	Parashu	*Vidvesha*
12	Chakra	Every Work/ *Ranjak*
13	Kulisha	*Utsāha*
14	Nārācha	*Sainya Bheda*
15	Bhushundi	*Mārana*
16	Padma	*Shānti Kārya*

Mantra Samskār

Janana, deepanam pashchād bodhanam tādanah-tathā;
Atha-abhisheko vimali-karan-āpyāyane punah;
Jeevan tarpanam guptih-darshatā mantra sanskriyā.

There are ten Mantra Samskāras which are being given below. The following charts will make many things clear.

S. No.	Samskār	Mantra for Samskār as examples	Number of Japa
1.	Janan	Worship Janan Chakra of 49 Trikonas.	
2.	Deepan	*Hansah shivāya namah so-aham.*	1000
3.	Bodhan	*Hung shivāya namah hung*	5000
4.	Tādan	*Phat shivāya namah phat*	1000
5.	Abhishek	*Ron hansah ong*	1000
6.	Vimali-karan	*Aum trong shivāya namah vashat trong Aum.*	1000
7.	Jivan	*Swadhā vashat shivāya namah vashat swadhā.*	1000
8.	Tarpan	Perform tarpan of the mantra with Milk, Ghee, Jala.	100 Tarpans
9.	Gopan	*Hring shivāya namah hring*	1000
10.	Āpyāyan	*Hrong shivāya namah hrong*	1000

Pranava Aum

Along with Aum aing; cling; hring and shring are also used before or after a Mantra.

Grihastha or householders should use Aum before every Mantra; otherwise, the Mantra will not be effective:

Prana-vādyam grihasthānām tat-shunyam nishphalam bhavet;
Āddyāntayoh van-sthānām yatinām mahatām-api.

1. Pranava Aum should not be chanted with

    i.   Vāgbeeja ainga;

    ii. Kāma-beeja cling;

    iii. Shakti-beeja hring; and

    iv. Shri beeja shring.

2. Chant Aum with Vaishanava Mantras;

    i.   Hring with Shiva Mantras;

    ii. Cling with Shakti Mantras;

    iii. Hringa before Surya and other Gods and

    iv. Shri before Shri Ganesh Mantras.

3. In Vashikaran; Ākardhan; Karma and Yagya add Swāhā.

4. In Shānti Mantras to pacify anger, etc. add Namah.

5. In Sammohan; Uddipan; Mrityu Japa, add Vaushat.

6. In separation Māran add Phat.

7. In Graha shānti and vighna-nāsh, to get rid of hurdles add Hung Phat.

8. In Mantra Uddipan and gain and loss, add Vashat.

9. If there is Namah or Swāhā at the end of a Mantra don't add Namah or Swāhā again.

❋❋❋

Mantras for Different Gods and Purpose

The following is yet another collection of classified Mantras which are very popular and commonly chanted in Yagyas and in personal Meditation.

Surya Mantra

Aum ghrinih surya ādityah! ॐ घृणिः सूर्य आदित्यः ।

Vishnu Mantra

Aum namo Nārāyanāya! ॐ नमो नारायणाय ।

Vakratunda Mantra

Shri Vakratundāya hung! श्री वक्रतुण्डाय हुं ।

Shakti Vināyak Mantra

Aum hring gring hring! ॐ ह्रीं ग्रीं ह्रीं ।

Lakshmī Vināyak Mantra

Aum shring gang soumyāya ganapataye;
Var-varada sarva-janam-mey vasham-ānaya swāhā!

ॐ श्रीं गं सौम्याय गणपतये ।
वर-वरद सर्व जन्मे वशं आनय स्वाहा ॥

Trailokya Mahan Ganesh Mantra

Shri Vakratundaik-dranshtrāya cling hring shring gang ganapataye
varvarada sarva-janma-mey vasham-ānaya swāhā!

श्री वक्रतुण्डैकद्रंष्ट्राय क्लीं ह्रीं श्रीं गं गणपतये
वरवरद सर्व जन्म मे वशमानय स्वाहा

Rinhartā Ganesh Mantra

Shree Ganesh rinam chhindhi varenyam hum namah phat!

श्री गणेश ऋणं छिन्दि वरेण्यं हुं नमः फट्।

Siddhi Vināyak Mantra

Shri namo siddhi-vināyakāya sarva-kāryakatre sarva-vighna
prashamanāya sarva-rājya vashya-karanāya sarva-jan
sarva-stri purush-ākarshanāya shring shri swāhā!

श्री नमो सिद्धिविनायकाय सर्व कार्यकर्ते सर्व-विघ्न
प्रशमनाय सर्व-राज्य वश्य करणाय सर्वजन
सर्वस्त्री पुरुष-आकर्षणाय श्रीं श्री स्वाहा।

Ashtākshari Shiva Mantra

Hring Aum Namah Shivāya Hring! ह्रीं ॐ नमः शिवाय ह्रीं।

Rudra Mantra

Aum namo bhagawate rudrāya! ॐ नमो भगवते रुद्राय।

Tvarita Rudra Mantra

Aum yon rudro-agnau yo psuya oshadhi-ashuyo rudro
vishwā-bhuvanā vivesh tasmai rudrāya namoastu.

ॐ यों रुद्रो-अग्नौ यो प्सय ओषधि-अशुओ रुद्रो
विश्वा-भुवना-विवेश तस्मै रुद्राय नमोऽस्तु।

Dvādashākshar Vishnu Mantra

Aum namo bhagavate vāsydevāya! ॐ नमो भगवते वासुदेवाय।

Shri Rāma Mantra

Aum rāng rāmāya namah! ॐ रां रामाय नमः।

Dashākshar Rāma Mantra

Hung jānaki ballabhāya swāhā! हुं जानकी वल्लभाय स्वाहा।

Shri Krishna Mantra

Kling krishnāya govindāya gopijana ballabhāya swāhā!

क्लीं कृष्णाय गोविन्दाय गोपीजन वल्लभाय स्वाहा।

Lakshmi Nārāyana Mantra

Aum hring hring shring shring lakshmi-vāsudevāya namah!

ॐ ह्रीं ह्रीं श्रीं श्रीं लक्ष्मी वासुदेवाय नमः।

Shri Lakshmi Mantra

The above given Mantra is the Lakshmi Nārāyana Mantra but there are many Lakshmi Mantras. '**Shring**' is her beeja mantra. There seems to be two reasons behind the Mantras of the Goddess of wealth and properity: one that people need wealth for themselves, their family and relatives and for others; and the second that Lakshmi never stays at a place for long. General people have to worship Mā Lakshmi to get wealth and riches for posterity. So, for different gains by different sections different Mantras were chanted.

O Mātā Lakshmi Live with us!

At least one story must be cited to open the eyes of all those who wish to be wealthy and prosper with wealth only. It must be kept in mind and the posterity must be taught its significance otherwise, Mahā Lakshmi will desert that family. Once deserted by Lakshmi, it is rather very difficult to get the past possessions easily but if Mātā Lakshmi pleases with anyone from the posterity then it will not take a lot of time and the prosperity and prestige of the family will be back.

Once, there was a rich merchant, named Sheetal Shroff, in the big and prosperous city of Ujjain. He was very kind and compassionate and worshipped Dhana Devi MahāLakshmi, the Goddess of wealth everyday. He would offer prayers to the earth before putting his feet on the floor; remember Jala Devatā, Indra and Varuna before touching water. After having his bath, he would go directly for poojan and perform the poojā for an hour. When it is over, he would distribute prasād to all the persons inside and outside the big house. Only then, he would eat something.

After getting ready, he would pray to Dhana Lakshmi and proceed to the shop. Although, he had a coach and coachman he would go to the shop on foot with the hope to meet many persons on the way; talk to them kindly, and help them as far as practicable because he was very kind and compassionate. He would pray to many gods and bow to all the temples on the way without wasting time. Without fail he would pray to the gods and Lakshmi before opening the shop. He would get the shop cleaned and perform poojā before sitting at his usual place and posture.

After finishing the day, dealing with people honestly, diligently, with sweet tongue and giving something in charity; he would offer prayers and then call it a day; come out of the shop and pray outside too before turning towards his residence. Everything was going on in a healthy and happy way.

One day, when he finished his morning poojan; Sheetal felt increased light and the presence of a person. He looked up and found the Dhana Lakshmi ready to fly off. He saluted her and started a Devi Stuti. When he finished the stuti, Lakshmi said:

'O Bhakt, I'm pleased with you. But I'm leaving you forever.'

Sheetal said with folded hands: "Mātā! Whatever I remember about myself, I'm sure I've done nothing wrong in my life. I have done whatever the Scriptures, Pandits and the Guru say. Yet you are ready to leave me? I can't understand it. Please tell me what is my fault that you are punishing me."

The mother said: 'O Bhakt! There is nothing wrong with you but your family members are doing so many things that I don't like. They are repeatedly doing it and it has become very difficult for me to breathe in such an atmosphere. So, I'm leaving you.'

Again with folded hands Sheetal prayed: 'O Mātā! I think, I must have missed something somewhere. Please give me one day. If I fail to mend the ways and means then you can do whatever you like.'

Mother Lakshmi agreed.

Before going to his work place, he talked to many family members and enquired about so many general things. There was nothing very unusual about it. But Sheetal was thinking and praying to the Gods to give him wisdom to come out of the dense darkness. Throughout the day he kept on gathering information, thinking over them and digesting. Before he was ready to return to his residence, he had come to a conclusion. With determined steps and at ease, he came to the house, stayed outside and asked each member of the household, including the servants, to come out of the house. It was something strange for the family members, servants and passers-by. Many outsiders also stopped to see what was happening.

He had decided to talk with the members of his family. When everyone was there, he addressed them loudly and confidently: 'Mātā Lakshmi has informed me that some among you have ego, lust etc. and are doing something unethical, immoral and irreligious. Now, it is my plain order; I'll not explain it and it will not be changed. So, listen carefully. As a religious man, I know the Gods will not tolerate anything irreligious, immoral, un-ethical. Those who can change themselves, can re-enter the house but those who can't must leave the place for ever and return only when they are able to be pure and lead a pure life. The impurities should be shed now and here or carry it to other place. It is for all who are here. No more words! Decide and follow!'

He was silent. For a few minutes, all expected him to say something more, then slowly a tense silence overpowered them. After looking around, at the faces of each one, his wife smiled, raised her folded hands, murmured something inaudible and turned back. She entered the house.

Then his putra-vadhu (daughter in law) stepped out came to him, touched his feet with a part of sāri and with crossed hands. He blessed her. She went inside. Slowly and slowly all of them followed her. Each one looked determined to lead a pious life. The merchant was happy. He went inside, took bath and straight way went to Poojā-room. He performed the poojan and chanted many Lakshmi Mantras. He looked at the deity. She was smiling. He stood up and found all the others standing silently behind him with folded hands. He picked up the pot of charanāmrit and gave two small spoons to each of them.

The metamosphosis was complete.

Purity in thinking, words and deeds and religiosity are all that count and bless one with health, wealth, prosperity, contentment and happiness.

Chaturākshar Lakshmi Beeja Mantra

Aing shring hring kling! ऐं श्रीं ह्रीं क्लीं ।

Dashākshar Lakshmi Mantra

Aum namah kamal-vāsinyai swāhā! ॐ नमोकमलवासिन्यै स्वाहा ।

Dvādashākshar Lakshmi Mantra

Aing hring shring kling soun jagat-prasutyai namah!

ऐं ह्रीं श्रीं क्लीं सौं जगत्प्रसूत्यै नमः ।

Siddha Lakshmi Mantra

Aum shring hring kling shring siddha-lakshmyai namah!

ॐ श्रीं ह्रीं क्लीं श्रीं सिद्धलक्ष्मयै नमः ।

Mahālakshmi Mantra

Aum shring hring shring kamala kamalālaye prasida prasida;
Shring hring shring Mahālakshmyai namah!

ॐ श्रीं ह्रीं श्रीं कमले कमलालये प्रसीद प्रसीद
श्रीं ह्रीं श्रीं महालक्ष्मयै नमः ।

Jyesthā Lakshmi Mantra

Aing hring shring jyeshthā Lakdhmi swayam-bhuve hring
jyeshthāyai namah!

ऐं ह्रीं श्रीं ज्येष्ठ लक्ष्मी स्वयम्भुवे ही ज्येष्ठायै नमः ।

Vasudhā Lakshmi Mantra

Aum gloung shring annam mahyannam mey dehyanna-
adhipataye mamānnam pradāpaya swāhā shring gloung Aum.

ॐ गलौं श्रीं अन्नं महानं मे देहयानः अधिपतये ममानं
प्रदापय स्वाहा श्री गलौं ॐ ।

Nrisingh Mantra

Aum ugra-veeram mahā-vishnum jvalantam sarvato mukham;
Nrisingh bheeshanam bhadram mrityu mrityum namāmyaham.

ॐ उग्रवीरं महाविष्णुं ज्वलन्तं सर्वतो मुखम्।
नृसिंह भीषणं भद्रं मृत्युमृत्यं नमाम्यहम्॥

Vārāha Mantra

Aum namo bhagawate vārāha rupāya bhur-bhuvah swah
syātpate bhu-patitvam dehyate dadāpaya swāhā!

ॐ नमो भगवते वराह रूपाय भूर्भवः स्वः
स्यात्पते भू पतित्वं देहयते ददापय स्वाहा।

Another Surya Mantra

Aum hring ghrinih surya āditya shring!

ॐ ह्रीं घृणिः सूर्य आदित्य श्रीं।

Shri Hanumān Mantra

Houng hra-srphem hra-sang hra-sra-ruphren
gra-son hanumate namah!

हौं ह स्फें ह स्त्ररूफ्रें ग्रसों हनुमते नमः।

Ashta-dashākshar Shri Hanumān Mantra

Aum namo bhagawate ānjaneyāya mahā-balāya swāhā!

ॐ नमो भगवते आन्जनेयाय महाबलीय स्वाहा।

Dvādashākshar Shri Hanumān Mantra

Hang hanumate rudrātmakāya hung phat!

हं हनुमते रूद्रात्मकाय हूं फट।

Chatur-dashākshar Shri Hanumān Mantra

Aum namo hari markat markatāya swāhā!

ॐ नमो हरि मरकट मरकटाय स्वाहा।

Kāma Deva Mantra

Kling kāmadevāya namah! क्लीं कामदेवाय नमः।

Varun Mantra

Aum dhruvāsutvāsu sannishanam kshiyamtovya
Asmat-pāsham varuno mumochat;
Avo-vanvānā adite rupasyā dyuyampāta Swastibhih sadānah swah!

ॐ धुवासुत्वासु सन्निषणं क्षीयन्तोव्य अस्मत् पाशं वरूणो मुमोचत
अवोवनवाना अदिते रूपस्या द्युयंपात स्वस्तिभिः सदानः स्वः।

Kuber Mantra

Aum Yakshāya kuberāya vaishravanāya dhan-dhānya-ādipataye
Dhan-dhānya samriddhi mey dehi vāpaya swāhā!

ॐ यक्षीय कुबेराय वैश्रवणाय धन धान्यधिपतये।

Shodashākshar Kuber Mantra

Aum shring Aum hring shring hring kling
shring kling vitteshwarāya namah!

ॐ श्रीं ॐ ह्रीं श्रीं ह्रीं क्लीं वित्तेश्वराय नमः।

Chandra Mantra

Aum Saung somāya namah! ह्रीं सों सोमाय नमः।

Mangal Mantra

Aum hāng hansah khang khah! ॐ हां हंसः खं खः।

Brihaspati Mantra

Aum bring brihaspataye namah! ॐ बृं बृहस्पतये नमः।

Shukra Mantra

Aum vastram mey dehi shukrāya swāhā!

ॐ वस्त्रं मे देहि शुक्राय स्वाहा।

Dharmarāja Mantra

Aum kong hring āng vaing vaing vaivasvatāya
dharmarājāya bhakta-anugrah krite namah!

ॐ कां ह्रीं अं वैं वैं वैवस्वताय धर्मराजाय भक्त अनुग्रह कृते नमः ।

Santān Gopāl Mantra

Aum devaki putra govindam vāsudeva jagat-pate;
Dehi mey tanayam Krishna tvām-aham sharanam gatah!

ॐ देवकी पुत्र गोविन्दं वासुदेव जगत्पते।
देहि मे तनयं कृष्ण त्वामहं शरणं गतः ॥

Putra Prāpti Mantra

Aum hwāng hwing hung putram kuru kuru swāhā!

ॐ ह्वां ह्रीं हं पुत्रं कुरु कुरु स्वाहा।

Shani Mantra

Shani is one of the Navagraha, nine planets in Indian astrology. A day, Shanivār, Saturday, is fixed for him. The name Shani comes from his slow movement; *Shanaih Kramati Sah Shani*; as it takes 30 earth years to complete its one revolution round the Sun.

Shani, the elder brother of Yama, the god of death; is the son of Surya Deva and his wife Chhāyā. That gives him another name Chhāyā Putra.

It is said that when Shani opened his eyes as a baby for the very first time, the Sun went into an eclipse. When Pārvati forced him to look at her son Shri Ganesh, Ganesh's head was cut off. When Rāvana called him, he turned towards Lankā and the houses started shaking. Rāvana requested him to go back. Once, when he was passing through Ayodhyā, drought hit the whole country hard. These few examples are enough to show the effect of Shani Drishti which lasts either two and half years or seven and half years.

According to legend, Shani is a devotee of Lord Shiva. According to the *"Navagraha Pidāhara Stotram"* of Brahmānda Purāna, the following stotra relieves the communicant from all the ill effects of Shani:

Nilānjana samābhāsam raviputram yama-agrajama,
chāyāmārtandam sambhutam tam namāmi Shanaishcharam.
Om Shanaischarāya Namah!
Surya Putro Dheergh Deho Vishālākshah Shivapriyah!
Mandacharah Prasannātma Peedam Haratu Mey Shanih!
Konasta Pingalo Prabhoo Krishno Rudro Dantako Yamah!
Sauriah Shanaischaro Mandah Pippalodatah Samstutah!
Yetāni Dashanāmāni Prātah Utthāya Ya Pathet!
Shanaischar Kritā Peedā Na Kadāchit Bhavishyati!

नीलान्जन समाभासं रविपुत्रं यमाग्रजम्।
छायामार्तण्डसम्भूतं तं नमामि शनैश्चरम्॥
ॐ शनैश्चराय नमः।
सूर्यपुत्रो दीर्घदेहो विशालक्षः शिवप्रियः।
मन्दचार प्रसन्नात्मा पीड़ांहरतु मे शनिः।
कोणस्थः पिन्गलो बभ्रुः कृष्णो रौद्रोऽन्तको यमः।
सौरिः शनैश्चर मन्दः पिप्पलादेन संस्तुतः॥
एतानि दशनामानि प्रातरुत्थाय यः पठेत्।
शनैश्चर कृता पीड़ान कदाचित् भवष्यिति॥

A common mantra for drawing the support of Shani Bhagavān is:

Om Sham Shanaischaryai Namah. ॐ शं शनैश्चरयै नमः।

A mantra for propitiating Shanaishchara:

Aum prāng preeng proung sah Shanaye namah.

ॐ प्रां प्रीं प्रौं सः शनये नमः।

Saturn's shloka from Navagraha Sukta, according to Vedic texts:

Om Shanno Devirabhishtāya Āpo Bhavantu Peetaye
Shanyoh-abhi-shravantumah Shanaishcharāya Namah.

ॐ शन्नो देवीरभिष्टय आपो भवन्तु पीतये।
शंयोः अभिश्रवन्तु मः शनैश्चराय नमः॥

❀ ❀ ❀

9

All Gāyatri Mantras

Gāyatri is the greatest Mantra, although it is popular as Chhanda too. The first Gāyatri Mantra is from the Vedas. It is present in all the three Veda Mantra Samhitās called Veda trai.

Aum bhur-bhuvah swah tatsaviturvarenyam bhargo devasya dheemahi. Dhiyo yo nah prachodayāt.

ॐ भूर्भुव: स्व: तत्सवितुर्वरेण्यं
भर्गो देवस्य धीमहि धियो यो न: प्रचोदयात्।

(We meditate on the absolute God who is in all the three worlds: Prithvi Loka; Bhuva Loka and Swaloka, who may guide our mind towards pious deeds.)

(We meditate on that glow of the absolute form of that Savitri Dev, who is worshipped by all; who may lead our mind towards virtuous deeds.)

Gāyatri Mantra composed in the Gāyatri Chhand or metre is the most popular Mantra. Gāyatri means: One that protects him who chants: *Gāyat trāyate.* This eulogy Mantra has so deep and intrinsic relation with Gāyatri Chhand that this Mantra is known as Gāyatri.

This Mantra in Gāyatri Chhand is found in each Mantra Samhitā: Rigveda 4:10:3:62; Yajurveda 3:35; Sāma Veda has its Sāvitri Upanishad; it is in the Surya Upanishad of Atharva Veda. It is the 35 Mantra of Nārāyana Upanishad. The Chhāndogya and Brihadāranyaka Upanishads have vehemently praised the Gāyatri Mantra. Manusmriti 2:81-82 claims that Sāvitri Mantra Gāyatri along with the Vyāhrities, is the most convenient way to reach Brahman. Krishna declares in the Gitā:

Brahatasāma tathā sāmnām Gāyatri Chhanda-sāmaham.

बृहत्साम तथा साम्नां गायत्री छन्दसामहम् ।

Among the Chhandas I'm Gāyatri. Bhavishya Purān claims that Gāyatri cleans all the sins: *Sarve pāpāni nashyanti Gāyatri japato nripa.* सर्वे पापानि नश्यन्ति गायत्री जपतो नृप: ।

As in other Mantras so also in the beginning of Gāyatri Mantra, Brahma-vāchak Aum is chanted. Aum stands for the absolute God. Aum is called Pranava which is another word for Brahma. In the Brihad Nāradeeya Upanishad A U M stands for Brahmā, Vishnu and Shiva. The Gītā says that AUM is One Word Brahma: *Omityekāksharam Brahma.* ॐ इत्येकाक्षरं ब्रह्म ।

Aum is followed by three Mahā Vyāhriti: Bhuh Bhuvah and Swah. These are the beeja, seeds of Gāyatri. The Mantra must always be chanted along with these four: Aum Bhuh Bhuvah Swah.

Gāyatri Rahasya makes it clear that Gāyatri is Saraswati:

Gāyatrayāh Sāvitri abhavat. गायत्र्या: सावित्री अभवत् ।

Gāyatri is Sāvitri.

Sāvitryah Saraswati abhavat. सावित्र्या: सरस्वती अभवत् ।

Sāvitri is Saraswati.

Saraswatyāh sarve Vedāh abhavan. सरस्वत्या: सर्वे वेदा: अभवन् ।

Saraswati is all the Vedas.

Sarvebhyoh vedebhyah sarve lokāh abhavan.

सर्वेभ्यो: वेदेभ्य: सर्वे लोका: अभवन् ।

All the Vedas contain all the worlds.

Sarvebhyo lokebhyah sarve prānino abhavan.

सर्वेभ्यो: लोकेभ्य: सर्वे प्राणिनो अभवन् ।

All the worlds contain all the beings.

Savitā is the Devatā of Gāyatri Mantra so it is also called Sāvitri. Vishwāmitra is generally accepted as the Rishi of Gāyatri Mantra but in fact all the 24 Varnas of Gāyatri were envisioned separately by 24 Rishis. Each one is the Rishi of one Varna. Āngirasa Vishwāmitra is the Rishi of the 24th Varna so, he is mentioned as the Rishi of Gāyatri Mantra. The following are the 24 Rishis given in the sequence of the Varnas they envisioned:

1.	Vasishta Rishi	2.	Bhāradwāj Rishi
3.	Maharishi Garga	4.	Rishi Upamanyu
5.	Bhrigu Rishi	6.	Shāndilya Rishi
7.	Lohit Rishi	8.	Maharishi Vishnu
9.	Maharishi Shatātap	10.	Sanat Kumār
11.	Veda Vyās	12.	Shukadeva
13.	Parāshar	14.	Pondra Karma
15.	Kratu	16.	Yaksha
17.	Maharishi Kashyap	18.	Maharishi Atri
19.	Agastya	20.	Udālak
21.	Āngirasa	22.	Nāmaketu
23.	Mudagal	24.	Vishwamitra

Maharishi Vālmiki completed his epic Rāmāyana in 24,000 Shlokas. The first Varna of each 1,000 Shlokas is a Varna of Gāyatri Mantra in sequence. The last Varna completes the Gāyatri Mantra.

Whatever is good, divine, sublime, pure and respectable, is Gāyatri and the essence of the Vedas. The greatness of this Mantra has been accepted by Shruti, Smriti and Purānas. It is said that Gāyatri is the mother of the Vedas; she is one who destroys the sins; there is nothing else that can purify so much and so many as Gāyatri can:

> *Gāyatri veda-janani gāyatri pāpa nāshini;*
> *Gāyatryā paramam nāsti divi cheha cha pāvanam.*

गायत्री वेद-जननी गायत्री पापनाशिनी ।
गायत्रया: परमं नास्ति दिवि चेह च पावनम् ॥

As Saraswati Gāyatri is jagan-mayi. She pervades the whole of the Universe. She possesses all the three gunas. The outer world is her immense form. As Saraswati she possesses the traya-shakti. So she is Brāhmni, Vaishnavi and Rudrāni. She is both the *karma kānda* and *gyān kānda*. She is Shri Tripur Sundari of Tantra Shāstra.

The Gāyatri mantra; for that matter all the Mantras, should be chanted in solitude and at a serene place with determination, dedication, concentration and devotion. Any of the three Japas: Mānasika; Upānshu or Vāchika is allowed. But the best one is Mānasika Japa. One must keep the meaning in mind while chanting the Mantra.

This Mantra is so popular that the Stuti of many Gods have been composed on its pattern and in the Gāyatri Chhand. All such Mantras are being given below:

1.   **Gāyatri Mantra**

Aum bhur-bhuvah swah tatsaviturvarenyam
bhargo-devasya dhimahi. Dhiyo yo nah prachodayāt.

ॐ भूर्भुवः स्वः तत्सवितुर्वरेण्यं भर्गो
देवस्य धीमहि । धियो यो नः प्रचोदयात् ॥

2.   **Hans Gāyatri Mantra**

Aum param-hansāya vid-mahe mahā-tattvāya dhimahi.
Tanno hansah prachodayāt.

ॐ परमहंसाय विद्महे महातत्त्वाय धीमहि । तन्नो हंसः प्रचोदयात्।

3.   **Brahma Gāyatri Mantra**

Aum vedātmane cha vid-mahe hiranya-garbhāya dhimahi.
Tanno brahmā prachodayāt.

ॐ वेदात्मने च विद्महे हिरण्यगर्भाय धीमहि । तन्नो ब्रह्मा प्रचोदयात्।

4.   **Saraswati Gāyatri Mantra**

Aum aing vāga-devyai cha vidmahe kāmarājāya dhimahi.
Tanno devi prachodayāt.

ॐ ऐं वागदेव्यै च विद्महे कामराजाय धीमहि तन्नो देवी प्रचोदयात्।

5. Vishnu Gāyatri Mantra

Aum dhri vishnave cha vid-mahe vāsudevāya dhi-mahi.
Tanno vishnu prachodayāt.

ॐ ध्री विष्णवे च विद्महे वासुदेवाय धीमहि । तन्नो विष्णुः प्रचोदयात् ।

6. Tralokya Mahan Gāyatri Mantra

Aum trailokya mohanāya vid-mahe ātmārāmāya dhi-mahi.
Tanno Vishnu prachodayāt.

ॐ त्रैलोक्य मोहनाय विद्महे आत्मारामाय धीमहि । तन्नो प्रचोदयात् ।

7. Lakshmi Gāyatri Mantra

Aum mahā-devai cha vid-mahe Vishnu-patnyai cha dhi-mahi.
Tanno lakshmi prachodayat.

ॐ महादेव्यै च विद्महे विष्णु पत्नयै च धीमहि । तन्नो लक्ष्मी प्रचोदयात्।

8. Nārāyan Gāyatri Mantra

Aum nārāyanah vid-mahe vāsudevāya dhi-mahi.
Tanno nārāyanah prachodayāt.

ॐ नारायणाय विद्महे वासुदेवाय धीमहि । तन्नो नारायणाय प्रचोदयात् ।

9. Rām Gāyatri Mantra

Aum dāsharathaye vid-mahe sitā-ballabhāya dhimahi.
Tanno rāmah prachodayāt.

ॐ दशरथये विद्महे सीतावल्लभाय धीमहि । तन्नो रामः प्रचोदयात् ।

10. Jānaki Gāyatri Mantra

Aum janak-jāyau vid-mahe rāma-proyiāyai dhi-mahi.
Tanno sitā prachodayāt.

ॐ जनकजायै विद्महे रामप्रयोजायै धीमहि । तन्नो सीता प्रचोदयात् ।

11. Lakshman Gāyatri Mantra

Aum dāsharathaye vid-mahe albelāya dhi-mahi.
Tanno lakshaman prachodayāt.

ॐ दशरथये विद्महे अलबलाय धीमहि। तन्नो लक्ष्मणः प्रचोदयात्।

12. Hanumān Gāyatri Mantra

Aum anjani-jāya vid-mahe vāyu-putrāya dhimahi.
Tanno hanumān prachodayāt.

ॐ अन्जनीजाय विद्महे वायुपुत्राय धीमहि। तन्नो हनुमान् प्रचोदयात्।

13. Garuda Gāyatri Mantra

Aum tatpurushāya vid-mahe suvarna-varnāya dhimahi.
Tanno garudah prachodayāt.

ॐ तत्पुरुषाय विद्महे सुवर्ण वर्णाय धीमहि। तन्नो गरुण: प्रचोदयात्।

14. Krishna Gāyatri Mantra

Aum devaki-nandanāya vid-mahe vāsudevāya dhimahi.
Tanno krishnah prachodayāt.

ॐ देवकीनन्दनाय विद्महे वासुदेवाय धीमहि। तन्नो कृष्ण: प्रचोदयात्।

15. Gopāl Gāyatri Mantra

Aum gopālāya vidmahe gopijana-ballabhāya dhimahi.
Tanno gopālah prachodayāt.

ॐ गोपालाय विद्महे गोपीजन-वल्लभाय धीमहि। तन्नो गोपाल: प्रचोदयात्।

16. Rādhikā Gāyatri Mantra

Aum vrish-bhānu-jayai vidmahe Krishna-priyāyai dhimahi.
Tanno prachodayāt.

ॐ वृषभानुजायै विद्महे कृष्णप्रियाय धीमहि। तन्नो प्रचोदयात्।

17. Parashurām Gāyatri Mantra

Aum jāmadagnyāya vid-mahe mahā-virāya dhimahi.
Tanno parashurāmah prachodayāt.

ॐ जमदग्न्याय विद्महे महावीराय धीमहि। तन्नो परशुराम: प्रचोदयात्।

18. Nrisingh Gāyatri Mantra

Aum ugra-nrisinghāya vidmahe vajra-nakhāya dhimahi.
Tanno nrisinghah prachodayāt.

ॐ उग्रनृसिंहाय विद्महे वज्रनखाया धीमहि। तन्नो नृसिंह: प्रचोदयात्।

19. **Shiva Gāyatri Mantra**

> *Aum mahādevāya vid-mahe rudra-murtaye dhimahi.*
> *Tanno shivah prachodayāt.*

ॐ महादेवाय विद्महे रूद्रमूर्तये धीमहि। तन्नो शिवाः प्रचोदयात्।

20. **Rudra Gāyatri Mantra**

> *Aum tatpurushāya vid-mahe mahādevāya dhimahi.*
> *Tanno rudrah prachodayāt.*

ॐ तत्पुरुषाय विद्महे महादेवाय धीमहि। तन्नो रूद्राय प्रचोदयात्।

21. **Gauri Gāyatri Mantra**

> *Aum subhagāi cha vid-mahe kāmalāyai dhimahi.*
> *Tanno gauri prachodayāt.*

ॐ शुभगायै च विद्महे कमलायै धीमहि। तन्नो गौरी प्रचोदयात्।

22. **Ganesh Gāyatri Mantra**

> *Shri tatpurushāya vid-mahe vakra tundāya dhimahi.*
> *Tanno danti prachodayāt.*

श्री तत्पुरुषाय विद्महे वक्रतुण्डाय धीमहि। तन्नो दन्ती प्रचोदयात्।

23. **Shanmukha Gāyatri Mantra**

> *Aum tatpurushāya vid-mahe mahā-senāya dhimahi.*
> *Tanno shanmukhah prachodayāt.*

ॐ तत्पुरुषाय विद्महे महासेनाय धीमहि। तन्नो सन्मुखः प्रचोदयात्।

24. **Nandi Gāyatri Mantra**

> *Aum tatpurushāya vid-mahe vakra-tundāya dhimahi.*
> *Tanno nandi prachodayāt.*

ॐ तत्पुरुषाय विद्महे वक्रतुण्डाय धीमहि। तन्नो नन्दी प्रचोदयात्।

25. **Surya Gāyatri Mantra**

> *Aum bhāskarāya vid-mahe mahā-tejāya dhimahi.*
> *Tanno suryah prachodayāt.*

ॐ भाष्कराय विद्महे महातेजाय धीमहि। तन्नो सूर्यः प्रचोदयात्।

26. Chandra Gāyatri Mantra

Aum ksheer-putrāya vid-mahe amrit-tattvāya dhimahi.
Tanno chandrah prachodayāt.

ॐ क्षीरपुत्राय विद्महे अमृततत्वाय धीमहि। तन्नो चन्द्रः प्रचोदयात्।

27. Bhauma Gāyatri Mantra

Aum angārkāya vid-mahe shaktih hastāt dhimahi.
Tanno bhaumah prachodayāt.

ॐ अंगारकाय विद्महे शक्तिः हस्तात् धीमहि। तन्नो भौमः प्रचोदयात्।

28. Prithivi Gāyatri Mantra

Aum prithivi devyai cha vid-mahe sahasra-murtyai cha dhimahi.
Tanno mahi prachodayāt.

ॐ पृथ्वी दैव्यै च विद्महे सहस्र मूर्त्यैं धीमहि। तन्नो मही प्रचोदयात्।

29. Agni Gāyatri Mantra

Aum mahā-jwālāya vid-mahe agni madhnyāya dhimahi.
Tanno agnih prachodayāt.

ॐ महाज्वालाय विद्महे अग्नि मध्याय धीमहि। तन्नो अग्निः प्रचोदयात्।

30. Jala Gāyatri Mantra

Aum jala-bimbāya vid-mahe neela-purushāya dhimahi.
Tanno ambu prachodayāt.

ॐ जल बिम्बाय विद्महे नीलपुरुषाय धीमहि। तन्नो अम्बु प्रचोदयात्।

31. Ākāsha Gāyatri Mantra

Aum ākāshāya cha vid-mahe nabho devāya dhimahi.
Tanno gagnam prachodayāt.

ॐ आकाशाय च विद्महे नभोदेवाय धीमहि। तन्नो गगनं प्रचोदयात्।

32. Vāyu Gāyatri Mantra

Aum pavan purushāya vid-mahe sahasra murtyai cha dhimahi.
Tanno vāyuh prachodayāt.

ॐ पवन पुरुषाय विद्महे सहस्र मूर्तयै च धीमहि। तन्नो वायुः प्रचोदयात्।

33. **Indra Gāyatri Mantra**

Aum tatpurushāya vid-mahe sahasra-ākshāya dhimahi.
Tanno indrah prachodayāt.

ॐ तत्पुरुषाय विद्महे सहस्र अकाशाय धीमहि। तन्नो इन्द्रः प्रचोदयात्।

34. **Kāma Gāyatri Mantra**

Aum manmatheshāya vid-mahe kāma-devāya dhimahi.
Tanno ananga prachodayāt.

ॐ मन्मथेशाय विद्महे काम देवाय धीमहि। तन्नो अनंग प्रचोदयात्।

35. **Guru Gāyatri Mantra**

Aum guru devāya vid-mahe para brahmāya dhimahi.
Tanno guruh prachodayāt.

ॐ गुरुदेवाय विद्महे परब्रह्माय धीमहि। तन्नो गुरुः प्रचोदयात्।

36. **Tulasi Gāyatri Mantra**

Aum tripurāya vid-mahe tulasi-patrāya dhimahi.
Tanno tulasi prachodayāt.

ॐ त्रिपुराय विद्महे तुलसीपत्राय धीमहि। तन्नो तुलसी प्रचोदयात्।

37. **Devi Gāyatri Mantra**

Aum devyai brahmānyai vid-mahe mahā-shaktyai cha dhimahi.
Tanno devi prachodayāt.

ॐ देव्यै ब्रह्माण्यै विद्महे महाशक्त्यै धीमहि। तन्नो देवी प्रचोदयात्।

38. **Shakti Gāyatri Mantra**

Aum sarva sammohinyai vid-mahe vishwa-janayai dhimahi.
Tanno shakti prachodayāt.

ॐ सर्वसमोहिन्यै विद्महे विश्वजनन्यै धीमहि। तन्नो शक्ति प्रचोदयात्।

39. **Annapurnā Gāyatri Mantra**

Aum bhagawatyai cha vid-mahe māheshwaryai cha dhimahi.
Tanno annapurnā prachodayāt.

ॐ भगवतै च विद्महे माहेश्वरायै च धीमहि। तन्नो अन्नपूर्णा प्रचोदयात्।

40. Kāli Gāyatri Mantra

Aum kālikāye cha vid-mahe shmashān-vāsinyai dhimahi.
Tanno aghorā prachodayāt.

ॐ कालिकाये च विद्महे श्मशानवासिन्यै धीमहि। तन्नो अघोरा प्रचोदयात्।

41. Tārā Gāyatri Mantra

Aum tārāyai cha vid-mahe mahogrāyai cha dhimahi.
Tanno devi prachodayāt.

ॐ तारायै च विद्महे महोग्रायै च धीमहि। तन्नो देवी प्रचोदयात्।

42. Tripur Sundari Gāyatri Mantra

Aum tripura devyai vidmahe kling kāmeshwarāi dhimahi.
Saustannah klinnai prachodayāt.

ॐ त्रिपुर दैव्यै विद्महे क्लीं कामेश्वरायै धीमहि। सौसतनः
क्लिन्नै प्रचोदयात्।

43. Bhuvaneshwari Gāyatri Mantra

Aum nārānyai cha vid-mahe bhuvanesharyai dhimahi.
Tanno devi prachodayāt.

ॐ नारायण्यै च विद्महे भुवनेश्वरयै धीमहि। तन्नो देवी प्रचोदयात्।

44. Bhairavi Gāyatri Mantra

Aum tripurāyai cha vid-mahe bhairavāyai cha dhimahi.
Tanno devi prachodayāt.

ॐ त्रिपुरायै च विद्महे भैरवायै च धीमहि। तन्नो देवी प्रचोदयात्।

45. Chhinnamastā Gāyatri Mantra

Aum vairochanyai cha vid-mahe chhinnamastāyai dhimahi.
Tanno devi prachodayāt.

ॐ वैरोचन्यै च विद्महे छिन्नमस्तायै धीमहि। तन्नो देवी प्रचोदयात्।

46. Dhoomāwati Gāyatri Mantra

Aum dhoomāvatyai cha vid-mahe sanhārinyai cha dhimahi.
Tanno dhoomā prachodayāt.

ॐ धूमावत्यै च विद्महे सन्हारिन्यै च धीमहि। तन्नो धूमा प्रचोदयात्।

47. Baglāmukhi Gāyatri Mantra

Aum bagalā-mukhyai cha vid-mahe stambhinyai cha dhimahi.
Tanno devi prachodayāt.

ॐ बगलामुख्यै च विद्महे स्तभिन्यै च धीमहि तन्नो देवी प्रचोदयात्।

48. Mātangi Gāyatri Mantra

Aum mātangyai cha vid-mahe uchhista-chāndālyai cha dhimahi.
Tanno devi prachodayāt.

ॐ मातंग्यै च विद्महे उच्छिष्टचाण्डाल्यै च धीमहि। तन्नो देवी
प्रचोदयात्।

49. Mahishasur Mardini Gāyatri Mantra

Aum mahisha-mardinyai cha vid-mahe durgāyai cha dhimahi.
Tanno devi prachodayāt.

ॐ महिषासुर मर्दिन्यै च विद्महे दुर्गायै च धीमहि। तन्नो देवी
प्रचोदयात्।

50. Tvaritā Gāyatri Mantra

Aum tavaritā devyai cha vid-mahe mahā-nityāyai dhimahi.
Tanno devi prachodayāt.

ॐ त्वरिता दैव्यै च विद्महे महानित्यायै धीमहि। तन्नो देवी प्रचोदयात्।

✿ ✿ ✿

10

Chanting and Repetition of Mantras

Japa Mālā and Mantra Jāp

Mantra Jāpa is done on a Japa Mālā or rosary. It has 108 beads and a Meru/Sumeru which is escaped and not counted. There are three types of Japa Mālā: Kar Mālā; Varna Mālā and Mani Mālā. The Japa that is done and counted on fingers are called Kar Mālā. In it, the Japa is counted either on the fingers or on the phalanage of the fingers. When the Japa is counted with Varnas, it is called Varna Mālā. Mani Mālā are special Mālā, painstakingly prepared out of Rudrāksha; Tulasi; Shankha; Padma Beej; Jiva-putrak; Moti; Sphatika; Mani; Ratna; Swarna; Mungā; Chāndi; Chandan; roots of Kusha. Equal beads of only one type are used.

Counting Japa

On the phalanage the counting starts from (1) the 2nd phalanage of ring finger (2) to first of ring finger; then (3) 1st, (4) 2nd and (5) 3rd of little finger; then (6) the third of ring finger; (7) 3rd of middle finger; (8) 3rd (9) 2nd, and finally (10) the 1st of index finger. The total comes to ten. Two phalanage of the middle finger are left for the *Sumeru*. The hand is kept at the height of heart. Japa mālā is covered with a cloth, which is called *gomukhi*. In this way, by rotating one bead at a time 108 mantras are counted. When the worshipper reaches the Sumeru (which is not counted) the Japa Mālā is reversed.

Varna Japa Mālā

Starting with 'a' and bind, i.e., '*ang*' chant the Mantra with each *Varna* (16 of *Avarga*; 25 i.e five each of *Kavarga, Chavarga, Tavarga, Tavarga* and *Pavarga*; 8 of *Yavarga* and *La* again), which comes to 50. Then reverse the order and starting from *La* return back to the first '*ang*'. This will add up to hundred. Then add eight of Shakār (the first letter of each *varna*: *ang; kang; chang; tang; tang; pang; yang* and *shang*). 108 of one rosary is complete. '*Ksha*' is treated as *Sumeru/Meru* and hence, it is not counted. These *Akshars* are treated as Akshar Brahman and the beads of rosary. They are embedded with *Kundalini* from *Mulādhār* to *Āgyā Chakra*. The worshipper has to ascend up through and descend down (*āroha* and *awaroha*). Such *japa* gives immediate results.

Mālā or Rosary and Mantra Counting

In *Baikhari* and *Upānshu* chanting or recitation, counting of the Mantras is needed, at least in the beginning and definitely during Mantra *Anushthān* but when a person identifies with the Mantra such outer aides are not required, at least not in the *mānasika japa*. Then onwards, Mantra recitation becomes a part of daily life, a second nature and the Sādhak recites the Mantras regularly without counting or even without being conscious of the fact that he is chanting the Mantras. They are a part and parcel of living, utterances and thinking. Then on, a rosary is not required. The seeker has transcended such needs. Some practice it without knowing the theory or result of it. They are the best seekers.

Eventually, the identification with the mantra dimnishes and then erases the need of rosary or counting as the practitioner enters a state of divine bliss in which he has forgotten the need of physical aides to perform spiritual deeds. He/She chants the Mantras unknowingly, without being conscious of the chanting. Such a seeker has already been over powered by divine bliss that he/she enjoys.

Scientific Meaning

1. The number of chanting of repetition of Mantras is the rotation of the Yantra, machines.

2. Sphatik is the quartz and chips.

3. The Diagrams on Mantras are the wire connections.

4. Three Nādis are the flow of power: positive, negative and neutral.

5. Mantra anushthān is the act of activating a machine.

Mantra Anushthān

Mantra means 'secret suggestion', *gupta mantranā*. When mantra is obtained from a Guru after formally performing the rituals and then it is again purified and absorbed. It is believed that only then the Mantra shows all its effect: the worldly and spiritual. This complete process is known as *mantra anusthān*. Faith, devotion and performance of the prescribed rituals are its requirements. During that long period of *Mantra-Jāpa-Anushthān* austerity has to be maintained and the following twelve rules are to be followed:

Bhumi-shayan	*Brahmacharya*
Maun	*Guru Sevan*
Trikāl Snān	*Pāpa-karma-parityāg*
Nitya Poojā	*Nitya Dān*
Stuti-Kirtan	*Naimitika Poojā*
Ishtadeva āsthā	*Japa-nishthā*

Types of Anushthāns

There are three types of japa performed as a part of *Mantra Anusthān*. There are *Vāchika Japa; Upānshu Japa* and *Mānas Japa*. During the Japa one must concentrate on and think of only the *Ishta Devatā*, the presiding duty. Usually, one thousand Japas are chanted every day for a month for *Siddhi*. Three *Prānāyāms* are done each before and after the *Japa*. *Japa, Hoam, Tarpan, Abhisheka* and *Brāhman Bhojan* are done every day. At the end of a month or the *anushthān* studying Brāhmans are given *bhoja* or meal.

1. ***Vāchika Japa:*** *Vāchika Japa* is repeated recitation or chanting of Mantra making audible sound that can be heard by many.

2. ***Upānshu Japa:*** *Upānshu Japa* is repeated recitation or chanting of Mantra without making loud sound but the lips and tongue can move and there is audible sound only for the self.

3. ***Mānas Japa:*** *Mānas Japa* is repeated recitation or chanting of Mantra without making audible sound.

Things Needed for Mantra Anushthān

Many things are needed for *Mantra Anushthān*. First, a guru is needed; in the absence of a guru a learned Brahmin can do it; or **the duties or tasks of a guru can be done by the wife of the person performing that *Anushthān*, provided that she has a son**. It must be a pious place: *Siddha Peetha*; pilgrimage; bank of a river; cave; mountain peak; religious place; *Sangam*; forest; garden; *Bilva Briksha* (a tree of stone apples); the foot of a hill; *Goshālā; Devālaya*; banyan tree; in water or near *Kula Devatā*; any place where a person feels fresh and apparently there is nothing to disturb him. Fresh, pure and healthy food is also required to complete the agreed number of *Mantra Jāpa* during a fixed period.

Benefits from Mantra Anushthān

Bhagwān Shiva has said in the *Kulārnava Tantra* that there is no sense in performing *Mantra Siddhi* if one's mind is somewhere else, the Gods at another place Shakti at a different place and Prān at yet another place. All the four should be brought at one place. Only then utmost attention and concentration could be achieved and the *Mantra Siddhi* will be fruitful.

As far as the benefits and fruits are concerned, all other yagyas are not even 16 percent of the *Vāchika Japa; Upānshu Japa* is a hundred times more fruitful than *Vāchika Japa* ; and *Mānas Japa* is one thousand times more fruitful than *Vāchika Japa*.

Cleaning and Starting Anushthān

The seeker must rise in Brāhma Muhurta, around 4.30 in the morning. After getting fresh and finishing bath, he should enter the worshipping room or place. He should salute the deity/deities present there; bow to them and perform *manglā ārti*; offer water for brushing and washing mouth. Only then can he sit. Then he must remember and mentally salute the Guru— Brahma, Trideva, and Trishakti; salute them and feel that he is their creation and is like them with: *Aham Brahāsmi*! This is not to demonstrate one's ego but to absorb their celestial power.

Sacred Ash

Anointing with the sacred ash taken from *hawan-kunda* or *hawan agni* is not as easy as it appears. One must recite the following mantra before anointing one's body with the sacred ash:

> *Agnih iti bhasma vāyu iti bhasma jalam iti bhasma sthal iti bhasma vyom iti bhasma sarva ha vā idam bhasmam yetāni chakshushi tasmād vratam yetat pāshupatam yad bhasma angāni sansprishet.*

Then take the Bhasma and chant Mahāmritunjaya Mantra:

> *Aum hong Aum jung sah Aum bhurbhuvah swah trayambakam yajā-mahe sugandhim pushti vardhanam; Urvā-rukmiva bandhanān mrityore-mukshiya mā mritāt. Aum bhurbhuah swarong jung sah houng Aum.*

ॐ हौं ॐ जूं स: ॐ भूर्भुव: स्व:
त्र्यम्बकं यजामहे सुगन्धिं पुष्टिवर्द्धनम् ।
ऊर्वारूकमिव बन्धान-मृत्योर्मुक्षीय मामृतात्
ॐ भूर्भुव: स्वरों जूं स: हौं ॐ ॥

Then with the following Mantras anoint the part of body mentioned against it.

Head: *Aum tatpurushāya namah!* ॐ तत्पुरुषाय नमः।
Right shoulder: *Aum aghorāya namah!* ॐ अघोराय नमः।
Left shoulder: *Aum 'sadyojātāya namah!* ॐ सद्योजाताय नमः।
Abdomen: *Aum vāma devāya namah!* ॐ वामदेवाय नमः।
Chest: *Aum Ishānāya namah!* ॐ ईशानाय नमः।
Then Vedic Sandhyā and Mantra Sandhyā both are performed.

The original Mantra that one has selected for repetition should be chanted once and a bit of water should be taken thrice as *āchaman*; then chant that Mantra seven times and cleanse the body. Then give *arghya* to Surya with the following Mantra after chanting the original Mantra:

Aum ravi mandal sandhyā devāya arghyam kalpayāmi!

ॐ रवि मंडल संध्या देवाय अर्घ्यं कल्पयामि।

Antar Poojan Vidhi

Chant the original Mantra 108 times and offer water 28 times during that period. Then salute the Teerthas; Lokapālas and own deity God, Ishtadeva. Return to the prayer-place, wash the feet, sip *āchaman*, then take the seat either in Swastiksan; Padmāsan or Veerāsan. Then chant the 12 lettered mantra for safety: *Aum namah sudarshanāya astrāya phat!*

After that perform Bhuta shuddhi; Prāna Pratishthā; Matrikā Nyās and other Nyāsas; mānas poojan; vāhya poojan. After doing all these, the seeker can start chanting the Mantra and perform poojan when the determinent number of chanting is over. At the end, one can leave the seat with salutations.

Vāhya Poojan Vidhi

Although the saints, sanyāsi and brahmachāris can do only antar yāga, the grihsthās have the right to perform, both anter and vāhya yāga. In the antar yāga, heart is the vedikā where the worshipping is done, flowers and other things along with the japa are offered; and the inner amrit is poured.

The seeker should worship the guru in the left and Shri Ganesh in the right. On the Yantras prepared with sandal powder, the devatās should be worshipped in all the eight directions and Peeth Shaktis at the centre.

From one inch to eighteen inches idols can be worshipped at home. Shāligrām; Jewel-idols; Yantras; and gold-idols must be worshipped everyday. Burnt; broken; imbalanced; unshapely idols should not be worshipped.

Āvāhan can be performed in worshipping at home including the Shiva Linga but āvāhan or visarjan is strictly prohibited of Shāligrām and fixed idols. In āvāhan chant the following Shiva Mantra:

> *Ātma sansthātmaj shuddham-tvām-aham;*
> *Aranyam-eva havyānsham murta-āvāvāgyāpya-aham.*

आत्म संस्थात्मज शुद्धंत्वामहम् अरण्यमेव हव्यांशं मूर्त अवावाज्ञाप्यहम्।

Panchāyatan Sthān Kram Yantra

In Panchāyatan, the following gods are worshipped in that sequence. The Panchāyatan Sthān Kram Yantra will make everything clear:

The following things are performed in that sequence:

Āvāhan Mudrā	Sthāpani Mudrā
Āsan dān abd upa-veshan	Sannidhān
Sammukhikaran	Sakalikaran
Abagunthan	Amritikaran and paramikaran
Pādya samarpan	Āchaman
Arhjya dān	Madhupark dān
Punah āchaman	Snān
Abhishek	Vastra dān
Upavit and ābhushan dān	Gandh dān
Pushp samarpan	Dhoop dān
Naivedya samarpan	Ārati and tāmbul
Stuti	Pradakshinā

गणेश रवि विष्णु शिव शक्ति	शिव रवि गणेश विष्णु शक्ति	गणेश विष्णु रवि शिव शक्ति	शिव गणेश शक्ति विष्णु रवि	रवि गणेश शिव विष्णु शक्ति

चित्र क: पंचायत स्थान क्रम यन्त्र

Mantra Shodhan: Mantra Siddhi

For the selection of Mantra and anishthān it is essential to calculate it through the first letter of Janma Nakshatra or of popular name. The best is to prepare a Yantra.

Akathah Chakram

Prepare a replica of the following Yantra and fill it up with Mātrikā Varnas. The square that contains the first letter of the name of the seeker is called **Siddha Chatushtaya**; the next four squares are **Sār Chatushtaya**; the third set of four square is called **Susiddha Chatishtaya** and the remaining set is called **Shatru Chatushtaya**.

If the first letter of the seeker and the selected Mantra are in the square then it is called **Siddha-Siddha Yoga**. If the Mantra is in the next square after the square with the first letter of the seeker's name it is called **Siddha Sādhya Yoga**. If it is in the third square then it is called **Siddha-Susiddha Yoga** and if it is in the fourth square then it is called **Siddhāri Yoga**.

In the first Yoga Mantra shows results in normal time; in the second Yoga it shows results in double time; if it is in the third square then it is perfected after chanting half number of Mantras but if it is the fourth Yoga then it destroys the seeker along with his family and relatives.

Other Yoga Mantras are also destructive: The Ari Siddha Mantra destroys the son; ari-sādhya destroys the daughter; Susiddhāri

Mantra destroys the whole family while ari-susiddha is dangerous for wide and Ari-ari Mantra annihilates the seeker. So, be careful and think twice before opting for the venture.

Some Yoga Mantras are helpful: Susiddha-Sidha gives success after chanting only half the numbers of Mantras; Susiddha Yoga and Susiddha Mantra shows results immediatly after deekshā of the seeker.

अकथह १	उ ङ प २	आ ख द ३	ऊ च फ ४
ओ ड ब ५	लृ झ म ६	औ ढ श ७	लॄ ञ य ८
ई घ न ६	ऋ ज भ १०	इ ग ध ११	ॠ द व १२
अः त स १३	ऐ ठ ल १४	अं ण ष १५	ए ट र १६

चित्र ख: अकथहचक्रम

Akadam Chakram

Akadama Chakram is another way of Mantra Shodhan. In the sixteen squares, the Varnas are written as shown below.

Count from the first varna of name of the Chankra to the first letter of the Mantra, it is Sādhya; the next is Siddha; and the last is Ari. The results have been given above.

अकथह १	उ ङ प २	आ ख द ३	ऊ च फ ४
ओ ड ब ५	लृ झ म ६	औ ढ श ७	लृ ञ य ८
ई घ न ६	ऋ ज भ १०	इ ग ध ११	ऋ द व १२
अः त स १३	ऐ ठ ल १४	अं ण ष १५	ए ट र १६

चित्र ग: अकडमचक्रम

Siddha Ādi Shodhan Chakram

The Chakra should be prepared as shown below and the yoga should be calculated on the basis of the first letter of the seeker's name to the first letter of the Mantra as Siddha Yoga and so on.

अ उ लृ ओ क ङ झ ड थ प म व ह	आ ऊ लृ औ ख च ज ढ द फ य श ळ
ई ऋ ऐ अः प ज ठ त न भ ल स ज्ञः	इ ऋ ए अं ग छ ट ण ध ब र ष क्ष

चित्र घ: सिद्धादिशोधन चक्र

Nakshatra Shodhan Chakram

Prepare the Chakra as shown below and starting from the name-nakshtra of the seeker, calculate up to the Mantra Nakshatra.

Janma; Sampat; Vipad; Kshema; Pratyari; Sādhak; Badha; Mitra and Param Mitra in the sequence. Vipad; Pratyari and Badha are not acceptable.

अ	भ	क	रो	मृ	आ	पु	पु	आ
अ आ	इ	ईउऊ	ऋ ॠ लृ लॄ	ए	ऐ	ओऔ	क	खग
म	पू	उ	ह	चि	स्वा	वि	अ	ज्ये
घङ	च	छ ज	झ ञ	टठ	ड	ढण	तथद	ध
मू	पू	उ	श्र	ष	श	पू	उ ष	रे
मपफ	ब	भ	म	यर	ल	षश	सह	क्षअंअः

चित्र च: नक्षत्र शोधन चक्र

Rini Dhani or Rina Dhan Shodhan Chakra

It is yet another way of calculating the effective or ineffective relation between the seeker and the Mantra.

१४	२७	२	१२	१५	६	४	३	५	८	६
अ	इ	उ	ऋ	लृ	ए	ऐ	ओ	आ	अं	अः
क	ख	ग	घ	ङ	च	छ	ज	झ	ञ	ट
ठ	ड	ढ	ण	त	थ	द	ध	न	प	फ
ब	भ	म	य	र	ल	व	श	ष	स	ह
१०	१	७	४	८	३	७	५	४	१	७

चित्र छ: ऋणि-धनि चक्र

Calculate the numbers of all the vowels and consonants and divide with eight. The remainder is the Mantra Rāshi. The greater Rāshi is called Rini and the smaller remainder is called Dhani. The bigger Rāshi is to be accepted.

Mantra Shodhan Chakra

Prepare a Chakra as shown below. If the Mantrākshar is in the first triangle after name-letter then wealth gain; if it is second, then wealth loss; third then it's gain; fourth fight among relatives; fifth then diseases; if sixth then total destruction.

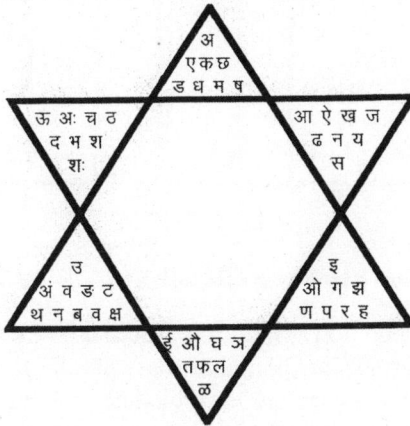

चित्र ज: मन्त्रशोधन चक्र

Kula-akula Chakra

The whole creation is based on the five gross elements; Panch Mahābhuta. 51 different sounds or Varnas also came out of it. Some Varnas belong to each of the five elements: Bhumi; Jala; Agni; Vāyu and Ākāsh. They are called 'Swa-kula', belonging to that element; others are akula, belong to other elements. There is friendship and enmity among them. The Varnas belonging to earth are friends to Jala; enemy to Agni and neutral to Vāyu. For the Varnas of Jala Tattva Prithvi Varnas are friends; Agni Varnas are enemy and Vāyu Varnas are neutral and so on. Swa Kula and Mitra Kula Varnas give easy attainment while neutral Varnas give nothing and the enemy ones bring ruin.

Make the Chakra as shown below and check the first letter of name and Mantra.

वायु	अग्नि	भूमि	जल	आकाश
अ आ	इ ई	उ ऊ	ऋ ॠ	लृ लॄ
ए	ऐ	ओ	औ	अं
क	ख	ग	घ	ङ
च	छ	ज	झ	ञ
ट	ठ	ड	ढ	ण
त	थ	द	ध	न
प	फ	ब	भ	म
य	र	ल	व	श
ष	क्ष	ळ	स	ह

चित्र झ: कुलाकुल चक्र

Exceptions for Mantra Shodhan

Some Mantras need no purification. Shodha is not for them. They are: Ekākshar; Tryākshar; Panchākshar; Shadākshar; Saptākshar; Ashtākshar; Navākshar; Ekādashākshar; Mantras having 23 Varnas; Hans; Kuta; Vedokta; Pranava; Swapna Prāpt Mantra (Mantra that came in dream); Stri Prāpt Mantra (received by wife); Mālā Mantra; Narsingh; Prasād, Hong Mantra; Ravi Mantra; Vārāha Mantra; Mātrikā; Parā, Hring; Tripurā; Āgyā-Siddha; Garuda Mantra; Boddha and Jain Mantras.

Important Note

It must be kept in mind that during childhood Beejākshar Mantras from 1 to 10 lettered Mantras are attained easily; during youth Mantra-varna 11 to 20 are attained but during old age Mālā Mantras; of more than 20 letters are attained easily.

Ten Types of Mantra Samskārs

1. **Janan Samskār**: Make a Janan Yantram (given at the end of Section IV). Starting from the Ishān Kone and purify

each Varna with Mātrikā Mantra. This is known as Janan Samskār, and the Yantra as Janan Yantram.

2. **Deepan Samskār**: Keep the Mantra between the Hans Mantra as Samputita, and chant one thousand times. It is known as Deepan Samskār; as for example: *Hansah rāmāya namah so-aham!* हंसः रामाय नमः सोऽहम्।

3. **Bodhan Samskār**: Nabha (ha); Vanhi (ra); Indu (Anuswār) and Arghish (Aum); Samputita Mantra if chanted for five thousand times, then, it is called Bodhan Samskār. *Hrung rāmāya namah hrung!* हुं रामाय नमः हुं।

4. **Tādan Samskār**: One thousand times chanting of a Mantra samputita with *astra*, weapon; Mantra phat is known as Tādan Samskār: For example: *Phat rāmāya namah phat!* फट् रामाय नमः फट्।

5. **Abhishek Samskār**: To annoit the Mantra with *Aing hansah Aum!* ऐं हंसः ॐ and chant for one thousand times with *abhimantrit* Jala, is called Abhishek Samskār.

6. **Vimalikaran Samskār**: If the Mantra samputita by *Aum trong vashat!* is chanted one thousand times it is called Vimalikaran, whitening. For example: *Aum trong vashat rāmāya namah vashat trong Aum!* ॐ त्रां वषट् रामाय नमः वषट् त्रां ॐ।

7. **Jivan Samskār**: To chant the Mantra one thousand times, samputita by vashat swadhā, is called Jivan Samskār. For example: *Swadhā vashat rāmāya namah vashat swadhā!* स्वधा वषट् रामाय नमः वषट् स्वधा।

8. **Tarpan Samskār**: If the Mantra is offered milk, ghee and water for hundred times, it is called Tarpan Samskār.

9. **Gopan Samskār**: To chant the Mantra with hring for one thousand times is called Gopan Samskār: For example: *hring rāmāya namah hring!* ह्रीं रामाय नमः ह्रीं।

10. **Āpyāyan Samskār**: To chant the Mantra hundred times samputita by ha sauh is called Āpyāyan Samskār. For

example: *Ha sauh rāmāya namah sauh ha!* ह सौः रामाय नमः सौः ह।

Types of Sādhanā

1. **Abhāvani Sādhanā**: In the absence of the articles needed for Sādhanā, when the seeker performs poojan with only water, it is called Abhāvani Sādhanā.

2. **Trāsi Sādhanā**: When a depressed individual who is afraid of many things, worships only in the mind; it is called Trāsi Sādhanā.

3. **Daurbodhi Sādhanā**: Worshipping performed by children, old ones, women, ignorant and fools, according to their physical, mental and economic strength is called Daurbodhi Sādhanā.

4. **Sautiki Sādhanā**: If one is attached then he should perform only mānasik poojan; if one is detached, he should do everything. For example: if a bed-ridden ill person offers a flower after chanting a mantra only once, it is enough for him. This is called Sautiki Sādhanā.

5. **Āturi Sādhanā**: If one completes the Yajan when he/she regains the health with the permission of the guru and elders; it is called Āturi Sādhanā.

It is worth mentioning here that despite one's personal knowledge and experience, one must seek the help of guru/expert pandit in worshipping and Sādhanā.

These four types of religious practices are sufficient proof in themselves that religious practices, religiosity and faith are essential and important. How are they performed is not very important.

However, the net result varies, if it is done with the core of the heart or done with the assistance of others, or if the seeker arranges the articles himself and sincerely performs the worshipping.

✿ ✿ ✿

11

Limbs of Mantras

For success and attainment it is essential to know the limbs or *angas*, of Mantras. According to *Mantra Yoga Samhitā* by Maharishi Bharadwāja, there are sixteen *angas* limbs of Mantras:

Bhavanti mantra yogasya shodash angāni nishchitam;
Yathā sudhānsho jāyante kalāh shodashah shobhanāh.
Bhaktih shuddhih-cha-āsanam cha panchānga-syāpi sevanam;
Āchār dhārane dvivya desh sevanam-iti-api.
Prānakriyā tathā mudrā tarpanam havanam balih;
Yāgo japah-tathā dhyānam samādhih-cha-iti shodashah.

भवन्ति मन्त्र योगस्थ षोडश अंगानि निश्चितम् ।
यथा सुधांशो जायन्ते कलाः षोडशः शोभनाः ॥
भक्तिः शुद्धिः च आसनं च पंचांगस्यापि सेवनाम् ।
आचार धारणे दिव्य देश सेवनं इति अपि ॥
प्राणक्रिया तथा मुद्रा तर्पणं हवनं बलिः ।
यागो जपः तथा ध्यानं समाधिः च इति षोडशः ॥

1. **Bhakti**

    Bhakti is divided in two categories: *Gauni*, the devotion during practicing stage and *Parā*, the devotion after attainment. The Gauni Bhakti has nine divisions called *Navadhā* Bhakti, and is further divided in two parts: the first five are the devotion of the primary stage and the other four are the devotion of advance stage and terminates in *Rāgātmikā.*

    The Sādhak or seeker must know all the nine types of Bhakti, called Navadhā Bhakti, and the ways it is performed. He should know, absorb and show deep devotion to the Ishta

Devatā, the designated deity through all, some or any one out of the following nine ways of bhakti:

i.   *Shravan*   ii.   *Kirtan*   iii. *Smaran*

iv. *Pāda Sevan*   v.   *Archan*   vi.   *Vandanā*

vii. *Sakhābhāva*   viii. *Ātma Bhāvanā*   ix.   *Nivedan*

The Rasatmikā Bhakti is solely based on the Bhakti, or pure Rasas: on the seven main rasas:

i.   *Dāsya*   ii.   *Sakhya*   iii. *Vātsalya*

iv. *Kāntā*   v.   *Ātma Nivedan*   vi.   *Guna-kirtan*

vii. *Tanmaya-āsakti*

and seven secondary, or mutilated Rasas, mostly used in everyday talk and behaviour and of course, in literature:

i.   *Hāsya*   ii.   *Veera*   iii. *Karuna*

iv. *Adbhuta*   v.   *Bhayānak*   vi.   *Bibhatsa*

vii. *Raudra*

2. **Shuddhi**

There are five types of Shuddhis:

i.   *Dik-shuddhi*: purity of the correct direction. One should sit either facing east or north.

ii. *Sthān*: the purity of the selected place. The place under a Peepal, Bargad, Ashok, Bilva or Amalā tree is always pure and suitable for mantra sādhanā or the place should be cleaned and sanctified with cow-dung.

iii. *Sharira*: The purity of the body. The purity of body is achieved by cleaning it well and taking any of the different baths. There are seven types of bath that are prescribed:

i)	*Mantra snān*	ii)	*Bhauma snān*
iii)	*Āgneya snān*	iv)	*Vāyavya snān*
v)	*Divya snān*	vi)	*Vārunya snān*
vii)	*Mānas snān.*		

iv. *Man Shuddhi*: The purity of the heart and mind. It depends only on the divine wealth that one collects through moral deeds and prayers.

v. *Āsan Shuddhi*: The purity of the seat. A mat of kush is always prepared though rough blanket or āsani is also accepted.

3. **Āsan:** For different type of Mantra Sādhanā different comfortable physical postures should be used, out of the main 84 āsanas. But the two most prescribed and followed āsanas are *Swastik* and *Padmāsan*.

4. **Panchānga Sevan**: In many Sādhanās, including mantra-sādhanā, the five anga sevan is performed:

i. *Ishta Sevā*   ii. *Sahasra-nām*   iii. *Stava*

iv. *Kavacha*   v. *Hridaya Nyāsa*

All these must be done everyday.

5. **Āchār**: To follow all religious, moral and social norms yamas and niyams must be observed for Mantra Sādhanā. The āchār has three divisions: *Divya; Dakshina* and *Vāma*.

6. **Dhāranā**: One must concentrate on a particular thing or idol or God for meditation on Mantras. It is of two types: *Antah Dhāranā* and *Bahir-dhāranā*.

7. **Divya-desh Sevan**: There are sixteen divine places in our body. They must be cleaned, strengthened and activated through *prānāyām*. They are:

i. *Agni*   ii. *Jala*   iii. *Linga*   iv. *Sthandila*
v. *Kundya*   vi. *Pata*   vii. *Mandal*   viii. *Vishikha*
ix. *Nitya-yantra*   x. *Bhāva-yantra*
xi. *Peetha*   xii. *Vigrah*   xiii. *Bibhuti*   xiv. *Nābhi*
xv. *Hridaya*   xvi. *Murdhā*.

8. **Prāna-kriyā**: Prāna Kriyā includes

i. *Prānāyāma*;   ii. *Kara-nyāsa*;

iii. *Anga-nyāsa*;   iv. *Mātrikā-nyāsa*; and *Rishyādi nyāsa*.

9. **Mudrā**: There are different postures which are created with hands, basically palms. Mudrās are created for the designated deity and for different sounds of **Mantras** and **Stotras**. 24 General Mudrās are:

Sumukha	Samput	Vitat	Vistrit
Dvimukha	Trimukha	Chaturmukha	Panchamukha
Shanmukha	Adhomukha	Vyāpakānjali	Shakat
Yama-pāsh	Grathita	Sanmukho-mukha	Pralamba
Mushtika	Matasya	Kurma	Vārāha
Singhākrānta	Mahākrānta	Mudagar	Pallava

10. **Agrima Advanced Mudrās**

Surabhi	Gyān	Vairāgya	Yoni
Shankha	Pankaj	Linga	Nirvāna

11. **Vishishta, special Mudrās**

Moolabandha	Uddiyān Bandha	Jālandhar Bandha
Mahābandha	Mahābedha	Mahāmudrā
Viparit-karani	Vajrajoli	Khechari
Shakti-chālini		

12. **Tarpan**: Water is poured for

   i.   own deity   ii.   other deities

   iii. for seers   iv. for forefathers

13. **Havan**: Many things are offered, poured and burnt in the havan, the sacred fire for Yagya and Poojā.

14. **Bali**: There are three sanctioned sacrifices:

   i.   *Ātma bali*; the sacrifice of ego or *ahankār*.

   ii. *Antah bali*, the sacrifice of passion, lust, anger, jealousy, etc.

   iii. *Vāhya bali*, the sacrifice or offering fruits etc.

15. **Yāga**: Yāga have two divisions: *antah yāga* and *vahir-yāga*.

16. **Japa**: To remember and chant the name or mantra related to one's own deity Japa. Its detail is given elsewhere. There are three types of Japa: *Vāchika*; *Upānshu* and *Mānas*.

17. **Dhyān**: To concentrate on the vigrah and vibhuti of one's own deity or Brahma or Aum. This is of two types: with *Bheda-bhāva* and with *Abheda-bhāva*.

18. **Samādhi**: Samādhi is Mahābhāva, illumined state. It is of two types: *Sabeeja* or *Sampragyāt Samādhi* and *Neerbeeja Asampragyāt Samādhi*. Asampragyāt Samādhi is further divided in four:

    i.   *Vitarkānugam*   ii. *Vichārānugam*
    iii. *Ānandānugam*   iv. *Asmitānugam*.

All these ways must be known and all the needed steps must be taken and all the instructions must be followed meticulously for safety and success.

✸✸✸

12

Indrājala Mantras

The following are the Mantras through which people try to deceive others. These are not tested Mantras and not even in traditional norm of Mantras. It is difficult to say when and how these Mantras crept into the fold. Yet, the pure Tāntriks kept these Mantras away and labelled them as "Indrajāla". There are many books available but their effectiveness is always questionable. Beware of such persons who are experts in influencing the mind for material gain and physical pleasure. It is a wonder that despite knowing these things to be false and non-effective people, even literate, educated and urban people fell prey to such things.

They lay down such impractical conditions that the interested and enchanted person will certainly fail to fulfill. Thus, they easily turn their prey into scapegoat.

In Indrajāla, the Mantras are divided into six Karmas; a Devatā for each; for performing the rituals one should sit in different directions; practice them in different seasons; at different hours and use different colours. The following chart will show all these very clearly:

Karmas	Devatā	Direction	Season	Time	Colour
Shāntikaran	Rati	Ishān Kona	Hemant	Before evening	White
Stambhan	Lakshmi	Purva	Shishir	After mid-day	Yellow
Vashikaran	Saraswati	Uttar	Vasant	Before mid-day	Red
Bair, enmity	Jyeshthā	Nairitya	Grish-ma	Mid-day	Red
Uchchātan	Durgā	Vāyavya	Varshā	Evening	Smoky
Māran	Bhadra Kāli	Agni Kona	Sharada	Night	Black

1. **Vashi Karan Mantra: Use of Supāri**

   Supāri (used in betel) should be infused 108 times with this mantra. Whosoever is offered this Supāri and eats it, will be under complete control. It is best to take sweet Supāri packets duly infused and kept safe for use.

   "Aum Dev namo Hrarye thah thah Swāhā!"

   ॐ देव नमो ह्रर्ये ठः ठः स्वाहा।

2. **Use of fruits:** The mantra should be recited ten thousand times to attain siddhi. After that take any good fruit and infuse it with mantra 108 times. Whosoever will take the fruit will remain under complete control.

   "Aum Hreeng Mohini Swāhā!" ॐ ह्रीं मोहिनी स्वाहा।

3. **Use of water:** Rise early in the morning and after your ablutions purify the water with 7 mantras and with the name of the person required to be brought under control. Drink this water. Repeat for 21 days. The person concerned will be under complete control.

   "Aum Chimi Chimi Swāhā!" ॐ चिमि चिमि स्वाहा।

   This mantra too can be used to control one's enemy. Procure 7 red chillies with their branch. Light a fire. Recite the above mantra adding name of the enemy before the word "Swāhā!" and put one chilly in the fire. Repeat 7 times for 11 or 21 days. For an enemy this should be started on a Saturday.

4. **To control husband:** Ladies can use this mantra to control their husbands who have gone astray, those who do not co-operate and are out of control. This mantra too can be used to control enemies, opponents, superiors and others.

   Mantra

   *"Aum namo mahārakshāya mam pati mum
   vashe kuru kuru swāhā!"*

ॐ नमो महारक्षाय ममपति ममवशे कुरु कुरु स्वाहा।

Recite the mantra 108 times duly performing Homa. The articles used in such mantra must be infused with 7 times recitation or be *Abhimantrit,* with the above mantra and given to the husband to eat in order to control him.

5. **Kām Gāyatri Mantra:** Kām gāyatri mantra is most effective in winning over one's husband or the boss.

     "Aum Manohavayai Vidmahe Karnapaye dhimahi
     Tantra Kāma Prachodyāt"

ॐ मनोहव्यै विद्महे कर्णपये धीमहि त्रन्त्र कामः प्रचोदयात्।

Recite this mantra 21 thousand times to attain siddhi and to appease Kām Devtā. After that use this mantra for any lady who will be infatuated and remain satisfied under your control.

6. **Kāmakhya Vashi Karan Mantra:** The most effective mantra for holding the desired person. This mantra is be recited eleven thousand times for siddhi. Replace the name of the female or male instead of word Amuka in mantra.

Mantra

     "Aum Namo Kāmākshi Devi (Amuka) (replace Amuka
     with name.) *mum Vashyam Kuru Kuru Swāhā!"*

ॐ नमो कामाक्ष देवी (अमुक) (अमुक के स्थान पर व्यक्ति के नाम
का उच्चारण करें) मम वश्यं कुरु कुरु स्वाहा ।

❀ ❀ ❀

Sounds Equivalent to
Mantras in other Religions

The research and the creation by the Drashtā Rishi is so powerful, great and effective that each religion of the world has its Mantras. But since, they don't like to accept this fact so they are not called mantras but be sure 'Āmin'; 'Yā Allāh'; 'Allāh O' Akbar' 'Wāhe Guru' are as powerful and effective as 'AUM'. They are neither called Mantras nor used in the same sense or with similar intentions but they have similar effect. Knowingly or unknowingly, they have the same derivatives. These things happened in such a remote past that nothing can be said with confidence about their origin and the way they gained popularity.

There is neither the need to change the concept nor the change will be advisable because since time immemorial or since their origin they have acquired a meaning and place in the minds of people and in the religions concerned. But none can deny that they are sacred words and have sacred effect.

Mantra and Meditation

Mantras may or may not be needed. It depends mostly on the individual and his/ her way of meditation. We meditate to adjust and absorb the freshly gained information, to retain their essence and reject the chaff, and to place it in the stored memory to use when needed. We don't possess the knowledge, wisdom, concentration and characters like that of the Rishis. We don't perform our duties with similar devotion, dedication, sincerity and concentration. We need and must make use of the Mantras in meditation, as Mantras easily give concentration and help one to concentrate for longer durations. One can focus better, with ease and for long if one chants Mantras. It is well known and established from the time of Pārvati to Paramhans and to the modern saint who uses and utilizes them.

It is well established that the Mantras generate powerful energies and imbue the seeker with positive and creative thoughts. If one knows the accurate meaning of the Mantras that he or she chants then the desired effect will become prominent sooner than expected, as the intentions become crystal clear. The greater the vigour and attention in chanting the Mantras the greater vigour and concentration will be achieved by the person chanting it.

For everyone: Open your mouth and produce a very long O sound and close your lips it will be the sound of **AUM**, the eternal sound. You can close both your ears and listen to the sound. It is clearly **AUM**. When Aum is pronounced from the navel, the source of life, energy increases and mind gets relaxed. Most of the mantras begin with Aum and hence, it connects one with one's being, with the root, to the source of life in the body and thus to universal source of life. The consciousness gets expanded.

Aum is the condensed and shortened way to universal life. It is for all, as it is directly related to the Almighty, the Brahma, as a humming sound. It comes from the centre of existence and expands to entire cosmos, returns to the centre and the — process goes on ceaselessly. Thus, it is the sound of the universe: *Nāda Brahma* that pervades all and is everywhere, Omnipresent like Him, vibrating in all, not as a symbol but as reality.

Hindus: Since Hindus believe in such recitations from time immemorial, there is no dearth of such Mantras for Hindus. A few examples are given here:

Common Mantras for Hindus:

AUM

Hari Aum Tatsat! हरि ॐ तत्सत्।
Aum Namah Shivāya! ॐ नमः शिवाय।
Jai Ganesh! जय गणेश।

Shri Ganeshāya Namah! श्री गणेशाय नमः।

Shri Ganapataye Namah! श्री गणपतये नमः।

Shri Namo Nārāyanāya! श्री नमो नारायणाय।

Mangalam Bhagawān Vishnu! मंगलं भगवान् विष्णु।

Hare Rām! Hare Krishna! हरे राम। हरे कृष्ण।

Sitā Rāma! Sitā Rāma! सीता राम। सीता राम।

Rādhey Shyāma! Rādhey Shyāma! राधे श्याम। राधे श्याम।

Aum Suryāya Namah! ॐ सूर्याय नमः।

Aum Chandrāya Namah! ॐ चन्द्राय नमः।

Aum Guruwe Namah! ॐ गुरुवे नमः।

Aham Brahmāsmi! अहं ब्रह्मास्मि।

Aum Shāntih Shāntih Shāntih! ॐ शान्तिः। शान्तिः॥ शान्तिः॥।

Tvameva Sarvam Mama Deva Deva! त्वमेय सर्वं मम देवदेव।

Alakh Niranjan! अलख निरंजन।

While in deep meditation or while learning meditation, recite whatever Mantra you choose. Some options are given below but it's not an exhaustive list. The follower of any religion or sect can select something of his/ her personal liking on the hints that one gets after reading and chanting Mantras quoted below.

Common Mantras for Buddhists: (any one or all of the following)

Aum Mani Padme Hum!

Buddham Sharanam Gachhāmi!

Dhamam Sharanam Gachhāmi!

Sangham Sharanam Gachhāmi!

Sabbe Satta Bhavanthu Sukhitattha!

Buddhāya Namo Namah!

Namo Samma Arhato Bhagavato Samma Buddhassa!

O Buddha! Grant me wisdom!

O Buddha! Keep me on the 'Right' Path

Common Mantras for Sikhs:

Ek Omkār!
Wāhe Guru!
Sat Shri Akāla!
Guru Di Kripā!

Common Mantras for Christians:

Amen!
"O God reform thy world beginning with me!"
O God Grant me Wisdom.
O God Grant me Compassion!
All are One!
Save me from degeneration, O Lord!

Common Mantras for Muslims:

Bismillāh!
Allāh hoo!
Bishmillāh hirrāhmānirraheem!
Inshā Allāh!
Sallallāho alaihe wasallam!
Lā Elāha Illalāh!
Allāh ho Akbar!
Allāh ki Maraji!
Allāh Mālika!
Allāh ki Nemat!
Allāh ki Nematton kā Shukra!
Allāh Meharwāni kar!
Maullā Gaphalat mein na rakh!

Muslims are more circumspect but if they form a habit of carrying a musalla or janamaz, a big towel size cloth, with them for Namāz then they can repeat loudly or silently the name of *Allāha.* They can easily perform all the five *Namāz: Salāt* or *Salwāt; or Salāt-o-Salawāt or Salāt-o-Salām:* **Fajar** at dawn; **Zuhar** at noon; **Asar** during afternoons, **Magharib** at sunset and **Ishā** after nightfall.

✸ ✸ ✸

14

Mantras Give Faith, Hope and Confidence

There is no need to show that you are remembering your god, and reciting His name. Repetition is all that is needed. There is no need to waste one's working hours or sleeping hours. Simply utilize your idle time, when you're neither doing anything nor in a position to do anything. Repeat any of mantras given in the previous chapter, when you are walking towards the bus stop or towards the office; ascending to or descending from a stair; sitting in a vehicle: rickshaw, auto, bus, car, train or metro; taking bath; waiting for someone to appear or for food or tea to be served; while marketing when you have left one shop and are going towards another; when searching a house or a place or waiting at bus stop or station or in some similar circumstances which may differ from person to person because of the nature and place of work. But *train you mind to repeat any of the above or a few of the above once, twice, thrice, five times or nine times depending on the time and place. This sort of repetition is a must. Do for some months and feel the effect.* **Faith, hope and confidence will grow manifold. We need them and these are our essential and basic needs.** Mantras give them all: Faith; Hope; Confidence; Courage; Ability and Wisdom.

Mantras Make us Grow

It is a sort of growing with Mantras. We can grow with Mantras because Mantras break the emotional, mental and physical knots and bring one out of the gyre in which he is turning incessant and going nowhere. The spiral movement in the gyre takes the sap out of life. Therefore, it is no wonder many wise people to refer the world as a sea, *jivan-sāgar*, where a person is beaten by and thrown away on the ever flowing currents without getting rest and respite.

The power of vibration of Mantras makes the spirit free flowing. The *japa* or chanting of the selected Mantra or the Mantra given by the guru, the preceptor, pervades the spiritual self and connects the spirit of the self to a powerful source of energy and intelligence by connecting one with either natural energy or cosmic or both (some may freely treat them as one). The *pratyāhār* leads to the journey within and *dhāranā* helps the mind to focus efficiently.

One does not have only to repeat the Mantra, but will have to understand its hidden, secret and mysterious meaning and allow the meaning to sink down the heart and mind and settle as a part of the being. Knowledge comes as a part of understanding and experience. We experience something in an isolated moment but the experience connects us to both time past and experiences gained earlier and to that of the future. If not, then it is not valuable or not an experience at all. Connectivity is the test. It forms or clicks at its right place in an imperceptible chain between one that preceeds and one that follows. The sequence would never be the same, and the experience never as easy as it appears in writing. Ironically enough, it is always peculiar, idiosyncratic and general. If it is not peculiar then it would lose its significance; if it's not novel and idiosyncratic then the time and energy spent over it would have been useless; and if it's not for all, for general use and benefit then it won't serve any purpose because the individual, experiencing it, is mortal and hence unable to use it. Experiences are meaningful and useful only because they become important property and active guides of the posterity. Posterity grows rich and aware. In the same fashion, our every action should be for the benefit and survival of the posterity. Our life and survival are not as important as the arrival and survival of new lives.

Time for Chanting

Those that are wise and conscious enough, distinguish between inactive or idle moments and creative or productive moments. Every moment, the atmosphere is not rich enough for creation and every moment, one is not ready to receive the boon or accept the fertility. There are moments of revelation and moments of creations. That is one reason that our forefathers thought of special and vibrant moments for fruition; for *Anushthān*, which is performed with all piety under command.

But modern human are so preoccupied with other matters that they cannot wait for the spiritually rich and peaceful productive moments. Yet they can add meaning to all the spare moments that they get by awkward and undefined movements. Modern humans can utilize the time in *Mānsika Jāpa* of Mantras while going up or descending down through stairs or lifts; going to and from a car; driving or sitting a car, bus or train or walking on pavements or taking tea, or when doing nothing at all. It's only a matter of training one's mind. If a person asks the mind to remind and recall the Mantras whenever one is idle, the Mantras will appear automatically for him or her to recite or chant. **Such chanting is for growth, safety, concentration and spirituality. Such chanting will not form a part or be counted as *Anusthān*.**

Mantras Reveal

The experiences are called revelation because they are not new they existed from before and will not cease to exist after the death of the person experiencing it because experiences and ideas are immortal. They are only collected and recollected or appear or disappear like life-being or the soul that never dies; that conceives its birth and death; that migrates to other bodies and other worlds or regions. Ideas and experiences too come and change form but they exist. We won't waste anything: neither life nor matter nor material if we think that our death is not our end, that we have to reappear in some form or body and would need them. The posterity feels its importance in that sense only when the children or grandchildren are compared to some deceased forefathers.

Timelessness

The Prāna, ideas and experiences are timeless in the sense that time — past, present and future are dissolved in them or they have dissolved into and exist in them: now was, now is and now will be. When it was being written it was now; when one is reading it is now and when someone else will read, it will be now. So, now never dies. Nothing dies. Matter too is immortal. It only changes form. You were and I was something, somewhere in the time past; we are something and somewhere in time present and would be something and somewhere in future. Our weakness is that 'something' or 'somewhere' is not known to us. The self existed before the birth of this body and will remain even after the death of this body.

Mantras Give in Abundance

Mantras imbibe both philosophy and psychology. They give both inner richness and silence, and help to see beautiful things, which is otherwise impossible to see and experience. They create silence and in the silence emerges the meaning through images that have become symbols.

Such persons feel established in the world. They neither feel nor can be uprooted. They have both '*vivek*' (wisdom) and '*vairāgya*' (detachment). These work as magnets to others and people are attracted towards that person. The man that started his journey from the physical body is now very close to his internal self, the spiritual body. Now, he understands life better, sees it in better and glowing light and knows the reality behind the apparent illusion. This new revelation is that of spiritual self that has been duly widened. There is no narrowness, no narrow feeling or narrow deeds. The blossom of a tree is its bliss, and it extends its bliss to others, to all living beings and non-living matter. It is the best example that feels and easily achieves 'Oneness' with all. Since man is not like a tree and cuts trees for petty gains, he is unable to know, feel and get Oneness and Bliss.

Man possesses more positive energy than he exhibits destructive energy. The Mantras bring forth what the most ancient Vedic Rishis thought and praised man in the following words:

"O, man thou hast wings of virtue and vitality, establish thyself on the surface of the earth, fill the firmament with thy radiance, cover the sphere with thy luster, and spread thy effulgence in all directions." Yajur Veda.

Mantras Help

Mantras help in many ways besides those that have already been discussed. Mantras make one spiritual and help in attaining spirituality. Spirituality in a person will ensure that there is no place for exploitation, oppression, arrogance, extremity and frenzy in his/her life. It has been replaced by propriety, truthfulness, simplicity, confidence and ethical behaviour. Whosoever has spirituality is invariably religious and leads a life full of moral values. Spirituality springs from religion and religion thrives on spirituality. Religion and spirituality first reflect in morality and eventually cover the soul of a being. He grows in stature and attains unfathomable depth. He cannot be displaced or won over. In his simplicity, humility and cordiality, he is always a winner. These are the ingredients that lay a strong and unshakable foundation on which the prosperity of a person stands tall, high and erect: un-shattered and stainless.

Whenever you are facing some crisis and there seems no way out, just sit relaxed and chant the Mantras. Before you finish them or just after finishing them, when you wash your face or take a glass of water, you are bound to get an idea, a sort of vision which would invariably be the answer to your immediate crisis. Follow it. Don't ignore it. You'll be out in the open and safe. Or, just keep on chanting the Mantras whenever you get time; you'll see the way clearly.

Information or knowledge comes in a flash: who are working against you? Who are to be tackled first? And who and what are to be ignored? Have faith inside your heart, and always keep God overhead. You are seriously ill and no medicine is working; start and keep on chanting the Mantras; any Mantra; whenever free; you'll unknowingly eat or start eating 'something' which will cure you. Mantras will definitely help you every time.

☆ ☆ ☆

15

Need of Mantras

In place of looking only at the physical body we may start feeling and enriching the Soul, our inner life element, and would immediately feel the surge just after switching preferences. That is the time to start meditation. There is no use of meditation if one is deeply engrossed in physical body only and is not ready to see and feel deeper beneath the skin. Include the living and sensitive soul in reckoning and then start meditation.

History of Mantras

Whatever sound is there in the words, all the sounds have immense power inherent in them. When these sounds are arranged in a rythmic way by a conscious and illuminated mind, they become Mantras. That must have been behind the origin of the Mantras. As far as the history of Mantras is concerned, it is all inductions, deductions, reasoning and dreaming. There have been so many Mantras and so many variations in them that is impossible for a man of the Kaliyuga or of any yuga to write correctly the chronicle of Mantras.

Like all other things, Mantras were conceived, created, absorbed and used intensively in India. The people of every age have shown admiration and respect towards them. It is a foolish idea to try to pin-point the time when the Mantras came into being; and even it is futile to try to collect all the Mantras that have been in use, more so when numerous books have been burnt by the invaders.

So, there is no authentic history available, but one thing can be said with utmost confidence that the Mantras were in use even before Vedas, and the Vedic Yuga. Veda Vyāsa edited and divided them in the Trivedas or Veda Chaturthi.

From then on, whatever scriptures have survived and are in human possession contain Mantras. There is not a single millennium in which these Mantras were not in vogue and use. Purity, concentration and sublimity were easily availed and used by the chanting of Mantras. In every Yagya and Poojan; in danger and suffering; in *Vratas* and *Tyohārs*, fasting and festivals Mantras were used by learned men, pundits and the masses. At least one person from almost every family chanted Mantras at appropriate times. That is the reason that Mantras have survived and rendered all the attacks futile.

Our Distance from Mantras

Even during this phase of Indian life, when the cold and unhealthy Western philosophy and way of life is being followed by most of the moneyed and powerful people, yet the Mantras are chanted and revered by all. It is so because the soul of Indian soil, culture, civilization and way of thinking is Mantra-maya, pervaded by Mantras. Mantras pervade all: the pandits, panchyat; Yagyas; Poojs; birth and death rites and rituals; festivals and functions. But the adoption of the material way of life has put all Indians into debt, irrespective of whether they are new born infants or old persons on their deathbeds. Life and progress cannot flourish in debt. Now, each citizen is under the debt of more than thirty three thousand. When we got freedom there was no debt on the country. The reason is that we have discarded the most balanced, healthy and controlled life of plain living and high thinking, we are now worried about material gain, physical pleasure and insane luxury. We have moved far away from our culture and civilization, from our knowledge and wisdom, from our tradition and patience because we have moved far away from the Mantras. We claim to be Indian but are destroying everything Indian; rather, we have already destroyed it. There is no possibity of survival without Indianness. Naturally, all are ill, suffering, and in tension; all are taking medicines yet are neither healthy nor happy.

That is not all. The devastating effects of foreign invasions continue. Not only our books were burnt; wise men, pundits and sādhak were also ruthlessly butchered. There was hardly any one left to guide the ignorant mass. The second string of the saints and sages tried to salvage whatever was possible but they lacked the depth and lofty height of their predecessors, so our loss continued; drift was not arrested and at present we have drifted far away from our own things. What are we doing? We are following the history, Scriptures and analysis of the great books written or compiled by foreigners whose main aim has been to destroy everything that could save India, Indianness and our ancient wisdom.

Controlling Speech

We hear almost everyday that some has denied the statement of the previous day or witness are committing perjury. Falsehood is rampant everywhere, truth does not come to the force. It is because of the fact that we have neither the māntrik piety nor the character to be honest and sincere to life, work and God. Mantra teaches first: what to say and how to say. That gives both piety and truthfulness. That is very important because falsehood leads to crime, and crime makes life miserable. Mantras are profusely used to get rid of misery and grief.

Once when the speech is under control then breathing will automatically be natural and rhythmic, which will help in performing better and lead a healthy and happy life. This is an important benefit from practicing Mantra chanting, but this advantage has not been mentioned clearly in the scriptures and classics.

When one proceeds on this path, one becomes fearless and both physically and mentally strong. That is the real reason that while teaching Devanāgari lipi and *uchchāran* of different varnas, half varnas and quarter sound of varnas are taught painstakingly. Every varna has its fixed pronunciation and fixed place of pronunciation. Neither the place nor the pronunciation changes, despite the fact that the last varna of one word gets mixed with the first varna of another word. This is the beauty of the most scientific alphabet, i.e. the Devanāgari script.

Our Fault

Puta Mantron mein shānti hai santosh hai;
Tuma nahin pātha karate yahi dosha hai.

पूत मन्त्रों में शान्ति है, संतोष है।
तुम नहीं पाठ करते, यही दोष है॥

(*There is peace and contentment in the pious Mantras. It is our fault that we don't chant them.*)

Mantras were created along with the sound, varnas and words. Ancient Rishis invisioned, recited, chanted, tested, taught, popularized and wrote them during a very long span of time. They have been there. They are light. They purify the inner and outer self and open, widen and keep the path clean to enable others to live happily in prosperity and finally depart after obtaining salvation.

But we have affection, lust, anger, jealousy and ego, and we have drifted far away from the Mantras. This is the time of crisis and there looms a danger of the extinction of all living beings. That is why the Mantras are needed. This is the time to return to Mantras to save whatever can be salvaged.

Sarve Subhe!

AUM

★★★

SECTION III

TANTRA

Tantra: Inside and Insight

- ➢ Tāntric Practices to Please Shiva-Shakti
- ➢ Tantra: A Mixed Practice
- ➢ Kula, Kaul or Kaulini in Tantra Shāshtra
- ➢ Important Things to Know
- ➢ Different Tāntrik Mantras
- ➢ All Yakshini Mantras
- ➢ Kundalini Shakti
- ➢ Tāntric Scriptures
- ➢ Kashmiri Shaivism
- ➢ Kulārnava Tantra
- ➢ Summary of Famous Tantra Shāstras

Tāntric Practices to Please Shiva-Shakti

The word "tantra" is derived from the combination of two words "tattva" and "mantra". "Tattva" means the science of cosmic principles, while "mantra" refers to the science of mystic sound and vibrations. Tantra, therefore, is the application of cosmic sciences with a view to attain spiritual ascendancy. In another sense, tantra also means the scripture by which the light of knowledge is spread:

Tanyate vistāryate gyānam aṇeṇṇa iti tantram.

तनयते विस्तार्यते ज्ञानं अनेन इति तन्त्रम्।

Tantra is the Sanskrit word. It is a tradition of worshipping the Eternal Energy called Mā Shakti, Since it is the energy which created the universe and all the living beings and fosters all, it has infinite number of forms and names. It is the energy that gave life to all and the universe, the big and small bodies that move and made procreation possible, hence, Mā Shakti is regarded as the creatrix, equal to the creator or even more powerful than Him, the Brahma whose manifest form is Shiva or Sadāshiva. Since, it is different in form, content and effect there are many different ways of Her worship for different effects, and for each different form there are different Mantras and different Yantras.

Because Tantra elaborates, **tan** or copious and profound matters, especially relating to the principles of reality, **tattva**, elements or essence; and sacred mantras, and because it provides **tra** or salvation; so, it is called **Tantra**. In short: *Tantra is a divinely revealed body of teachings, explaining what is necessary and what is a hindrance in the practice of the worship of Shiva and Shakti; and also describing the specialized initiation and* *purification ceremonies that are the necessary prerequisites of Tantric practice.*

There are 18 "*Āgamas*", which are also referred to as Shiva Tantras, and they are ritualistic in character. There are three distinct Tāntrik traditions — Dakshinā, Vāma and Madhyamā. They represent the three "shaktis" or powers of Shiva and are characterised by the three "gunas" or qualities — "sattva", "rajas" and "tamas". The Dakshina tradition, characterised by the "sattva" branch of tantra is essentially for good purpose. The Madhyamā, characterised by "rajas" is of mixed nature, while the Vāma, characterised by "tamas" is the most impure form of tantra.

Village Tāntriks

In Indian villages, *Tāntriks* are still not quite hard to find. Many of them help the villagers solve their problems. Every person, who has lived in the villages or has spent his childhood there, has a story to tell. What is so easily believed in the villages might appear illogical and unscientific to the rational urban mind, but these phenomena are realities of life.

Desire for Worldly Pleasures

Tantra is different from other traditions because it takes the whole person, and his/her worldly desires into account. Other spiritual traditions ordinarily teach that desire for material pleasures and spiritual aspirations are mutually exclusive, setting the stage for an endless internal struggle. Although most people are drawn into spiritual beliefs and practices, they have a natural urge to fulfill their desires. With no way to reconcile these two impulses, they fall prey to guilt and self-condemnation, or become hypocritical. Tantra offers an alternative path.

The Tāntrik Approach to Life

The *Tāntrik* approach to life avoids this pitfall. Tantra itself means "to weave, to expand, and to spread", and according to

Tāntrik masters, the fabric of life can provide true and ever-lasting fulfillment only when all the threads are woven according to the pattern designated by Nature. When we are born, life naturally forms itself around that pattern. But as we grow, our ignorance, desire, attachment, fear, and false images of others and ourselves tangle and tear the threads, disfiguring the fabric. Tantra "sādhanā" or practice reweaves the fabric, and restores the original pattern. This path is systematic and comprehensive. The profound science and practices pertaining to hatha yoga, prānāyāma, mudrās, rituals, kundalini yoga, nāda yoga, mantra, mandala, visualization of deities, alchemy, ayurveda, astrology, and hundreds of esoteric practices for generating worldly and spiritual prosperity blend perfectly in the *Tāntrik* disciplines.

The Tāntrik way of life and practice is the best in the eyes of Tāntrik Yogis. It is their foremost path as they claim that: wherever there is material and physical pleasure, there is no salvation; wherever there is penance and salvation, there is no pleasure of life; but those who serve and worship Bhagawati Tripur Sundari, there is both physical pleasure as well as salvation:

> *Yatra-asti bhogo na cha tatra moksho*
> *Yatra-asti moksho na cha tatra bhogah;*
> *Shri-Sundari-sevan-tatparā*
> *Bhogah-cha mokshah-cha karastha yeva.*

> यत्र अस्ति भोगो न च तत्र मोक्षो।
> यत्र अस्ति मोक्षो न च तत्र भोग: ॥
> श्री सुन्दरी सेवन तत्परा: ।
> भोग: च मोक्ष: च करस्थ एव॥

Ten Names of Tāntrik Practice

The Tāntrika practice is popular as Vāma Mārga. It is also popular as Kaul Vidyā, Kaulārnava. This practice has ten names. The names may be treated as different stages. All these ten names are called 'Prashasya'; one who should be praised or one who is

wise, pragyāvān. The Pragyāvān Prashasya Yogi is called Vāma.
In the words of Durgāchārya: *ya yeva hi pragyāvantasta yeva hi
prashasyā bhavanti.* The following are the ten names given in the
Nirukta:

Asnem; Anena; Anedya; Unvadya; Un-abhishapta; Ukathya;
Suneetha; Pāka; Vāma; Vayunam.

> *Asnemah anenah anedyah unvadyah unabhishaptah;*
> *Ukathyah suneethah pākah vāmah*
> *vayunam-iti dasha prashasya nāmāni.*

अस्नेमहः अनेहः अनेद्यः उन्वद्यः उनभिशप्तः।
उक्थ्यः सुनीथः पाकः वामः वायुनं इति दश प्रशस्य नामानि॥

The Meaning of Kaul

According to the Swachahand Tantra, the word Kula is the symbol
of Shakti. It represents the original and perennial Cosmic Energy.
The word Akula symbolizes Shiva. The integral inseparable entity
and the relation between Shiva and Shakti, Akula and Kula are
called Kaul:

> *Kulam shaktih-iti proktam akulam shiva uchyate;*
> *Kula-akulasya sambandhah kaulam-iti-abhidhiyate.*

कुलं शक्तिः इति प्रोक्तं अकुलं शिव उच्यते।
कुल अकुलस्य सम्बन्धः कौलं इति अभिधीयते॥

Tantra and the Presiding Deity

Brahma Yāmala declares that the Devi created Tantra; she is
worshipped by Tantra; she owns Tantra; she accepts Tantra; she
knows Tantra; she is attained through Tantra and she has the form
of Tantra:

> *Tantra-krit tantrā-sampujyā tantric-vesh tantric sammatā;*
> *Tantreshā tantric-vitta tantric-sādhyā tantric swaroopini.*

तन्त्र कृत तन्त्रा सम्पज्या तान्त्रिक वेश तान्त्रिक सम्मता।
तन्त्रेषा तान्त्रिक वित्त तान्त्रिक साध्या तान्त्रिक स्वरूपिनी॥

Meaning thereby: the Tantra is the way to amass energy and power as Shakti is herself Tantra and in tantric who accepts the worship through Tantra. There are two main paths of Tantra: one is the Bhāvanā and the other is the upward movement of Kundali coiled as a snake. It is claimed by Rudra Yāmal that by ideas and emotions, inspiration and imagination one gets everything including the nearness of the God; with that we get the best and maximum knowledge. We can't get anything with extreme penance if we lack inspirational ideas:

> *Bhāvena labhate sarvam bhāvena deva-darshanam;*
> *Bhāvena paramam gyānam tasmād bhāva-avalambanam.*

भावेन लभते सर्व भावेन देव-दर्शनम्।
भावेन परमं ज्ञानं तस्मात् भाव-अवलम्बनम्॥

A similar idea is expressed even in Bhāva Chudāmani:

> *Bahu-jāpāt-tathā homāt-kāyā klesha ādi vistaraih;*
> *Na bhāvena binā devo Yantra mantra phala pradah.*

बहु-जपातथा होमात्काया क्लेश-आदि विस्तरै:।
न भावेन बिना देवो यन्त्र मन्त्र फलप्रदा:॥

Who can Follow it?

Only that Brāhmin, pure, wise and a person of moral character and inner strength can follow this path; if he is blind to others' wealth; enuch for others' wives; dumb to others' scandal; and he who always keeps his sense organs under control:

> *Par-dravyeshu yo-andhah par-strisu napunsakah;*
> *Par-apavāde mookah sarvadā vi-jitendriya;*
> *Tasya-yevai brāhmanā-syātra vāme syād-adhikāritā.*

परद्रव्येषु योअन्ध: परस्त्रीषु नपुंसक: परअपवादे मूक: सर्वदा
विजिनेन्द्रिय: तस्यवै ब्रह्माणा स्याद्-वामे स्यादधिकारिता।

The person who wishes to enter into Tāntrik Sādhana must get an able guru, preceptor. There is one very subtle reason behind it that everything is kept secret. It is also the reason that very little is understood about the complete process and the Sādhanā itself cannot be performed by common men. Such great and tedious penance is not the cup of tea for common folk.

Two things must be taken for granted that this is a mystic practice and mysteriously given by the guru to his disciple on the condition that he would give it only to his able disciple and to none else. So, on the one hand the guru and shishya were meticulously selected. There are very tough terms and conditions for such selections. On the other hand, the disciples were taught this tough practice slowly and secretly. The teaching and practice continued side by side. This is a mystic art and science and the mystery is deliberately maintained. According to Vishwa-sār:

Prakāshāt siddhah hānih syādām-āchār-gatau priye;
Ato vāma pantham devi gopāyet tātrijārvat.

प्रकाशात सिद्धः हानिः स्यादम-आचारगतौ प्रिये।
अतो वामा पन्थम् देवी गोपायेत् तत्रीजार्वत॥

O Beloved Devi! When the process of Vāma Mārga is made public, the loss of Siddhis is the ensuing result. So, it is kept secret as the physical relations of the mother with another person is kept secret.

Modern Superfluity

Modern scholars have also provided definitions of Tantra as 'Tantra is based on the key principle that the universe we experience is the concrete manifestation of the divine energy that creates and maintains it'. Tantric practice seeks to contact and channel that energy within the human microcosm by means of rituals in order to achieve creativity and freedom. This is a superfluous view as the persons dishing out such definitions have not themselves practised it and have not realized the tempestuous flow of energy in one's artery, veins and at the centres, which are like many transformers combined together.

Westerners either could not feel the essence of this sort of worship or tried to belittle it, or did not have an equivalent word. So, they started calling it **tantrism** or **tantricism**, akin to a religious and spiritual cult. They wrongly claimed it to have started as a later movement though the worshipping tradition is as old as worshipping itself, as the worship of Shiva; Shaivism or Vishnu, Vaishanavism. The Mantras are Vedic Mantras taken from Veda Vāngamaya. Among the Siddha Yogis the tradition is different while among the farmers and householders it is again different. In some form it has continued in almost every village of the Indian sub-continent but in some parts or regions this or that form was worshipped. During certain periods in history, certain forms in certain regions acquired prominence which the Westerners were unable to grasp and digest. For them, it is only a movement, while for the practitioners it is everything and perhaps more essential than their life. The Western view seems to hurriedly formed, immature and misleading. They have not concentrated on its mystic nor on its scientific meanings and psychological effects.

Tantra worships the Eternal Mother as Ten Mahāvidyās; Shakti of 51 Shakti Peethas along with the male counterparts called Bhairavas; 108 Shakti Peethas; Sahasra Rupā, in Her 1000 forms and the villagers worship her as Mātā, their local deity or family deity.

Tāntric Practice

Years of training are generally required to master Tantric methods, into which pupils are typically initiated by a guru. *Yoga*, including breathing techniques and postures, *āsana*, is employed to subject the body to the control of the will. *Mudras*, or gestures, *mantras* or syllables, words and phrases, *mandalas* and *yantras*, symbolic diagrams of the forces at work in the universe or in a body or machine at their prayer places, are all used as aids for meditation and for the achievement of spiritual and magical power. During meditation the initiated identifies with any of the numerous Hindu gods and goddesses, visualizes and internalises them, a process likened to sexual courtship and consummation. The *Tāntric*, or tāntric practitioner may use visualizations of deities, identifying with the deity so that the aspirant "becomes" the *Ishta-deva* or meditational deity.

Expansion of Tantra

When the Greeks came to India they felt the impact of shakti started worshipping Her and have mentioned it at many places. So, the Europeans mislead themselves and declared that period as the period when Tantra started. It is not only the Greeks but all the invaders who felt the impact as the bond between Shakti of Tantra and Indian belief to be deep and powerful.

Buddhism and Jainism also developed a Tāntric cult which has developed on the traditional pattern and is practised in many countries including Europe and America. Even Islam in India was influenced by Tantra. The geographical impact of Tantric ideas and practices spread far outside of India, into Tibet, Nepal, China, Japan, Cambodia, Vietnam, and Indonesia. Today, it is Tibetan Buddhism and various forms of Hinduism that show the strongest Tantric influence, as well as the international postural yoga movement and most forms of American alternative spirituality grouped under the New Age Rubric.

Invaders and other foreigners could not maintain its purity as they were not dedicated, so Tantra got mixed up with many ordinary and esoteric traditions and gained notriety. Some may have/had hideous intentions and may have tried to get it uprooted by explaining it in different ways and including ascribing to it unsocial, immoral and inhuman activities which are not allowed in real Tantra. **The one basic concept, accepted everywhere, is that all the powers gained through Tantra are lost if used for personal gains or in immoral acts**.

The doctrines of Tantra vary too widely to summarize briefly as each Siddha Sādhak added something to replace something else. This way, many changes occurred and were termed as different

Tāntric Practices which are now claimed to be divisions. It may have been done to make the process easier or for quicker gains. The real reasons for the changes are not known as no Siddha ever explained why the changes were added while adding and teaching them to their disciples. At certain places where the Siddha attained *Samādhi* without teaching everything to his main disciple, the disciple started doing something on hearsay.

Some of the Siddhas wrote their Mantras and rituals without mentioning the reasons and their thinking or their personal experiences. It was the tradition to write only the important matter and to leave out everything extraneous. That way, many traditions and cults were created even in Tantra.

To be precise, this is not turning away from the tradition or breaking it, but the extension of the same tradition. These are all Tantras and Tāntric practices, and each one is rich and true enough to give success. Anyway, there is nothing called instant success in any such practice as all of them are parts of penance and not ready food to be eaten as and when needed. Penance is always tough and time consuming.

Some people compare the different versions and find dual and non-dual existence at the core. They forget that the non-dual entity is only the half. Its completness lies in the other half. That is the meaning of Ardha-nārishwar. One of its most salient features, they say, when compared with earlier forms of Indian religion is that its non-dual forms reject the renunciation values of classical yoga, offering instead a world-embracing vision of the whole of reality as the self-expression of a single, free and joyous Divine Consciousness; as the divine play of *Shiva* and *Shakti*. Actually, this is the main concept and has remained unchanged. From the very beginning it is accepted that Shivā is inseparable from Shiva; that Shiva and Shakti are one and the same.

The practical consequence of this view was that not only the Tāntrics but householders also could aspire to spiritual liberation in the Tāntric system. Furthermore, since Tantra dissolved the false dichotomy of spiritual versus mundane, practitioners could entail every aspect of their daily lives into their spiritual growth process, seeking to realize the transcendental in the mundane. Tāntric spiritual practices and rituals thus aim to bring about an inner realization of the truth that "Nothing exists that is not Divine" *na-ashivam vidyate kvachid*; bringing freedom from ignorance and from the cycle of suffering, *samsārikatā*; that gives pain and keeps suffering alive till the *Jiva* is not freed from the endless cycle of birth-death and re-birth. It is achieved with *Moksha*, or Salvation.

Shiva and Shivā and Tantra

Shivā is the integral power of Brahma, and Shiva is the manifest form of Brahma. There is no distinction between them other than that one is male and the other is female. To worship one is to worship the other. Most people worship both but some worship Shiva and others Shivā. All forms of worship are the same. This is the theory behind the creation. Power is inherent in the object and the object contains power. Throughout the cosmos whatever is male in nature is Shiva and whatever is female is Bhagawati Umā. The praise of one is the praise of the other.

Distinct and yet the same

Shivā or Umā or Bhagawati or Kāli has two forms Vyakta, concrete or worldly and Avyakta, subtle or cosmic. The following are the worldly 'Vyakta' forms of Shakti, the forms with attributes: Māyā, Mahāmāyā, Moolaprakriti, Avyakt, Avyākrit, Kundalini, Maheshwari. Ādishakti. Ādimāyā, Parāshakti, Parameshwari, Jagadishwari, Tamas, Agyān, Navadurgā, Kāli, Ashtalakshmi, Navashakti, Devi, Mahāshakti, Mahālakshmi, Mahāsaraswati, Mahākāli, Pārvati, Sitā, Rādhā, Rukmini, Sati, Tārā, Chandi, Dākini, (in Moolādhār Chakra), Rākini (in Swādhistān Chakra), Lākini (in Manipuraka Chakra), Kākini (in Anāhat Chakra), Shākini (in Vishuddha Chakra), Shushkā, Chandikā, Utpalā, Jayā, Siddhā, Jayanti, Vijayā, Aparājitā, Durgā, Umā, Gāyatri, Sāvitri, Saraswati, Gauri, Bhawāni and Kāli, and many more.

Shakti or Power is everything: the strength, the force, the action and the living element. Without Shakti we can neither move nor act, neither we can think nor speak, neither see nor listen to, neither touch nor taste, can neither know nor understand. Everything gives power, has power to generate power, attractions, repulsions, electrical, thinking and doing are all the expressions of power.

There is nothing in the universe that has no power. Everything great and small has some power, may be feeble, insignificant but it has energy and power. Mā Shakti is behind and in every creation. On that very system and process of energy and power, man has also created so many things.

Everything we say or do is the play of power. That power and energy is everywhere in the Cosmos and in abundance. They are powerful, skilled and accomplished that have absorbed more cosmic power and energy and are adept into using them to the best of ability and advantage. *They know Mā, the inherent source of eternal energy.*

Its form is not known, even to Brahmā, hence and is called **Agyeyā**, unknown and unknowable. (It must be mentioned here that for a long time now, Western and modern scientists have been trying hard to know it through Higgs-Boson particles.) No one can reach its end so it is called **Anantā**, Endless, one that has no end. One cannot perceive its aim, so it is called **Alakshyā**, unseen. One cannot understand its birth or it has no birth, so it is called **Ajā**, born without birth. It is everywhere alone, so it is called **Ekā**, and it is alone and everywhere, so it is called **Na ekā**. Thus Shakti is called _ *Agyeyā, Anantā, Alakshyā, Ajā, Ekā and Naekā.*

Shakti exists, may be as Kāli or Karāli; and others exist because of Shakti. It makes no difference whether one feels it or not, one experiences it or not. What can experiments do to it? Experiments are human deeds and whims but claimed to be for knowing the Truth. The truth is that experiments have created more veils and curtains, and covered Truth with mists. They have miscalculated and misrepresented the facts and misled the world.

This Shakti is the life force, the cause behind living and the force behind all activities. The Indian concept of Shakti, Shiva-Shakti, Brāhmani Shakti or Vaishnavi Shakti is purely scientific. But it is very complex and cannot be understood without a rich vocabulary and deep knowledge of the different connotations and denotations of the closely related words. The difference among them is so subtle that it becomes exceedingly difficult to immediately co-relate, in what context and meaning the word is used. But one thing is sure that Brahman or Shiva or Shakti are always considered to be the **life force** that resides in all: animate or inanimate. It is called *Ātmā* or the Soul. It is explained in the Niruttar Tantra that Prāna or life force enters as '*sah*' in the living beings and goes out as '*han*' making it '*hansah*', which is the '*Nād Brahman*' or the 'Perfect Mantra' that the living beings always and unknowingly chant. This 'chanting' is the cause of life, the moment it ceases, the body is dead and physical activities are stopped. The lines are:

Hankārena bahiryāti sah kārena vishet punah,
Hanseti paramam mantram jivo japati sarvadā.

हंकारेण बहिर्याति स:कारेण विशेत् पुन: ।
हंसोति परमं मन्त्रं जीवो जपति सर्वदा ॥

Vāmāchār

Though the vast majority of scriptural *Tantric* teachings are not concerned with sexuality, in the popular imagination the term tantra and the notion of superlative sex are indelibly, but erroneously, linked. It is the case that in the non-dual schools that advocated "left-handed" practice or *vāmāchāra*, sexual rituals were employed as a way of entering, intensifying and expanding awareness and dissolving mind-created boundaries.

✿ ✿ ✿

17

Tantra: A Mixed Practice

Tantra is a mixed practice. It takes many things from Vedas, Mantras and Yantras too. It is neither a true Vedic tradition nor a complete departure from it. As usual, like other things, Tantra also evolved out of Vedas or it was a Vedic practice which aquired a separate entity and acceptance.

Tantra is a part of many other doctrines and practices for supernatural powers. In other words it can be said that Tantra absorbed many things from different doctrines for sublimity and attainment. As so many things are required for growing from inside and for achieving something higher, many things from many places were borrowed and incorporated in it. Yet it has maintained its serparate entity since time immemorial because whatever others may say, Tāntric practices were there in India even when there was no civilization anywhere else in the world, what to say of subtle inner growth.

Relation with Vedic tradition

Various orthodox Brahmans routinely incorporate Tāntric rituals in their daily activities or Ahnikas. For example, *sarva-anga-nyāsa* and *kara-nyāsa,* Tāntric techniques for placing various deities, are part of chanting tracts such as the *rudra-prashna* of the Yajurveda and Vishnu-sahasra-nāma; and Gāyatri-āwāhanam. It is a common part of Sandhyā-vandanam in south India. Orthodox temple archakas of various sects profess to follow rules laid down in Tāntric texts. For example, priests of the Iyengar sect prefer to follow Pancharātra *Āgama*s. Nyāsa and Vinyāsa are Vedic practice used in all the three, Mantra, Tantra and Yantra. It helps in concentration and in clarifying the meaning.

Middle Ages saw the fall of man from the height of purity and morality. Many things related to luxury and physical pleasure crept into the Tantra Sādhanā. Most of the Indians disliked the fall and turned away from Tantra. It is not true that the orthodox Vedic traditions were antagonistic to Tantra as the Tāntric texts are not hostile to the Vedas. Some Tāntrics may regard the precepts of the Vedas as too difficult for them. They tried an easier cult and an easier doctrine for both pleasure and attainment. They are responsible that Tantra faced devaluation in the eyes of the mass. Many orthodox Brahmans who accept the authority of the Vedas reject the authority of the Tantras. Although, many Tāntric writers wanted to base their doctrines on the Vedas, some orthodox followers of the Vedic tradition invariably referred to Tantra in a spirit of denunciation, stressing its anti-Vedic character despite the fact that Vedic Mantras are recited in Tāntric practices.

Relation to Yoga

During the Middle Ages, it became exceedingly difficult to follow the original texts as wise Brahmins were killed and most of Nirukta and other books were burnt to ashes. It was at that time numerous analytical and explanatory books appeared, which also caused direct deviation from the grand old tradition. Shaiva Tantra gave Hathayoga Pradipikā and Gheranda Samhitā. It is from these manuals that most modern knowledge of Yoga and the subtle body emanates as these books are easier versions. Also, it is easier to find these texts, while it is very difficult to get older texts.

Yoga as it has been inherited in the modern world, comes from Yoga Vāshishta and Pātanjali Yoga but it also has its scattered hair roots in Tāntric rituals and in secondary passages, *pādas* within Tāntric scriptures. The practices of mantra, *āsana*, seat/pose; sense-withdrawal, *pratyāhāra*; breath-regulation, *prānāyāma*; mental or mantric fixation, *dhāranā*; meditation, *dhyāna; mudrā*, the subtle body, *sukshma sharira*; with its energy centres, *chakras, ādhāras, granthis,* etc. and channels, *nādis*, as well as the phenomenon of Kundalini Shakti are but a few of the tenets that are also integrated to Tantra and comprise Tāntric Yoga. Some of these derive from earlier, pre-Tāntric sources, such as the Upanishads, Āranyakas and the Yoga Sutras. They were greatly expanded upon, ritualized, and philosophically contextualized in these Tantras and mostly with a difference.

Relation to Buddhist Tantra

In Buddhism, particularly in Vajra-yāna, Tantra is assimilated and practised. It is claimed and defined as a scripture taught by the Buddha describing the Vajrayāna practices.

According to Tibetan Buddhist Tāntric master Lama Thubten Yeshe:

'Each one of us is a union of all universal energy. Everything that we need in order to be complete is within us right at this very moment. It is simply a matter of being able to recognize it. This is the Tāntric approach.'

It is not only a question of recognizing the Eternal Energy that an individual possesses but also of purifying it; awakening it; mastering it and using it for the good of living beings. Despite the fact that it is a personal possession yet it is cosmic and divine in nature and scope; it is for all. It must not be used selfishly or lustfully.

Ritual Practices

Statues of the Tāntric goddess Kālī from Dakshineswar, West Bengal, India; along with her Yantra, are placed for worship.

The Paths

The Tāntric aim is to sublimate rather than to negate relative reality. This process of sublimation consists of three phases: purification, elevation, and the "reaffirmation of identity on the plane of pure consciousness." The methods employed by *Dakshināchāra*, right-hand path, interpretations of Tantra are very different from the methods used in the pursuit of the *Vāmāchāra,* the left-hand path. Because of the wide range of communities covered by the term *tantra,* it is challenging and problematic to describe Tāntric practices definitively. Yet one can provide a useful dichotomy of the General Ritual and the Secret Ritual.

General Ritual

The general ritual or *pujā* may include any of the following elements:

Mantra and Yantra

As in other Hindu and Buddhist yoga traditions, *mantra* and *yantra* play an important role in Tantra. The *mantra* and *yantra* are instruments to invoke specific Hindu deities such as Shiva, Shakti, or Kali. Similarly, *pujā* may involve focusing on a *yantra* or *mandala* associated with a deity.

Identification with Deities

Tantra, as a development of early Vedic thought, embraced the gods and goddesses, especially Shiva and Shakti, along with the *Advaita* philosophy that each represents an *aspect* of the ultimate Parā Shiva, or Brahmna. These deities may be worshipped externally with flowers, incense, and other offerings, such as chanting names or mantras or both; singing and dancing. These deities are treated as *Ishta Devatā* for meditations, the practitioners either visualize themselves *as* the deity, or experience the *darshan,* the vision of the deity. These Tāntric practices the foundation of the ritual, temple dance of the *devadāsis,* and are preserved in the *Melattur* style of *Bhāratanātyam.*

Secret Ritual

Secret rituals are performed mostly in the Vāma-mārga, a branch of Tantra which departs from its conventional form or mantra and also from yoga. Secret rituals may include any or all of the elements of ordinary ritual, either directly or substituted, along with other sensate rites and themes such as a feast, representing food, or sustenance; coitus, representing sexuality and procreation; the charnel grounds, representing death and transition and defecation, urination and vomiting, representing waste, renewal, and fecundity.

Chakrapujā

Worship with the Pancha-tattva generally takes place in a Chakra or circle composed of men and women, sitting in a circle, the Shakti, or female practitioner, being on the Sādhaka's or male practitioner's left. Hence it is called *Chakrapujā*. There are various kinds of Chakra; productive, but with differing fruits for the participators therein.

There are a series of variations and substitutions of the *Pancha-tattva, Panchamakāra* "elements" or *tattva* encoded in the Tantras and various Tāntric traditions, and affirms that there is a direct correlation to the Tāntric Five Nectars and the *Mahābhūta*.

Sexual Rites

Sexual rites of the Vāma-mārga may have emerged from early Tantra as a practical means of catalyzing biochemical transformations in the body to facilitate heightened states of awareness. These constitute a vital offering to Tāntric deities. Sexual rites may have also evolved from clan initiation ceremonies involving transactions of sexual fluids. Here, the male initiate is inseminated or ensanguined with the sexual emissions of the female consort, sometimes admixed with the semen of the guru. The *Tāntrika* is thus transformed into a son of the clan, *kulaputra*, through the grace of his consort. The clan fluid, *kuladravya* or clan nectar, *kulāmrita,* is conceived as flowing naturally from her womb. Later developments in the rite emphasize the primacy of bliss and divine union, which replace the more bodily connotations of earlier forms. For many practicing lineages, these *maithuna* practices metamorphased into psychological symbolism.

When enacted as enjoined by the Tantras, the ritual culminates in a sublime experience of infinite awareness for both the participants. Tāntric texts specify that sex has three distinct and separate purposes, procreation, pleasure, and liberation. Those seeking liberation eschew frictional orgasm for a higher form of ecstasy, as the couple participating in the ritual lock in a static embrace. Several sexual rituals are recommended and practiced. These involve elaborate and meticulous preparatory and purificatory rites. The sexual act itself balances energies coursing within the *prānic idā* and *pingalā* channels in the subtle bodies of both participants. The **sushumnā** *nadi* is awakened and *kundalini* rises upwards within it. This eventually culminates in *Samādhi*, wherein the respective individual personalities and identities of each of the participants are completely dissolved in a unity of cosmic consciousness. Tāntrics understand these acts on multiple levels. The male and female participants are conjoined physically, and represent *Shiva* and *Shakti*, the male and female principles. Beyond the physical, a subtle fusion of *Shiva* and *Shakti* energies takes place, resulting in a united energy field. On an individual level, each participant experiences a fusion of one's own *Shiva* and *Shakti* energies.

✿✿✿

18

Kula, Kaul or Kaulini in Tantra Shāshtra

Tantra Shāshtra deals with the ways and means of worshipping various Gods, goddesses and deities. There are particular books for worshipping almost each of the gods and goddesses. There are many books on some of them. They follow a particular path and express particular opinion. On the basis of the path and opinions they are divided into three: Samaya Mat, Kaul Mat and Mishra Mat. Incidentally (or ironically, or happily), these are also the ways of vidyopāsanā or enlightenment.

1. Samaya Mat or Samayāchār Tantra follows the Vedic ways for attaining Shri Vidyā. They mostly follow the five books:

    i.   Vashishtha Samhitā

    ii.   Sanak Samhitā

    iii. Sanadan Samhitā

    iv.   Sanat Kumār Samhitā and

    v.   Shukra Samhitā. It is the right path or Dakshina Mārg of worshipping

2. The famous 64 Tantras, including Mahāmāyā Tantra and Shambar Tantra come under the classification of Kaul or Kula Mat. It is the left path or Vāma Mārga of worshipping.

3. The middle path between the two is called Mishra (Mixed) Mat. Many books are available on it. They try to bridge the gap between the Rightists and Leftists.

The Vāma Mārg incurred a lot of notoriety during the Middle Ages which only worsened during the British period. Things have not improved for it ever now. As a result, many despise with Tāntrika Sādhanā and it has touched its lowest ebb.

It was all due to wrong and degenerated analysis and explanation of the Panch Makār (five things beginning with letter M), *Madya, Mānsa, Matasya, Mudrā* and *Maithun*. The Tāntriks started following a filthy concept that was based totally on literal meaning but in Tantra Shāshtra all the five Makārs have symbolic meaning and significance. Since, the pioneer of Vāma Mārga is Bhagawān Shankar, who stands for Shiva-Tattva, Morality, hence there can never be anything immoral or unacceptable in it.

The Shāshtras should be analysed and understood correctly before it is followed. The following are the real meaning of Kaul and Panch Makār. It is all based on the Kundali and Nādi (Irā, Pingalā and Sushumnā). One should read Shri Lalit Sahasranāma in the Brahmānd Purāna and the commentaries on it.

Kula, Kaul *or* Kaulini

According to the 'Vishwakosha', country, home, people of same clan, similar gotra and body are called Kula. A sincere lady is called a Kula Vadhu. As she remains secure under curtain too so this science, called Shāmbhari Vidyā, has been kept under cover and mystery:

> *Anyāst sakalā vidyāh prakatā manika iwa,*
> *Eyam tu shāmbhavi vidyā guptā kula badhuh iwa.*

अन्यास्त सकला विद्या प्रकटा मणिक इव।
इयं तु शाम्भवी विद्या गुप्ता कुल-वधुः इव॥

Moral behaviour is also called Kula but in Tantrashāshtra Kula is mentioned only with reference to the basic cycle, *Mooladhār chakra* of *Kundalini* where the earth element is completely deluded:

> *Prithvi tattva-leeyate yatra tat kulam,*
> *Ādhār chakram tat sambandh alakshanayā sushumnā mārgo api.*

पृथ्वी तत्वालियते यत्र तत् कुलं
आधार चक्रं तत् सम्बन्ध अलक्षन्या सुषम्नाः मार्गो अपि।

Just below the **Brahman Randhra** there is a lotus with thousand petals. In it the *Kula Devi* and *Kula Shakti* reside. It is also called *kula*. According to *Swachhand Tantra Shakti* is called *kulam*, Shiva is called *akulam* and their relation is called *kaul*. The balancing of Shiva and Shakti is *kaula* and the presiding deity of that *kula* is called *kaulani*:

> *Kulam shaktih iti proktam akulm shiva uchyate,*
> *Kule akulasya sambandhah kaulam iti abhidhiyate.*

> कुलं शक्तिः इति प्रोक्तं अकुलं शिव उच्यते।
> कुल अकुलस्य सम्बन्धः कौलं इत्यभिधीयते॥

The way coming down the family tradition is called kaula:

Swa swa bansah paramparā prāpto mārgah kula sambandhitwāt kaulah.

With the kula and kaulani are related the *Tantra, Mantra* and *Yantra*. That which has such multipurpose Tantras, devices, as *Gyānārnava* and *Kulārnava* is called **Mahātantrā**. Swatantra is the related tantra. That which has *Bālā* and *Bagalā* like effective Mantras is called **Mahāmantrā**. *Shri Vidyā* is the most popular mantra. That who is worshipped with mystic mechanical formulas, Yantras, like *Poojā Chakra* and *Padma Chakra* is called **Mahāyantra**. *Siddhi Vajra* is the most effective Yantra.

Panch Makārs

Then comes the debatable *Panch Makār*: *Madya, Māns, Meena, Mudrā*, and *Maithun*. According to *Dakshināmurti Samhitā* it is also famous as *Vārāhi*. That Shakti is mostly called Panchami, the spouse of Sadāshiva, who is one among the five Devas. It mentions that Panch Makārs are five spots in the body: *Makāreshu panchamasya ānand rupatwā tad rupā*. In the form of *ānand* it is established in the body as stated in Kalpa Sutra. Those five corresponding places are expressed through Panch Makārs:

Ānandam brahmano rupam tat cha dehe vyawasthitam,
Tasya abhivyanjikā panch makārāh taih athārchanam.

आनन्दं ब्रह्माणो रूपं तच्च देहे व्यवस्थितम्।
तस्य अभिव्यन्जिका पन्च मकाराः तैः अथार्चनम्॥

Those persons, who are ignorant of the places and its real meaning follow the wrong path or dislike that wrong path. There is nothing wrong with Panch Makār if taken in its true form and meaning.

The symbolical meaning of the ancient time was deliberately changed to the popular meaning of the middle ages to malign it as it was done to almost everything great in Indian Sanskriti and Samskār or Gyān and Bhakti. When there is the question of worship of God, naturally, purity is essential. Keeping that purity in mind one should explain these words or fall down to degraded traditions of physical pleasure only.

Madirā: Amrit, Nectar

The Yogis, Hatha Yogis and others in deep penance aim at, try to and get the Nectar that oozes out from Sahsrār Chakra. It is intoxicating and gives immense satisfaction, strength and a sort of immortality or youthfulness to the Sādhaka, devotee. It is not the western, tribal or traditional Indian wine:

Brahma sthān saroj pātra lasitā brahmānd tripti pradā,
Yā shubhra anshu kalā sudhā vigalitā sā pāna yogya surā,
Sā hālā piwatā mana artha phaladā shri divya bhāva āshritā,
Yāmitwā munayah parārtha kushalā nirvāna mukti gatāh.

ब्रह्म स्थान सरोज पात्र लसिता ब्रह्मांड तृप्ति प्रदा।
या शुभ्रांशुकला सुधा विगलिता सा पान योग्य सुरा॥
सा हाला पिवता मन-अर्थ फलदा श्री दिव्य भाव अश्रित।
यामित्वा मुनयः परार्थ-कुशला निर्वाण मुक्ति-गताः॥

Madya or Madirā is the knowledge about the Brahma without attributes, Nirvikār and Niranjan:

Yad uktam paramam brahma nirvikāram niranjanam,
Tasmin pramadan gyānam tan madyam parikirtitam.

यदुक्तं परमं ब्रह्म निर्विकारं निरञ्जनम् ।
तस्मिन् प्रमादन ज्ञानं तन मद्यं परिकीर्तितम् ॥

Kulārnava Tantra 17: 63, 64; clarifies its spiritual value and effect. It says: Because Madya destroys all bondage of Māyā; shows the path of liberation; and parts away with eight afflictions; it is called Madya, madirā. It connotes great charity, Mahādāna; because the holy place of Yoga is the only place that calls for its use and because it generates the state of Shiva, so, it is called Madya:

Māyā-jāla-ādi-shamanān-moksha-mārga-nirupanāt;
Ashta-dukh-ādi-virahān-madyam-iti-abhidhiyate.
Mahā-dānārth-rupa-tvāt yoga-bhumi-ek-kāranāt;
Mad-bhāva-jananā-devi madyam-iti-abhidhiyate.

मायाजाल आदि शमनान मोक्ष मार्ग निरुपणात् ।
अष्ट दु:खादि विरहान मद्यमितिभिधीयते ॥
महादानार्थ रूपत्त्वात्योग भूम्येक कारणात् ।
मदभाव जनना देवी मद्यमितिभिधीयते ॥

Māns: To Get Rid of Physical Sensations

To eat *māns* or meat or flesh is to get completely detached from the sensations caused to and felt through body. It is the state of bodilessness. To eschew the craming or pleasure of meat-eating, means to get control over sex, anger, lust, affection, and other animal instinct. It is an essential act for success in Yoga. He is wise that succeeds in becoming completely detached from the physical longings. They are the virtuous persons that practise non-violence. Eating meat without being violent can mean only one thing, i.e., getting control over one's physical body:

Kām krodha sulobh moha pashukānschhitwā vivekāshnā,
Mānsam nirvishyam parātma sukhadam khādanti teshām budhāh.
Te vigyānparā dharātal surāste punya wanto narā,
Nāshrayiyat pashu mānsam vimate hinsā param sajjanah.

काम क्रोध सुलोभ मोह पशुकश्चछित्वा विवेकश्ना।
मनसं निर्विषयं परात्मा सुखदं खादन्ति तेषां बुद्धः॥
ते विज्ञानपरा धरातल सुरस्ते पुण्यवन्तो नराः।
नश्रायियत् पशु मांसं विमेत हिंसा परम् सज्जनः॥

O Rasanāpriye! Rasanā is a synonym to Mā. *Vākya*, sentence is a part of it. He that always devours his sentences and never utters them, is the silent yogi. Such yogis eat, chew and swallow their sentences. They keep mum. They are the *Māns-Sādhakas*:

Mā shabdād rasanā ksheyā tad anshān rasanāpriye.
Sadā yo bhakshaye devi sa yeva māns sādhakah.

माशब्दाद् रसना क्षेयातद् अंशान रसनाप्रिये।
सदायो भक्षये देवी सैव मांस साधकः॥

There must be a simple question: what is that *mānsa* which is always auspicious, *mangalya*; gives concentrated pleasure, *samvid-ānand* and is very dear to all the gods, *sarva-deva-priya-tvāt*. Naturally it is not the flesh. The explanation of *māns* in Kulārnava Tantra 17:69, gives these words which indicate purity:

Mānglya-jananā-devisamvidānand-dānatah;
Sarva-deva-proya-tvāt māns iti abhidhiyate.

Because it causes auspiciousness; because it gives ānand in consciousness and because it is dear to all gods; it is called *māns*.

Meena or Matsya: Breathing Control and Non-commitment

Our physical longings, ego, jealousy, pride, lust, affection and other animal instincts, the six enemies are the six fish. He succeeds in yoga who eats them and digests them with the inner heat:

Ahankāro dambho mada pishunatā matsar dweshah,
Shad yetān minān wai vishaya harjālena vidhritān.
Pachan sadviyā agnau niyamit kritih dhivar kritih,
Sadā khādet sarvānna ch a jalacharānām tu pishitam.

अहंकारो दम्भो मद पिशुनेत मत्सर द्वेष: ।
सदेतान् मिनानवै विश्व हर्जलेन विर्धितन ॥
पचन सदविया अंगनौ नियमित कृति: धीवर कृति: ।
सदाखादेत् सर्वना च अजलचरणान तू पिषितम् ॥

The Idā and Pingalā nadies in body are called Gangā and Yamunā
(the third one Sushumnā is called Saraswati). Incoming and
outgoing breaths are the two fish that always move in the rivers
Gangā and Yamunā. They are the Matasya Sādhakas that control
the breathe through Prānāyāma while performing Kumbhak:

Gangā yamunayoh madhye matsyau charatah sadā,
Tau matsyau bhakshayed yastu bhawen matsya sādhakah.

गंगा-यमुनयो मध्येमत्स्यौ चरत: सदा ।
तौ-मत्स्यौ भक्षयेद्-यस्तु भवेन मत्स्य साधक: ॥

One should be balanced in both pain and pleasure, neither too
much aggrieved nor excited. This knowledge of the fact and
practice in life is called Matasya:

Matsamānam sarve moole sukh dukham idam priye,
Iti yat sātwikam gyānam tan matsyah parikirtitah.

मतसमानं सर्वे मूले सुख दुखं इदं प्रिये ।
इति यत सात्विकं ज्ञानं तन् मत्स्य: परिकृतित: ॥

Mudrā: Different State of Mind or Feelings

Hope, desire, lust, fear, hatred, respect, shyness and anger are
eight Mudrās that cause a lot of pain throughout the life. He is a
great soul that controls them and burns them out:

Āshā trishnā jugupsā bhaya vishād ghrinā māna lajjā prakopah,
Brahma āgnāwasht mudrāh parāsu kritih janah pāchya mānāh samantāt.
Nityam sambhakshaye tānvahit manasā divya bhāvānurāgi,
Yo asau brahmānd bhānde pashuhat vimuksho rudra tulyo mahātamāh.

आशा तृष्णा जगप्सा भय विषाद घृणा मान लज्जा प्रकोपः।
ब्रह्म आग्नवश्त मुद्राः परासु कृतिः जनः पाच्यमानः समन्तात॥
नित्यं सम्भक्षये तान्वहित मन्सा दिव्य भावानुरागी।
यो असौ ब्रह्मांड भांडे पशुहत विमुक्षो रूद्रः तुल्यो महात्माः॥

O Deveshi! The soul, like pārad, resides in the lotus with thousand petals. In its brightness, it is like millions of suns but in coolness it is like millions of moons. That absolute element possesses the power of the Kundalini. The person that gets the revelation of this divine knowledge is the real Mudrā-Sādhak:

Sahasrāre mahāpadme karnikā mudritashcharet,
Ātmā tatraiva Deveshi kewalah pardosham.
Surya koti pratikāshah chndra koti sushitalah,
Ateeva kamaneeyashcha mahā kundalini yutah.
Yasya gyānodayah tatra Mudrā-Sādhak uchyate.

सहस्रारे महापदमे कर्निका मुद्रिताश्चरेत।
आत्मा तत्रैव देवसि केवलः परदोषं॥
सूर्यकोटि प्रतिकाशः चन्द्रकोटि सुशीतलः
अतीव कामनीयश्च महाकुंडलिनी युतः।
यस्य ज्ञानोदयः तत्र मुद्रासाधक उच्यते॥

Through the company of Saints one gets salvation but in the company of illiterates and immoral persons one gets tied to the world. To know this fact and to avoid the bad company is known as Mudrā:

Sat sangena bhaven mukti-ast sangeshu bandhanam,
Asat sang mudrānam yattu tan mudrā prakirtitā.

सत्-संगेन भवेन मुक्तिस्त संगेषु बंधनम्।
असत् संग मुद्रानं यतु तन् मुद्रा प्रकीर्तिता॥

When there has been ample stress on the purity and refinement in the whole of Sanatana Dharma then showing something dirty to God is never possible. Mudrā is both art and science in Vedic Culture. Almost every emotion and each variation is shown through different mudras, often called Nyāsa. It is very valuable.

Kularnāva Tantra (17:57), establishes it. When the Tantras give pious meaning to Panch Makār then it is a wonder how it descended to such an extent. Perhaps, because all the best Gurus were killed and the persons elevated to that high rank were under different influences and of little learning. They were given a luxurious life for creating doubts and mixing dirty things in pious deeds for liberation.

Mudra is such that pleases the gods— *mudam kurvanti devānām* and melts the mind— *manānsi drāvayanti* and that is why it is called Mudrā:

Mudam kurvanti devānām manānsi dravyanti cha;
Tasmān-mudrā iti khyātā dashitavyā kuleshwari.

मुदं कुर्वन्ति देवानां मनांसि द्रवयन्ति च।
तस्मान्मुद्रा इति ख्याता दशितव्या कुलेश्वरी ॥

Maithun: Union, Brahma Gyān

Sushumnā is the nādi that connects one with the Sahasrār chakra. So, she is the Vadhu that has to be decorated and kept closer. She is one's own and inside. For her, everything else should be rejected. One has to keep a smooth, soothing and closer relation with only her:

Yā nādi sukshma rupā parampadagatā sevaneeyā sushumnā,
Sā kāntā linga nārhā na manuja ramani sundari vār-oshit,
Kuryā chandrārk yoge yuvā pawangate maithunam naiva yonau,
Yogindro vishwa vandyah sukhamaya bhavane tām
prishvaya nityam.

या नन्दी सूक्ष्म रूपा परमपदगताः सेवनीया सुषुम्ना।
स कन्ता लिंगा नरहा न मनुजा रमानी सुन्दरी वरोसित॥
कुर्या चन्द्रार्क योगे युवा पवनगते मैथुनं नैवयोनौ।
योगिन्द्रो विश्व वंद्यः सुखमय भवने ताम् प्रिश्वै नित्यम्॥

'Ref', the upper 'r' sound, resides in the red reservoir. Makār resides in as a vindu, a spot in the Mahāyoni. When one takes the help of the swan in the form of '|', then the sacred union is

completed. It is known as Brahma gyān. He, who achieves it, is a
Maithun-Sādhak:

> *Refāstu kumkum ābhās kunda madhyevyvasthitah,*
> *Makārascha vindu rupah mahāyonau sthitah priye.*
> *Akār hansam ārudhya ekadtā cha yadā bhaveta,*
> *Tadā jāto mahānando brahma gyānam sudurlabham.*

रेफास्तु कुमकुम आभास कुंद मध्येव्यवस्थितः।
मकारश्च विन्दुरूपः महायोनौ स्थितः प्रियेः॥
अकारहंसं आरुध्येकदता च यदा भवेत।
तदा जातो महानन्दो ब्रह्म ज्ञानं सुदूरलभं॥

Kundali Shakti resides in every body as a coiled snake in the
Moolādhār Chakra. One who awakens it, clears ways, opens other
charkas, rises up, reaches Shiva, in the Sahasrār chakra and he
who succeeds in the union of Shiva and Shakti, is a Brahmagyāni.
It is called union, yoga or *maithun*:

> *Kula kundalini shaktih dehini dehadhārini,*
> *Tathā shivatwa samyogo maithunam parikirtitam.*

कुल कुंडलिनी शक्तिः देहिनी देहधारिणी।
तथा शिवात्वा समयोगो मैथुनम परिकीर्तितम्॥

No one should try to follow unholy, immoral and unethical path
because of some misunderstanding or for some personal gain. Life
at large is important. Human life is far superior and human beings
will have to prove to every living being that their superiority is
because of the immense knowledge and pious moral character.
They are to save everything and not to destroy because life depends
on numerous things; and because in life, and its inner growth, life
is the only thing important. The existence of 'one' is ephemeral.
Moreover, everyone should aim at and try to be purer and better
to pave the way for others, not for creating obstacles in the way or
life whether of human beings or of others: *paropakārāya punyāya*;
it is a virtue to help others.

Divisions of Shakti in Tantrashāshtra

In Tantrashāshtra, particularly in the Shākt Tantra, there are 94 divisions called Kalā. According to 'Saubhāgya Ratnākar' there are the following Kalā of different gods. They are all various forms of Shakti:

19 Kalā of Sadāshiva, 06 Kalā of Ishwar, 10 Kalā of Vishnu, 11 Kalā of Rudra,

10 Kalā of Brahmā, 10 Kalā of Agni, 12 Kalā of Surya, 16 Kalā of Chandramā,

According to 'Saubhāgya Ratnākar' the following are the names of the Kalā of different gods.

19 Kalā of Sadāshiva

S.N.	Name of Kalā	S.N.	Name of Kalā
1.	Nibritti	11.	Sukshma Amritā
2.	Pratishthā	12.	Gyān Amritā
3.	Shānti	13.	Amritā
4.	Vidyā	14.	Āpyāyani
5.	Indhikā	15.	Vyāpani
6.	Dipikā	16.	Vyomarupā
7.	Rechikā	17.	Moola Vidyā Mantra Kalā
8.	Mochikā	18.	Mahā Mantra Kalā
9.	Parā	19.	Jyotish Kalā
10.	Sukshmā		

06 Kalā of Ishwar

S.N.	Name of Kalā	S.N.	Name of Kalā
1.	Pitā	4.	Arunā
2.	Shwetā	5.	Asitā
3.	Nityā	6.	Anantā

10 Kalā of Vishnu

S.N.	Name of Kalā	S.N.	Name of Kalā
1.	Jadā	6.	Kāmikā
2.	Pālini	7.	Vardā
3.	Shānti	8.	Hrādini
4.	Ishwari	9.	Priti
5.	Rati	10.	Dikshā

11 Kalā of Rudra

S.N.	Name of Kalā	S.N.	Name of Kalā
1.	Tikshanā	7.	Krodhani
2.	Raudri	8.	Kriyā
3.	Bhayā	9.	Udgāri
4.	Nidrā	10.	Amāyā
5.	Tandrā	11-	Mrityu
6.	Kshudhā		

10 Kalā of Brahmā

S.N.	Name of Kalā	S.N.	Name of Kalā
1.	Srishti	6.	Lakshmi
2.	Riddhi	7.	Dyuti
3.	Smriti	8.	Sthirā
4.	Medhā	9.	Sthiti
5.	Kānti	10.	Siddhi

10 Kalā of Agni

S.N.	Name of Kalā	S.N.	Name of Kalā
1.	Dhrumrārchi	6.	Sushri
2.	Ushmā	7.	Surupā
3.	Jwalini	8.	Kapilā
4.	Jwālini	9.	Havywahā
5.	Visphulingani	10.	Kavyawahā

12 Kalā of Surya

S.N.	Name of Kalā	S.N.	Name of Kalā
1.	Tapini	7.	Sushumnā
2.	Tāpini	8.	Bhogadā
3.	Dhumrā	9.	Viswā
4.	Marichi	10.	Bodhini
5.	Jwālini	11.	Dhārini
6.	Ruchi	12.	Kshamā

16 Kalā of Chandramā

S.N.	Name of Kalā	S.N.	Name of Kalā
1.	Amritā	9.	Chandrikā
2.	Mānadā	10.	Kānti
3.	Pushā	11.	Jyotsanā
4.	Tushti	12.	Shri
5.	Pushti	13.	Priti
6.	Rati	14.	Angadā
7.	Dhriti	15.	Purnā
8.	Shashini	16.	Purna Amritā

✿✿✿

Important Things to Know

1. **Kula Path Bhedan:** While passing through different paths of Kula, at least twenty one elements are crossed over in the mind. They are:

Prithvi, Earth	Apa, Water	Agni, Fire
Vāyu, Air	Ākāsh, Space	Gandha, Fragrance
Rasa, Juice, Essence	Roopa, Body	Sparsh, Touch
Shabda, Sound	Nāsikā, Nose, Smell	Jihvā, Tongue, Taste
Chakshu, Eyes	Tvak, Skin	Shrotra, Ears
Vāk, Voice	Pāni, Hands	Pāda, Feet
Pāyu, Kidney	Upastha, Genitals	Mana, Mind

2. **There are other twelve elements which are beyond mana, mind. They are:**

Buddhi, Wisdom	Ahankār, Ego	Prakriti, Nature
Kalā, Art	Avidyā, Ignorance	Vidyā, Knowledge
Rāga, Attachment	Niyati, Fate	Māyā, Illusion
Shiva, Brahma, Absolute God		Shakti, Cosmic Power
Purusha, Chitta, Consciousness		

3. **Fifteen other elements are also accepted:**

i. Sapta Dhātu:

Tvak, Skin	Asrija, Blood	Mānsa, Flesh	Meda, Fat
Asthi, Bone	Majjā, Marrow	Shukra, Semen	

ii. Pancha Prāna:

Prāna	Apāna	Vyāna
Udāna	Samāna	

iii. Triguna:

Sattva   Rājas   Tamas

4.   Chakra Nyāsa of Tattva Beeja:

Place	Element	Chakra	Beeja Mantra
Trikona	Ākāsha	Āgyā	Hang
Ashta Kona	Vāyu	Vishuddha	Yang
Dashār-dvya	Agni+Vāyu	Hrit	Yang Rang = Yung
Chatuh-dashār	Agni	Nābhi	Rang
Asgta-dal Padma	Jala	Swādhishthān	Vang
Shodasha-dal Padma	Bhu	Mooladhār	Lang

In the Mahāshaktyā Bhupur

5.   Ashta Siddhis; Eight Attainments

Animā mahimā chaiva garimā laghimā tathā;
Prāptih prākāmyam ishitvam vashitvah-cha adhata sidhyah.

अणिमा महिमा चैव गरिमा लघिमा तथा।
प्राप्तिः प्राकाम्यं इशित्वं वशित्वः च अधत सिध्यः॥

i.   **Animā**: The power to reduce the body up to anu.

ii.   **Mahimā**: The power to enlarge the body as wished.

iii. **Laghimā**: The power to make the body weightless like air.

iv.   **Garimā**: The power to make the body heavy like mountains.

v.   **Prāpti**: The power to get the desired thing with only the wish.

vi.   **Prakāmya**: The power to keep the body young, healthy and handsome.

vii. **Ishitva**: The power to control all the living beings on the earth.

viii. Vashitva: The power to change worldly things into other things.

6. **Dasha Gauna Siddhi— Ten Minor Siddhis**

i. **Anurmi**: Victory over hunger; thirst; attachment; hobbies; old age and weaknesses.

ii. **Door Shravan Siddhi**: The power to hear distant sound and talk while sitting at own place.

iii. **Door Darshan Siddhi**: The power to see distant things, even under cover while sitting at own place.

iv. **Mano-Java Siddhi**: The power to reach anywhere with the speed of mind.

v. **Kāma-rupa Siddhi**: The power to change the body to youth, old or that of a child.

vi. **Para-Kāyā Pravesh**: The power to enter others' dead or living body.

vii. **Swachhanda Maran**: The power to die as and when wished.

viii. **Deva-Kripā-anudarshan**: The power to see the play of the Gods and perform in the same manner.

ix. **Yathā-Samkalpa-Sansiddhi**: The power to get whatever one wishes.

x. **Apratihat-gati**: The power to go anywhere one likes.

7. **Pancha Kshudra Siddhis; Five Negligible Attainments**

i. **Trikālagyatā**: The power to know the past, present and future.

ii. **Advandvatā**: The power to feel and live at ease in any season and climate.

iii. **Para-chitta-aghyabhigyatā**: The power to read anyone's mind and know what is there in.

iv. **Pratishtambha**: The power to nullify the effect of poison, fire, air, heat, etc.

v. **Aparājeyatā**: The power to remain unbeaten in any debate, fight, battle, etc.

8. **Ashta Mātarah; Eight Mothers**

Brāhmni	Māheshwari	Kaumāri
Vaishanavi	Vārāhi	Indrākshi
Chāmundā	Mahālaxmi	

9. **Dasha Mudrā**

Sarva-Krodhini	Sarva-Vidrāvini	Sarva-Ākarshani
Sarva-Vashamkari	Sarva-Unmādani	Sarva-Mahā-Ankushā
Sarva-Khechari	Sarva-Beejā	Sarva-Yoni
Sarva-Trikhandā		

10. **Bhairavi in the Shodasha-dal**

Kāma-ākarshani	Budhayākarshini	Ahankār-karshini
Sparshākarshini	Shabdākarshini	Rupākarshini
Rasākarshini	Gandhākarshini	Chitākarshini
Dhairyākarshini	Smrityākarshini	Nāmākarshini
Beejākarshini	Ātmākarshini	Amritākarshini
Sharirākarshini		

11. **Bhairavi in Ashtadal**

Anaga-Kusumā	Anaga Mekhalā	Anag Madan
Anag Madanāturā	Anag Rekhā	Anag Vegani
Anag-Ankushā	Anag-Mālini	

12. **Bhairavi in Chatuh-Dashār**

Sarva-Sankshobhini	Sarva Vidrāvini	Sarva Ākarshini
Sarva Ahlādini	Sarva Sammohini	Sarva Stambhini
Sarva Jivrini	Sarva Vashamkari	Sarva Ranjini
Sarva Unmādini	Sarvārth Sādhini	Sarva Sampatipurani
Sarva Mantramayi	Sarva Dvanda Kshayamkari	

13. Bhairavi in Bahir Dashār

Sarva Siddha Pradā	Sarva Sampat Pradā
Sarva Priyankari	Sarva Mangal Kārini
Sarva Kāma Pradā	Darva Saubhāgya Dā
Sarva Mrityu Prashamini	Sarva Vighna Nivārini
Sarva Dukha Vimochani	Sarvānga Sundari

14. Bhairavi in Antah Dashār

Sarvagyā	Sarva Shakti Pradā
Sarva Aishwarya Pradā	Sarva Gyān Mayi
Sarva Vidyā Vikāsini	Sarva Ādhār Swaroopā
Sarva Pāpa Harā	Sarva Ānand Mayi
Sarva Rakshā Swarupini	Sarvepsita Phala Pradā

15. Bhairavi in Ashtār

Vashini	Kāmeshi	Modini
Vimalā	Arunā	Jayani
Sarveshi	Kaulini	

16. Bhairavi in the Triangle

Kāmeshwari	Vrajeshi	Bhaga Mālā

17. As Bindu the Point:

Shri Tripur Sundari

18. Eight Tantras of Chandra Kalā Vidyā

Chandra Kalā	Jyotishmati	Kalānidhi
Kulārnava	Kuleshwari	Bhuvaneshwari
Bārhaspatya	Durvā Samat	

19. Navātman Shiva

Kāla	Kula	Nām	Gyān	Chitta
Nād	Bindu	Kalā	Jiva	

20. **64 Mānas Mayukhāyen**— Mentally Lighted Lustre: Para-Shambhunāth Chitta Parāmbarā is worshipped with 64 Mānas Mayukhāyen.

Par	Parā	Bhar
Bharā	Chitta	Chittaparā
Mahāmāyā	Mahāmāyāparā	Srishti
Sristiparā	Ikshā	Ikshāparā
Stithi	Stithiparā	Nirodha
Nirodhaparā	Mukti	Muktiparā
Gyān	Gyānparā	Sat
Satparā	Asat	Asatparā
Sad-sat	Sad-sat-parā	Kriyā
Kriyāparā	Ātmā	Ātmā-parā
Indriyāshraya	Indriyāshra-parā	Godhar
Gochar-parā	Loka Mukhyā	Loka Mukhyā Parā
Vedavat	Vedavatparā	Samvid
Samvidparā	Kundalini	Kundalini Parā
Saushumni	Saushumniparā	Prāna Sutrā
Prāna Sutrā Parā	Spand	Spand Parā
Mātrikā	Mātrikāparā	Swarod-bhavā
Swarod-bhavā Parā	Varnajā	Varnajāparā
Shabdajā	Shabdajā Parā	Varnāgyā
Varnāgyā Parā	Vargajā	Vargajā Parā
Sanyogajā	Sanyogajā Parā	Mantra Vigrahā
Mantra Vigrhā Parā		

21. **18 Vidyās**

Rig Veda	Yajur Veda	Sāma Veda
Atharva Veda	Shikshā	Kalpa
Vyākaran	Nirukta	Chhanda
Jyotish	Mimāmsā	Nyāya
Sānkhya	Dharma Shāstra	Āyurveda
Shalya	Dhanurveda	Gāndharva Veda

22. Trees which can be used in Tāntrik Havans

Kadamba	Ashok	Agastya	Punnāga
Āma	Madhuka	Champā	Palāsa
Bilva	Pātala	Kapittha	Mālati
Mallikā	Jāti	Bandhuka	Kamal
Mandār	Yuthi	Kunda	Japā
Nārikela	Kadali	Drākshā	Ikshu
Prithuka	Chandan	Agaru	Kapura
Rochanā	Kum kum		

23. Shatakarma

i.   For Brāhmins

Adhyayan	Adhyāpan	Yajan
Yājan	Dānam	Pratigrah

ii.   For livelihood

Uchchham	Pratigrah	Vānijyam
Pashupālanam	Krishi-karma	Bhikshātanam

iii. As Tāntrik Vidyā

Shānti	Vashikaran	Stambhan
Vidwesh	Uchchātan	Māran

iv.   For purification

Dhauti	Vasti	Neti
Trātak	Kapāl-bhāti	Nauliki

Gurus in Yantra Shāstra

24. **Twelve Divyaugha Gurus:** One should Namah or Parama Shiva at the end of the name of the Gurus of this status.

   i.   1/2 Ādinath and His Shakti
   ii.   3/4 Sadāshiva and his wife
   iii. 5/6 Ishwar and his Bhāryā
   iv.   7/8 Rudra and his Vadhu
   v.   9/10 Vishnu and his beloved
   vi.   11/12 Brahmā and his wife

25. **Eleven Siddhaugha Gurus:** One should suffix Namah and Mahā Shiva at the end of the name of the gurus of this status.

Sanak   Sanandan   Sanātana   Sanat Kumār
Sanat Sujāt   Ribhukshaja   Dattātreya   Raivataka
Vāmadeva   Vyāsa   Shuka

26. **Six Mānavaugha Gurus:** One should suffix Namah and Sadā Shiva at the end of the name of the gurus of this status.

Nrisinha   Mahesha   Bhashkar
Mahendra   Mādhava   Vishnu

27. **Ten places of worship of Devi**

Linga, Symbol   Sthandila, altar
Vahni, fire   Jala, water
Vastra, garments   Surpa, winnowing fan
Phalak, plank   Murdhani, head
Mandala, ritualistic circle   Hridaya, heart

28. **Kulāshtak**: Eight Kula Shaktis which should be worshipped.

Chandāli   Charmākari   Mātangi   Pukkasi
Swapachi   Khattaki   Kaivarti   Vishwa Yosjitā

29. **Akulāshtak**: Eight non-kula Shaktis which should not be worshipped.

Kanduki   Shaundiki   Shastrajivi   Ranjaki
Gāyaki   Rajaki   Shilpi   Kauliki

30. **Seven Ullāsa, Exhilarations**

Ārambha, Childhood   *Taruna*, Juvenile
Yauvana, Youth   *Praudha*, Mature
Praudhānta, Post-maturity   *Unmanā*, Excited
Manollāsa, Hearty Exhilaration

31. **Eight Avasthās**

Kampana, trembling   *Romāncha*, thrill
Sphurana, throbbing   *Sved*, perspiration
Hāsya, laughter   *Premāshru*, tears of love
Lāsya, dance   *Gāyana*, singing

32. **Six kinds of Gurus**

    Prerak, impeller   *Suchak*, indicator
    Vāchak, explainer   *Darshak*, demonstrator
    Shikshak, teacher   *Bodhak*, illuminator

33. **Three kinds of Shishyas**

    Ādiyogya, competent in the beginning;
    Madhyayogya, competent in the middle;
    Antayogya, competent till the end, the best Shishya.

34. **Seven kinds of initiation** that gives liberation:

    Samayā, initiation through rituals;
    Sādhikā, initiation through letter;
    Putrikā, initiation through special emanation;
    Vedhakā, initiation through touch;
    Purnā, initiation through speech;
    Charyā, initiation through sight;
    Nirvāna, initiation through thought.

35. **Five grades of Kalā Dikshā**

    Nivriti Kalā: from feet to the knee;
    Pratishthā Kalā: from knee to navel;
    Vidyā Kalā: from navel to neck;
    Shanti Kalā: from neck to forehead;
    Shāntyāpit: from forehead to head.

36. **Six conditions of Vedha by Tivratar Diksha**

    Ānand, joy;   *kampa*, tremor;   *Udabhava*, new birth
    Ghurnā, reeling;   *Nidrā*, sleep;   *Murchhā*, swooning.

37. **Ashta Beeja**

Guru Beeja	Shakti Beeja	Ramā Beeja
Kāma Beeja	Yoga Beeja	Tejo Beeja
Shānti Beeja	Rakshā Beeja	

38. **Four Peethas**

Shamshān Peetha	Shava Peetha	Aranya Peetha
Shyāmā Peetha		

39. Five Shaktis in the body

  i.   Nivritti Shakti: Lower part of body up to thigh;

  ii.   Pratishthā Shakti: From thighs to navel;

  iii. Vidyā Shakti: From navel to neck;

  iv. Shānti Shakti: From throat to temple;

  v.   Shāntyāteeta Kalā Shakti: From temple to the upper centre of head.

40. Six types of Deekshā

Kriyāvati   Varnamayi   Kalāvati

Vedhamayi   Panchāyatani   Krama Deekdhā

41. Pancha Panchikā— five sets of five Devis each:

  i.   Panch Mahālakshmi
      Shri Vidyā; Lakshmi; Mahālakshmi; Trishakti; Sarva Sāmrājyā

  ii.   Panch Kosha
      Shri Vidyā; Par-jyoti; Par-nishkal-shāmbhavi; Ajayā; Mātrikā

  iii. Pancha Kalpa latā
      Shri Vidyā; Tvaritā; Pārijāteshwari; Triputā and Bāneshi

  iv. Pancha Kāma Dhenu
      Shri Vidyā; Amrit Pāteshi; Sudhāshri; Amriteshwari; Annapurnā

  iv. Pancha Ratna
      Shri Vidyā; Siddha Lakshmi; Mātangi; Bhubaneshwari; and Vārāhi

✸✸✸

Different Tāntrik Mantras

The following are some important Tāntrik Mantras which have not been included in the Mantra section, although some general Mantra practitioners also use it.

Navārna Mantra

Aum aing hring kling chāmundāyai vichche!

ॐ ऐं ह्रीं क्लीं चामुण्डायै विच्चे।

Navārna Māran Mantra

Aum aing hring kling chāmundāyai vichche (add name of person to be given) rang rang khe khe māraya māraya rang rang sheeghram bhasmi kuru kuru swāhā!

ॐ ऐं ह्रीं क्लीं चामुण्डायै विच्चे
रं रं खे खे मारय मारय रं रं शीघ्रं भस्मी कुरु कुरु स्वाहा।

Navārna Mohan Mantra

Aum aing hring kling chāmundāyai vichche (add name of the person) *kling kling mohanam kuru kuru kling kling swāhā!*

ॐ ऐं ह्रीं क्लीं चामुण्डायै विच्चे
क्लीं क्लीं मोहनं कुरु क्लीं क्लीं स्वाहा।

Navārna Uchchātan Mantra

Aum aing hring kling chāmundāya vichche (add name of the person) *phat uchchātanam kuru kuru swāhā!*

ॐ ऐं ह्रीं क्लीं चामुण्डायै विच्चे
फट उच्चाटनम कुरु कुरु स्वाहा।

Navārna Vashikaran Mantra

Vashat aing hring kling chāmundāya vichche (add name of the person) *vashat mey vashyam kuru kuru swāhā!*

वषट् ऐं ह्रीं क्लीं चामुण्डायै विच्चे
वषट् में वश्यं कुरु कुरु स्वाहा।

Navārna Stambhan Mantra

Aung thang thang aing hring kling chāmundāya vichche (add name of the person) *hring vācham mukham padam stambhaya hring jihvā keelaya hring buddhim vināshaya vināshaya hring thang thang swāhā!*

ॐ थैं थैं ऐं ह्रीं क्लीं चामुण्डायै विच्चे ह्रीं वाचं मुखं पदं स्तम्भ ह्रीं
जिह्वा कीलय ह्रीं बुद्धिं विनाशय ह्रीं थैं थैं स्वाहा।

Navārna Vidveshan Mantra

Aum aing hring kling chāmundāya (add name of the person/ persons) *vidveshanam kuru kuru swāhā!*

ॐ ऐं ह्रीं क्लीं चामुण्डायै विद्वेषनं कुरु कुरु स्वाहा।

Navārna Mahāmantra

Aum aing hring kling mahādurge navākshari nava durge navātmike nava chandi mahāmāye mahāmohe mahāyoga nidre jaye madhu-kaitabha vidrā-vini mahishāsur mardini dhumra-lochan sanhatri chand-munda vināshini raktbeejāntake nishumbha dhvanshini shubha darpaghni devi ashtādash-bāhuke kapāla khat-wānga shool, khadag khetak dhārini chhina-mastak-dhārini rudhir-mānsa bhojini samasta bhuta preta ādi yoga dhvanshini brahmendra ādi stute devi mām raksha raksha mam shatrun nāshāya hring phat hung phat Aum aing hring kling chāmundāya vichche!

ॐ एं ह्रीं क्लीं महादुर्गे नवाक्षरी नवदुर्गे नवात्मिके
नव चण्डी महामाये महामाये महायोग नींद्रे जये
मधुकैटव विद्राविनी महिसासुर मर्दिनी धूम्रलोचन संहत्री
चण्डमुण्ड विनाशिनि रक्तबीजान्तके निशुम्भध्वंशिनि
शुभ दर्पघ्नी देवि अष्टादश बहुके कपाल खटबांग
शूल खड्ग खेटक धरिणि छिन्नमस्तक धारिणी रुधिर
मांसभोजिनि समस्त भूत प्रेत आदियोग ध्वंशिनि ब्रह्होन्द्रादि
स्तुते देवि मां रक्ष रक्ष मम शत्रुं नाशाय ह्रीं फट हं फट
ॐ ऐं ह्रीं क्लीं चामुण्डाय विच्चे ।

Dakshina Kāli Mantra

*Aum kring kring kring hring hring hung hung dakshine kālike
kring kring hring hring hung hung swāhā!*

ॐ क्रीं क्रीं क्रीं ह्रीं ह्रीं हं हं दक्षिणे कालिके
क्रीं क्रीं ह्रीं ह्रीं हं हं स्वाहा ।

Neela Saraswati Mantra

*Aing hring shring kling soung kling hring aing blung string
neela tāre saraswati drāng dring kling blung sah!
Aing hring shring kling soungah soungah hring swāhā!*

ऐं ह्रीं श्रीं क्लीं सौं क्लीं ह्रीं ऐं ब्लं स्ट्रीं नील तारे सरस्वती द्रां द्रीं
क्लीं बलं सः । ऐं ह्रीं श्रीं क्लीं सौंः सौंः ह्रीं स्वाहा ।

Saraswati Mantra

Aum vad vad vāgvādini swāhā! ॐ वद् वद् वाग्वादिनी स्वाहा ।

Vāgdevi Mantra

Aum hring aing hring Aum saraswatyai namah!

ॐ ह्रीं ऐं ह्रीं सरस्वत्यै नमः ।

Vidyā Mantra

*Aum hring shring aing vāgvādini bhagawati arhan-mukha nivāsini
saraswati mamāsye prakāsham kuru kuru swāhā aing namah!*

ॐ ह्रीं श्रीं ऐं वाग्वादिनी भगवती अर्हनमुख
निवासिनी सरस्वती ममास्ये प्रकाशं कुरु कुरु स्वाहा ऐं नमः ।

Shodashi Mantra

Shring hring kling aing souh Aum hring kling aimg yee la hring Ha-sa-ka-ha-la hring sa-ka-la hring souh aing kling hring shring!

श्रीं ह्रीं क्लीं ऐं सौः ॐ ह्रीं क्लीं ऐं यी ल ह्रीं
हसकहल ह्रीं सकल ह्रीं सौः ऐं क्लीं ह्रीं श्रीं।

Bālā Tripurā Mantra

Aum kling souh! ॐ क्लीं सौः।

Bhuvaneshwari Mantra

Aing hring shring! ऐं ह्रीं श्रीं।

Chhinnamastā Mantra

Aum shring hring hring kling aing vajra-vairochaneeyae hring hring phat swāhā!

ॐ श्रीं ह्रीं ह्रीं क्लीं ऐं वज्र वैरोचनायै ह्रीं ह्रीं फट स्वाहा।

Dhoomāvati Mantra

Dhung dhung dhoomāvati swāhā! धुंग धुंग धुमावती स्वाहा।

Bagalāmukhi Mantra

Aum hring bagalāmukhi sarva dushtānām vācham mukham padam stambhaya jihvām keelāya vriddhim vināshāya hring Aum swāhā!

ॐ ह्रीं बगलामुखी सर्व दुष्टानं वाचं मुखं पदं स्तम्भय जिह्वा कीलाय
वृद्धिं विनाशय ह्रीं ॐ स्वाहा।

Mātangi Mantra

Aum hring aing shring namo bhagawati uchhista chāndāli shri mātangeshwari sarvajana vashangkari swāhā!

ॐ ह्रीं ऐं श्रीं नमो भगवती उच्छिष्ट चाण्डाली
श्री मतंगेश्वरी सर्वजन वशंकरी स्वाहा।

Getting the Mahāmantra: Drishtānta

If and when one fails to follow the right moral values, downfall is certain. Then, he remembers the forgotten words of his Guru: Tell the truth as falsehood destroys.

A seeker went to a preceptor and learnt many things for many years. He returned home to lead the life of a householder. He kept following the dictates of his guru and prospered well and quickly. He had everything that was needed for a rich, happy, healthy and satisfied life. He had an obedient wife; two sons, a daughter; many relatives, a few good friends and a large contigent of skillful workers. He was righteous and followed the moral path. This gave him prosperity, name, fame and respect beyond imagination.

The king appointed him a minister. Then ego and lust crept into his mind and life. He started committing misdeeds and accumalating wealth. The lust has a habit of showing itself. His wife casually mentioned when you have everything more than you need then why are you bringing in more wealth and more sins. He did not go to the court next day. He thought over all the aspects of different values. Rightous deeds are more valuable than anything else. He decide to follow old and tested ways and gained the peak again.

It is the lust and pride that is the chief cause of the fall and misery. Lust and pride always mean enmity: enmity to friends, relatives, dependents and finally to God.

Pride and lust erase common sense, character, morality, love, kindness, compassion and of course, contentment.

Power gives pride but if power is used for the common good; in serving the people, then it is humility and lust. Don't demand service; be a servant to God; serve all His creation; you would be always served well.

Annapurnā Mantras

Annapurnā is the Goddess who fulfills all wishes. For such fulfillments there are many Annapurnā Mantras. Four among them have been given below.

Aum hring shring kling namo bhagawati māheshwari annapurnāyai swāhā!

ॐ ह्रीं श्रीं क्लीं नमो भगवती माहेश्वरी अन्नपूर्णाय स्वाहा।

Aum hring shring kling namo bhagawati māheshwari Mam-abhimatam-annam dehi dehi-annapurne swāhā!

ॐ ह्रीं श्रीं क्लीं नमो भगवती माहेश्वरी
मम अभिमातं देहि देहि अन्नपूर्णे स्वाहा।

Aum shring hring namo bhagawati prasanna pārijāt-aishwarya-annapurne swāhā!

ॐ श्रीं ह्रीं नमो भगवती प्रसन्ना पारिजात ऐश्वर्य अन्नपूर्णे स्वाहा।

Aum hring hring namo bhagawati māheshwari prasanna-var-de annapurne swāhā!

ॐ ह्रीं ह्रीं नमो भगवती महेश्वरी प्रसन्नवरदे अन्नपूर्णे स्वाहा।

Manikarnikā Mantra

Aum aing hring kling Aum manikarnike namah!

ॐ ऐं ह्रीं क्लीं ॐ मणिकर्णिके नमः।

Sheetalā Mantra

Aum Hring shring sheetalāyai namah!

ॐ ह्रीं श्रीं शीतलाये नमः।

Swapna Siddhi Mantra

Dreams are natural and so is the desire of individuals to know the meaning of the numerous dreams that come to them. That is the reason that there are different dream Mnantras. A few have been collected below.

Aum hring namo vārāhi aghore swapanam darshāya thah thah swāhā!

ॐ ह्रीं नमो वाराही अधोरे स्वप्नं दर्शाय ठः ठः स्वाहा।

Swapneshwari Mantra

Aum shring swapneshwari kārya mey vad swāhā!

ॐ श्रीं स्वप्नेश्वरी कार्य मे वद स्वाहा।

Swapna Devi Mantra

Aum hring mānase swapneshwari vichāram vidye vad vad swāhā.

ॐ ह्रीं मानसे स्वप्नेश्वरी विचारं विद्धे वद् वद् स्वाहा।

Swapna Chakreshwari Mantra

Aum namah swapna chakreshwari avatar avatar gatam vartmānam kathaya kathaya swāhā.

ॐ नमः स्वप्न चक्रेश्वरी अवतार-अवतार गतं वर्तमानं कथय कथय स्वाहा।

Swapna Mātangi Mantra

Aum yakshini ākarshini ghantākarne ghantākarne vishāle Mam swapnaam darshaya darshaya swāhā.

ॐ यक्षिणी आकर्षिणि-घण्टाकर्णे घण्टाकर्णे विशाले मम स्वप्नं दर्शय दर्शय स्वाहा।

All Karna Pishāchini Mantras

Aum namah karna pishāchini matta-kārini praveshe-atita-anāgat vartamānāni satyam kathaya mey swāhā!

ॐ नमः कर्ण पिशाचिनि मत्तकारिणि प्रवेशे अतीत-अनागत
वर्तमानानि सत्यं कथय मे स्वाहा।

Aum hring sah namo shakti bhagawati
karna-pishāchini chandra-rupini vad vad swāhā!

ॐ ह्रीं सः नमो शक्ति भगवती
कर्ण पिशाचिनि चंद्र रूपनि वद् वद् स्वाहा।

Aum hanso-hansah namo bhagawati
karna-pishāchini chandra-vegini swāhā!

ॐ हंसो-हंसः नमो भगवती कर्णपिशाचिनि चंद्र वेगिनि स्वाहा।

Aum bhagawati chand karna pishāchini swāhā!
Aum hring ching chichini pishāchini swāhā!

ॐ भगवती चंद्रकर्ण पिशाचिनि स्वाहा।
ॐ ह्रीं चीं चिचिनि पिशाचिनि स्वाहा॥

Aum hring āgachchhāgachchha chāmunde shri swāhā!
Aum namo bhagawate rudrāya karna-pishāchai swāhā!

ॐ ह्रीं आगच्छागच्छ चामुण्डे श्री स्वाहा।
ॐ नमो भगवते रूद्राय कर्ण पिशाचै स्वाहा॥

✿ ✿ ✿

21

All Yakshini Mantras

Yakshini Sādhan Mantra Vichitrā

Aum vichitra rupe siddhim kuru kuru swāhā!

ॐ विचित्र रूपे सिद्धिं कुरु कुरु स्वाहा।

Hansi Yakshini Mantra

Hansi hansa hāng neng hing swāhā!

हंसि हंस हां नें हीं स्वाहा।

Vibhramā Yakshini Mantra

*Aum hring vibhram rupe vibhramam kuru kuru aihyehi
bhagawati swāhā!*

ॐ ह्रीं विभ्रम रूपे विभ्रमं कुरु कुरु ऐह्येहि भगवति स्वाहा।

Bhikshini Yakshini Mantra

Aum aing mahānāde bhikshini hāng hring swāhā!

ॐ ऐं महानादे भिक्षिणी हां हीं स्वाहा।

Jana Ranjani Yakshini Mantra

Aum kleng jana ranjini swāhā!

ॐ क्लें जन रंजिनि स्वाहा।

Vishālā Yakshini Mantra

Aum aung vishāle hrāng hring kling swāhā!

ॐ औं विशाले हां हीं क्लीं स्वाहा।

Madanā Yakshini Mantra

Aum madane madane devi māmālinaya sangam dehi dehi swāhā!

ॐ मदने मदने देवि मामालिनय संगं देहि देहि स्वाहा।

Ghantā Yakshini Mantra

Aum aing puram kshobhaya
bhagawati gambhir sware klaing swāhā!

ॐ ऐं परं क्षोभ्य भगवती गम्भीर स्वरे क्लैं स्वाहा।

Lālakarni Yakshini Mantra

Aum tveng kālkarnike tah tah swāhā!

ॐ त्वें कालकर्णिके तः तः स्वाहा।

Mahāmāyā Yakshini Mantra

Aum hring mahābhaye hung phat swāhā!

ॐ ह्रीं महाभये हं फट स्वाहा।

Māhendri Yakshini Mantra

Aum aing kling aundri māhendri kuru kuru chulu chulu swāhā!

ॐ ऐं क्लीं अन्द्र महेन्द्रि कुरु कुरु चुलु चुलु स्वाहा।

Shankhini Yakshini Mantra

Aum shankh dhārini shankh-ābharane hrāng hring kling kling
shrih swāhā!

ॐ शंखधारिणि शंख-आभरणे ह्रां ह्रीं क्लीं क्लीं श्रीः स्वाहा।

Chandrikā Yakshini Mantra

Aum hring chandrike hansah kling swāhā!

ॐ ह्रीं चन्द्रिके हंसः क्लीं स्वाहा।

Shashāni Yakshini Mantra

Aum hung hring sphung shamshān-vāsini shamshāne swāhā!

ॐ हं ह्रीं स्फूं श्मशानवासिनि श्मशाने स्वाहा।

Vat Yakshini Mantra

*Ahyehi yakshi yakshi mahā yakshi vat-vriksha niwāsini
sheeghram mey sarvam saukhyam kuru kuru swāhā!*

एह्येहि यक्षि यक्षि महायक्षि वटवृक्ष निवासिनि
शीघ्रं मे सर्व सौख्यं कुरु कुरु स्वाहा।

Mekhalā Yakshini Mantra

Aum kong madan-mekhale namah swāhā!

ॐ कौं मदनमेखले नमः स्वाहा।

Vikalā Yakshini Mantra

Aum vikale aing hring shring klang swāhā!

ॐ विकले ऐं ह्रीं श्रीं क्लैं स्वाहा।

Lakshmi Yakshini Mantra

Aum shring hring kling mahālakshmai namah!

ॐ श्रीं ह्रीं क्लीं महालक्ष्मै नमः।

Mānini Yakshini Mantra

*Aum aing mānini hring ahyehi
sundari has has mih sangmahah swāhā!*

ॐ ऐं मानिनि ह्रीं एह्येहि सुन्दरी हस हस मिः संगमहः स्वाहा।

Shatpatikā Yakshini Mantra

Aum hrāng shat-patrike hrāng hring shring swāhā!

ॐ हैं शतपत्रिके हां ह्रीं श्रीं स्वाहा।

Sulochanā Yakshini Mantra

Aum klaung sulochanādi devi swāhā!

ॐ क्लौं सुलोचनादि देवि स्वाहा।

Sushobhanā Yakshini Mantra

Aum ashok pallavā kār-ker tale
shobhane devi shring kshah swāhā!

ॐ अशोकपल्लवा कारकेरतले शोभने देवि श्रीं क्षः स्वाहा।

Kapālini Yakshini Mantra

Aum aing rupālini hrāng hring kling kleng klaung
ha-sa-ka-la hring phat swāhā!

ॐ ऐं रूपालिनि हां हीं क्लीं क्लें क्लैं हसकल हीं फट स्वाहा।

Vilāsini Yakshini Mantra

Aum virupāksha vilāsini āgachchha-āgachchha hring
priyā mey bhava priyā mey bhava kleng swāhā!

ॐ विरूपाक्ष विलासिनि आगच्छागच्छ हीं
प्रिया मे भव प्रिया मे भव क्लें स्वाहा।

Nati Yakshini Mantra

Aum hring natini swāhā! ॐ हीं नटिनि स्वाहा।

Kāmeshwari Yakshini Mantra

Aum āgachchha kāmeshwari swāhā! ॐ आग्छ कामेश्वरी स्वाहा।

Swarna-Rekhā Yakshini Mantra

Aum varka-shalmile suvarna rekhe swāhā!

ॐ वर्कशाल्मिले सुवर्ण रेखे स्वाहा।

Sur-sundari Yakshini Mantra

Aum āgachchha sura-sundari swāhā!

ॐ आग्छ सुरसुन्दरी स्वाहा।

Manoharā Yakshini Mantra

Aum hring āgachchha manohare swāhā!

ॐ हीं आगच्छ मनोहरे स्वाहा।

Pramadā Yakshini Mantra

Aum hring premade swāhā! ॐ ह्रीं प्रेमदे स्वाहा।

Anurāgini Yakshini Mantra

Aum hring āgachchha anurāgini maithun priye swāhā!

ॐ ह्रीं आगच्छ अनुरागिनि मैथुनप्रिये स्वाहा।

Nakha Keshikā Yakshini Mantra

Aum hring nakha-keshike kanakāwati swāhā!

ॐ ह्रीं नखकेशिके कनकावति स्वाहा।

Nemini Yakshini Mantra

Aum hring mahāyakshini bhāmini priye swāhā!

ॐ ह्रीं महायक्षिणि भामिनिप्रिये स्वाहा।

Padmini Yakshini Mantra

Aum hring āgachchha padma-mani ballabhe swāhā!

ॐ ह्रीं आगच्छ पद्ममणि वल्लभे स्वाहा।

Swarnāwati Yakshini Mantra

Aum kanakāwati maithun priye swāhā!

ॐ कनकवति मैथुनप्रिये स्वाहा।

Rati-priyā Yakshini Mantra

Aum hring āgachchha rati-sundari swāhā!

ॐ ह्रीं आगच्द रतिसुन्दरी स्वाहा।

Kuber Yakshini Mantra

*Aum yakshāya kuberāya dhan-dhānya-adhipataye
dhan-dhānya-samvriddhi mey dehi dāpaya swāhā!*

ॐ यक्षाय कुबेराय धनधान्य-अधिपतये
धनधान्य समृद्धि मे देहि दापय स्वाहा।

Bilva Yakshini Mantra

Aum kling hring aing ong shring mahā-yakshinyai
Sarva aishwarya pradātryai;
Aum namah shring kling aing Aum swāhā!

ॐ क्लीं ह्रीं ऐं ओं श्रीं महायक्षिणियै
सर्व ऐश्वर्य प्रदात्र्यै ॐ नमः श्रीं क्लीं ऐं ॐ स्वाहा।

Chandra-dravā Vat Yakshini Mantra

Aum hring namah Chandra-drave karnākarna kārane swāhā!

ॐ ह्रीं नमः चन्द्रद्रवे कर्णाकर्ण कारणे स्वाहा।

Dhandā Pippal Yakshini Mantra

Aum aing kling dhanam kuru kuru swāhā!

ॐ ऐं क्लीं धनं कुरु कुरु स्वाहा।

Putradā Āmra Yakshini Mantra

Aum hring hring hrung putram kuru kuru swāhā!

ॐ ह्रीं ह्रीं हं पुत्रं कुरु कुरु स्वाहा।

Ashubha Kshayakari Dhātri Yakshini Mantra

Aum aing kling namah! ॐ ऐं क्लीं नमः।

Vidyā Dātri Nirguni Yakshini Mantra

Aum saraswatyai namah! ॐ सरस्वत्यै नमः।

Vidyā Yakshini Mantra

Aum hring shring shāradāyai namah! ॐ ह्रीं श्रीं शारदायै नमः।

Jayārka Yakshini Mantra

Aum aing mahā-yakshinyai sarvakārya sādhanam kuru kuru
swāhā!

ॐ ऐं महायक्षिणियै सर्वकार्य साधनं कुरु कुरु स्वाहा।

Santoshā Sweta Gunjā Yakshini Mantra

Aum jaganmātre namah! ॐ जगन्मात्रे नमः।

Rājyadā Tulasi Yakshini Mantra

Aum kling kling namah! ॐ क्लीं क्लीं नमः।

Kusha Yakshini Mantra

Aum wānga-mayāyai namah! ॐ वां मायायै नमः।

Apāmārga Yakshini Mantra

Aum hring bhārtyai namah! ॐ ह्रीं भारत्यै नमः।

Ksheerrārnavā Yakshini Mantra

Aum namo jwālā mānikya bhushanāyai namah!

ॐ नमो ज्वालामाणिक्य भूषणायै नमः।

Uchhista Yakshini Mantra

Aum jagat-traya mātrike padminibhi swāhā!

ॐ जगत्रय मात्रिके पदमिनिभि स्वाहा।

Chandrāmrit Yakshini Mantra

*Aum gulu gulu chandrāmat avajātitam
hulu hulu chandra-neere swāhā!*

ॐ गुलु गुल चन्द्रमात अवजातितं हुलु हुलु चन्द्रनीरे स्वाहा।

Swāmishwari Yakshini Mantra

Aum hring āgachchha swāmishwari swāhā!

ॐ ह्रीं आगच्छ स्वामीश्वरी स्वाहा।

Mahāmāyā Bhoga Yakshini Mantra

Aum namo mahā-māyā mahā-bhoga-dāyini hung swāhā!

ॐ नमो महामाया महाभोगदायिनि हं स्वाहा।

Tyāga Sādhan Yakshini Mantra

Aho tyāgi mahā-tyāgi artha-dehi mey
vittam veer sevitam hring swāhā!

अहो त्यागी महात्यागी अर्थ देहि मे वित्तं वीरसेवितं ह्रीं स्वाहा।

Sarvānga Sulochanā Yakshini Mantra

Aum kuvalaye hili hili kuru kuru siddhim
siddheshwari hring swāhā!

ॐ कुवलये हिली हिली कुरु कुरु सिद्धिं सिद्धेश्वरी ह्रीं स्वाहा।

Bhuta Lochanā Yakshini Mantra

Aum bhute sulochane tvam! ॐ भूते सुलोचने त्वं।

Jala-pāni Yakshini Mantra

Aum hring jala-pānini jwal jwal hung labung swāhā!

ॐ ह्रीं जलपाणिनि ज्वल ज्वल हं ल्बुं स्वाहा।

Mātangeshwari Yakshini Mantra

Aum hring shring kling mātang-aishwaryāi namo namah!

ॐ ह्रीं श्रीं क्लीं मातंग ऐश्वर्यै नमो नमः।

Hatele Kumāri Yakshini Mantra

Aum namo hatele kumāri swāhā! ॐ नमो हटेले कुमारी स्वाहा।

ॐ ॐ ॐ

22

Kundalini Shakti

Kunadalini is visualized as a sleeping snake in three and half coils. It is illumined with its own light. It resides like a snake at the lowest Chakra and is famous as the *beeja nāma* of Vāgadevi. It is the energy and power of Vishnu. It is fearless and bright golden in colour. It is the creation centre of Triguna, the three qualities: Satoguna; Rajoguna and Tamo guna. The scriptures describe Kundalini in the following way:

> *Suptā nāgopamā hyeshā sphuranti prabhayā swayā;*
> *Ahivat-sandhi sansthānā vāgadevi beeja sangyakā.*
> *Gyeyā shakti-riyam vishnuh nirbhayā swarna bhāswarā;*
> *Sattvam rajah tamah cha-iti guna-traya prasutikā.*

सुप्ता नागोपमा ह्येषा स्फुरन्ति प्रभयास्वया
अहिवत्सन्धि संस्थाना वाग्देवी बीज संज्ञयका।
ज्ञेया-शक्ति-रियं विष्णुः निर्भया स्वर्ण-भास्वरा
सत्त्वं रजः तमः चेति गुणत्रय-प्रसूतिका॥

The Kundalini shakti is the fundamental and original power, and creator of all other energies. The only difficult question before every seeker is: how to awaken it? How to control it and how to make it work for? The Rishis have shown us many ways according to the inner strength of the seekers, as for example Mantra Yoga; Bhakti Yoga; Dhyān Yoga; Bindu Yoga; Nāda Yoga; Hatha Yoga; Rāja Yoga, etc. Despite the fact that the details are available in different scriptures, an able preceptor is needed; and one should venture for its awakening only under the guidance of the guru.

Some other things are also needed:

1. The foremost important thing is the inner and outer purity.

2. One should take healthy and digestible, balanced and pure vegetarian food at fixed hours.

3.　One should not do anything that can create depression.

4.　One should follow only the righteous path; moral ethics and religious rules.

5.　One should read the scriptures regularly.

6.　One should meticulously follow instructions given by the preceptor.

7.　One should sit in meditation early in the morning or late at night, when there is no disturbance.

·8.　Night after ten o'clock or around three in the morning is most suitable for meditation.

9.　One must possess control over one's sense organs.

10.　One should neither think ill of others nor speak ill nor harm others.

11.　One should always think oneself to be a part of the Brahma Shakti.

12.　One should think that the soul is all powerful and immortal.

13.　One must regard Kundalini to be one centre of all powers.

14.　One should have confidence in the self and faith in God.

15.　One should treat all women as mothers and never indulge in sensuous talks or deeds.

16.　Yoga Sādhanā is a must for strength, willpower and sustenance.

17.　These precautions must definitely be taken before continuing the real sādhanā.

18.　With *Shradhā*, dedication and devotion; *Tatparatā*, readiness; and *Indriya Sanyam*, control over the sense organ, one can open *Trividha Gyāna Dwār*, three doors of knowledge.

19.　One must keep away from *Kāma*, sex; *Krodha*, anger and *Lobha*, lust as these are Trividha Narak Dwār, three doors to hell.

Inner and Outer Purity

One can get rid of the impurities by following different limbs of
Yoga which prescribes many ways and systems to cleanse the
organs. *Shatkarma* are different cleansing activities to purify the
body and mind and to prepare it for *Yoga Kriyā*. It includes: (1)
Dhauti (2) *Vasti* (3) *Neti* (4) *Nauli* (5) *Kapālbhāti* (6) *Trātaka*. (a)
Gajakarni (b) *Nyoli* (c) *Dhaukani* (d) *Bāghi* and (e) *Shankhapāla*
are also parts of *Shatkarma*. Some Yogis prefer one to another and
hence the activities; and its one list differs from another.

1. **Dhauti:** Take a 4 inches wide and 22 feet long clean and wet
    cloth, drink water and then slowly swallow 18 feet of that
    cloth, then pull it slowly out. It clears the stomach and takes
    kapha and pitta out. Such cleaning is called *Dhauti*. Some
    people use green and well cleaned branch of a bamboo, *koin*.
    Following the lead, scientists use a rubber pipe for cleaning
    purposes.

    Chaturang vistāram hastapancha dashāyatam;
    Gurudishta mārgena siktam vastram shanaiha graseta;
    Punah pratyāharechaita duditam dhauti karma tat.

    चतुरंग विस्तारं हस्तपंच दशायतम्।
    गुरुदृष्ट मार्गेण सिक्तं वस्त्रं शनै: ग्रसेत्।
    पुन: प्रत्याहरेच्चैत दुहितं धौति कर्मतत्॥

    (All the quotations are from *Hathayoga Pradipikā*)

2. **Vasti:** *Vasti* is a red organ near the *Mulādhār Chakra*. It is
    cleaned in two ways: *pavan vasti*, through air; and *jala vasti*
    through water. Through *nauli karma apāna vāyu* is inhaled
    well, and in *mayurāsan* it is exhaled.

    Nābhi daghdha jale pāyo nyasta nālot katāsanah;
    Ādhār kunchanam kuryāt kshālanam vasti-karma-tat.

    नाभि दग्ध जलेपायो न्यस्त नालोत्कटासन:।
    आधार कुन्चनं कुर्यात् क्षालनं वस्ति-कर्मतत्॥

3. **Neti**: *Neti* can be performed only after brushing the teeth. About half a liter water is taken through one nostril after closing the other one; then that water is thrown out through the other nostril. After it, a feet of wet cotton prepared with wax as a thread should be taken in though one nose and pulled out. It is called *gharshan neti*.

    Kapāl shodhani chaiva divya drishti pradāyani;
    Jatra urdhva jāta rogaidam netirāshu nihanti cha.

    कपाल शोधिनी चैव दिव्य दृष्टि प्रदायनि।
    यत्र ऊर्ध्वजात रोगैदं नेतिराषु निहन्ति च॥

4. **Nauli**: *Nauli* is known by many names: *Nauli; Naulika; Nala Kriyā; Nyoli*. After bowing the shoulders moving fast the abdomen from right to left is known as *Nauli*. *Gajakarani* is a variation of *Nauli* in which a lot of water is taken in and with the help of fingers vomitted out deliberately. It is repeated till clean water comes out.

    Amand āvarta vegena tundam savyāp savyatah;
    Natānso bhrāmayedeshā nauli siddhaih prachakshyate.

    अमन्द आवर्त वेगेन तुन्दं सवयाप सवयतः।
    नतान्सो भ्रामयेदेशा नौलि सिद्धेः प्रचश्यते॥

5. **Kapālbhāti**: To perform inhaling and exhaling; *Purak* and *Rechak Prānāyām* as *Lohār ki Bhāthi;* like the furnace of an ironsmith; is called *Kapāl Bhāti*.

    Bhasrāva lohakārasya recha purau sasambhramam;
    Kapāl bhāti vikhyātā kapha dosha visheshani.

    भस्राव लोहकारस्य रेच पूरौ ससम्भ्रमम्।
    कपाल भाटि विख्याता कफ दोष विशेषनी॥

6. **Trātaka**: One should look at a designated thing with concentrated eyes till the tears start rolling down. It is known as *Trātaka*.

Mochanam netra rogānām tandrādinām kapātakam;
Yatnatah trātakam gopyam yathā hātaka petakam.

मोचनं नेत्र-रोगानां तन्त्रादीनां कपाटकम्।
यत्नतः त्राटकं गोप्यं यथा हाटक पेटकम्॥

What the Vedic Rishis have stated is very true — the whole of Brahmānd is inside our body. Naturally, there is a solar centre or solar plexus and many transformers like centres called Chakra, wheels. There are tri-granthis or three important glands in our body called *Brahma Granthi*; *Vishnu Granthi* and *Rudra Granthi*. There are *Tri-shakti* or three powers, also called *Urdhva Shakti* in the throat; *Adhah Shakti* in the kidney and *Madhya Shakti* in the navel.

Movements of the Kundalini

Unneya Bhumikā: The rise of awakened Kundalini through the middle Sushumnā Nādi is called Unneya Bhumikā.

Pratyā-vritti Bhumikā: After moving through all the chakras, the return journey of the Kundalini to the first Moolādhār Chakra and to fall asleep after turning into three and half coils is called **Pratyā-vritti Bhumikā:** It is the toughest task. When it is achieved after returning from the top, the Sahasrā Chakra, the person gets Divinity and Wisdom. It is winning the Kunadalini in the body only but if the Cosmic Kunadalini is attained then the person can do anything and go to any place.

Chakras in Kundalini Sādhanā

Many different ways are followed in Kundalini Yoga and Sādhanā. Some follow *Pipplikā Mārga*, the path of an ant; others prefer *Vihangam Mārga*, the path of birds and some selected few prefer *Markat Mārga*, the path of a monkey.

The number of Chakras also differs in different divisions. The Chakras in our body are divided into three sets: Shata Chakra;

Sapta Chakra and Nava Chakra. Another Chakra is added to Shat Chakra to make it Sapta Chakra and two more are added to make it Nava Chakra. The following chart will make it clear and provide their names:

Shat Chakra

1. *Moolādhār Chakra*
2. *Swādhistān Chakra*
3. *Manipur Chakra*
4. *Anāhat Chakra*
5. *Vishuddha Chakra*
6. *Āgyā Chakra*

Sapta Chakra

7. *Sahasrār*

Nava Chakra

8. *Lalanā Chakra*
9. *Guru Chakra*

Kunadalini is Shakti which has different forms and is known by four names. During material and physical pleasure, she is called Bhavāni; during battle she is Durgā; when in anger she is Kāli and when in male form, she is Vishnu. The names differ; the qualities also change because she is all and does everything from creation to destruction. With the help of Prānāyāma and Bandha, the Prāna-vāyu is controlled and Kundalini is awakened. Then it is made to move upwards through Sushumnā Nādi to activate the latent energy of each chakra finally to reach Sahasrār. When Kundalini is reached there, it is called union with the soul or the *Brahma-milan*.

Details about Kundalini, Chakras and Beeja Akshar Mantras

Chakras	Moolādhār	Swādhisān	Manipur	Anāhat	Vishuddhi	Āgyā Chakra	Sahasrār
Place/in backbone	Near Anus	Above sex organ	Navel	Heart	Throat	Between brows	Back of head
Petals	4	6	10	12	16	2	1000
Mātrikā	*Va, Sha, Sha, Sa*	*Ba, bha, ma, ya, ra, la*	*Da, dha, na, ta, tha, da, dha, na. pa, pha*	*Ka, kha, ga, gha, anga, cha. Chha, ja, jha, jna, ta, tha*	*A, ā, e, ee, u, u:, ye, ai, o, au, ang, ah*	*Ha, ksha, sa*	
Tattva/Guna	*Prithivi; sakali-karana; gandhavāh*	*Āpa; ākunjan; rasa-vāh*	*Teja; prasaran; ushna-vāh*	*Vāyu; gati; sparsh-gyān*	*ākash*	*Mana*	*Ātmā*
Colour	yellow	white	red		white		
Shape	chatushkona	Ardha chandra	Trikona	Shata-kona	Vartul		
Beeja	*Lang*	*Vanga*	*Rang*	*Shang*	*Hang*	*Aum*	*Pranava*
Vāhan	*Airāvat*	*Makar*	*Mesha*		*hasti*		

Table continue....

Devatā	Brahmā	Vishnu	Rudra	Isha	Sadāshiva	Shambhu	Kāmeshwari/Kāmanāth
Devavāhan	Airāvat	Garuda	Nadi				
Shakti	Dākini	Shākini	Lākini	Kākini	Sākini	Hākini	
Quality	Gandha	Rasa	Roopa	Sparsha	Shabda	Mahat	
Organ	Pāda	Hasta	Gudā	Linga	Mookha	Hranya Garbha	Guru Pādukā
Linga	Swayambhu		Vāna		Pātāl		
Devi	Tripurambā	Tripurshi	Tripur Su-nadari	Tripur Vāsini	Shri Chakra Adhishwari	Tripur Mālini	Shri Lalitā
In Tantra	Trailokya Mohan	Sarva-āshā-paripurnā	Sarva Sankshopini	Sarva Saubhāgyā	Sarvārtha Sādhikā	Sarva Rakshikā	Sarva Ānanadmayā

Union or Salvation

Salvation is the result of the purity, virtue and power of our deeds. All the efforts of a person combined together must give the following qualities discussed in the Mahābhārat (19:2-4); only then can he or she get salvation or freedom from the endless cycle of birth and rebirth.

Sarvamitrah sarvasah shame rakto jitendriyah;
Vyapet-abhayam-anyushcha ātmawāna-muchyate narah.

सर्वमित्रः सर्वशः शमे रक्तो जितेन्द्रियः।
व्यपेतभयमन्युश्च आत्मवानम्-उच्यते नरः॥

The virtuous Purush or Stri, man or woman must become a friend to all; endure everything and sustain through all calamities; have control over mind and senses; be fearless and without anger; self-restrainted and self-dependent. Only then can he/she think of freedom; such men and women are free without a shred of doubt.

Ātmawat sarvabhuteshu yashcharenniyatah shuchih;
Amāni nirabhimānah sarvato muktah yewa cha.

आत्मवत्सर्वभूतेषु यश्चरेन्नियतः शुचिः।
अमानी निरभिमानः सर्वतो मुक्तः एव च॥

That man or woman who follows the scriptures, social customs and ethics; religious rites, rituals and tenets; and behaves well with all and treat others as a projection of the self; has no lust for fame or reward; is not conceited and has no ego-problem; can think of freedom or such men and women are free without a shred of doubt.

Jivitam maranam chobhe sukhdukhe tathaiwacha;
Lābhālābhe priyadwesh yah samah sa cha muchyate.

जीवितं मरणं चोभे सुखदुःखे तथैव च।
लाभालाभे प्रियद्वेषे यः समः स च मुच्यते॥

That man or woman who is detached and has no deep involvement in life and death, in pleasure or pain, in loss or gain, in happiness and sadness; can think of freedom or such men and women are free without a shred of doubt.

In nutshell it is the power, result and effect of wholesome deeds. It can be achieved by following the dictates of the scriptures. The essence of all the effort, activities and deeds that are performed is that a person is able to live a complete life, a meaningful one, and his life is not a waste. He gets united with the self, which is Moksha.

While yet in life, a person feels the inner pleasure which is incomparable. Such a person can easily deny the kingdom of Indra. For him, the worldly kings have nothing, and are like insects:

> *Brahmānand-rasam pitvā ye tu unmattāh yoginah;*
> *Indro-api rank-vat-bhāti kā kathā nripa-kitakah.*

ब्रह्मानन्द-रसं पीत्वा ये तु उन्मत्ताः योगिनः।
इन्द्रोऽपि रंकवत्भाति का कथा नृपकीटकः॥

ॐ ॐ ॐ

23

Tāntric Scriptures

The primary sources of written Indian Tantric theory and practice are the *āgama*, which generally consist of four parts, delineating metaphysical knowledge, Gyāna; contemplative procedures, *yoga*; ritual regulations, *kriyā*; and ethical and religious injunctions, *charyā*. Schools and lineages affiliate themselves with specific *āgamic* traditions. The whole Tantra exists in *Shaiva*, *Vaishnava*, *Ganapataya*, *Saurya* and *Shākta* forms, amongst others, so that individual Tāntric texts may be classified as *Shaiva Āgamas*, *Vaishnava Pāncharātra Samhitās* and *Shākta Tantras*, though there is no clear dividing line between these works. The expression *Tantra* generally includes all such works.

The following are the available books for Tantra. But most of the books, which were written at a later date and are not accepted as scriptures, have not been included in the list.

The List of Important Books on Shakti

1.	Devi Purāna	8.	Harivansh Purāna
2.	Devi Bhāgawat	9.	Rewati Tantra
3.	Padma Purāna	10.	Kunjikā Tantra
4.	Mārkandeya Purāna	11.	Saurabh Ratnākar
5.	Kālikā Purāna	12.	Rahasya Tantra
6.	Vārāh Purāna	13.	Meru Tantra
7.	Brahman Vaivart Purāna	14.	Kātyāyani Tantra

15.	Vārāhi Tantra	37.	Durgopāsanā Kalpadruma
16.	Har-Gauri Tantra	38.	Sitā Upanishad
17.	Krodha Tantra	39.	Adhyātma Rāmāyana
18.	Rudra Yāmal	40.	Shakti Darshan
19.	Shakti Āgam Sarvaswa	41.	Kāli Tantra
20.	Shabda Mālā	42.	Bhāva Chudāmani
21.	Gupta Rahasya	43.	Samayāchār
22.	Devi Rahasya	44.	Kumāri Tantra
23.	Shārdā Tilak	45.	Gyān-deep
24.	Tantra Sār	46.	Viswa-sār
25.	Mantra Mahodadhi	47.	Sarvollās
26.	Anushthān Prakāsh	48.	Kāmākhyā
27.	Shākt Pramod	49.	Kubjikā Tantra
28.	Shri Tatwa Nidhi	50.	Mahānirvāna Tantra
29.	Māricha Kalp	51.	Āchār Tantra
30.	Kulārnava		
31.	Kalpwalli		
32.	Shānti Sār		
33.	Shwetāshwtar Upanishad		
34.	Sapta Padārtha Sangrah		
35.	Prapancha Rahasya		
36.	Durgā Saptshati		

The List of 64 Tantra Granthas

S.N.	Tantra Grantha	S.N.	Tantra Grantha
1.	Mahāmāyā or Māyottar	33.	Tantra Bheda
2.	Shambar or Mahāsāraswat	34.	Guhya Tantra
3.	Yogini Jālashambar	35.	Kāmika
4.	Tattva Shambar	36.	Kalāvāda
5.	Bhairvāshataka- Asitāng	37.	Kalāsāra
6.	Bhairvāshataka- Charu	38.	Kubjikāmat
7.	Bhairvāshataka- Chand	39.	Tantrottar
8.	Bhairvāshataka- Krodha	40.	Veenā Tantra
9.	Bhairvāshataka- Unmat	41.	Trodal
10.	Bhairvāshataka- Kapāli	42.	Trodalottar
11.	Bhairvāshataka- Bhishana	43.	Panchāmrit
12.	Bhairvāshataka- Samhār	44.	Surya Bheda
13.	Bahurupāshataka- Brāhmani	45.	Bhutoddāmar
14.	Bahurupāshataka- Māheshwari	46.	Kulasāra
15.	Bahurupāshataka- Kaumāri	47.	Kuloddisha
16.	Bahurupāshataka- Vaishnavi	48.	Kula Chudāmani
17.	Bahurupāshataka- Vārāhi	49.	Mahākālimata
18.	Bahurupāshataka- Māhendri	50.	Mātribheda
19.	Bahurupāshataka- Chāmundā	51.	Mahālakshmi Mata
20.	Bahurupāshataka- Shiva-Duti	52.	Siddha Yogeshwari Mata
21.	Brahman Yāmala	53.	Kurupikāmat
22.	Āishnu Yāmala	54.	Devarupikāmat
23.	Rudra Yāmala	55.	Sarva Veera Mata
24.	Lakshmi Yāmala	56.	Vimalā Mata
25.	Umā Yāmala	57.	Āmnāya: Purvāmnāya, Pashchimāmnāya, Dakshināmnāya, Uttarāmnāya
26.	Skand Yāmala	58.	Niruttar
27.	Ganesh Yāmala	59.	Vaisheshika
28.	Graha Yāmala	60.	Shānārnava
29.	Mahochchraya	61.	Veerā Vali
30.	Vātula	62.	Arunesh
31.	Vātulottar	63.	Mohinisha
32.	Hrid Bheda	64.	Vishuddheshwar

✿ ✿ ✿

Kashmiri Shaivism

Among the various Hindu philosophies, **Kashmir Shaivism** is a school of Shaivism consisting of *Trika* and its philosophical articulation *Pratyabhigya*.

Kashmir Shaivism is categorized by various scholars as monistic idealism, absolute idealism, theistic monism, realistic idealism, transcendental physicalism or concrete monism.

Its particular stance is that Consciousness is the underlying stuff of the universe. It differs from the Advaita Vedānta of Shankarāchārya, who also gave primacy to Universal Consciousness *Brahmna*, but held that the phenomenal world is an illusion, *māyā*. It does not call the phenomenal world unreal, but sees it as a play of Consciousness, meaning that everything exists and has its being in Consciousness. Thus, the philosophy of Kashmir Shaivism, also called the Trika, can be seen as a refinement or adjustment of Shankara's Advaita.

The goal of Kashmir Shaivism is to merge in Shiva or Universal Consciousness, or realise one's already existing identity with Shiva, by means of wisdom, yoga and grace.

Origin

Kashmiri Shaivism is a householder religion. It is based on a strong monistic interpretation of the *Bhairava Tantras,* and its subcategory the *Kaula Tantra*, which were written by Kapalikas. In addition to this, there was a revelation of the *Shiva Sutras* to Vasugupta. Kashmir Shaivism claimed to supersede Shaiva Siddhānta, a dualistic tradition which scholars consider normative Tāntric Shaivism. The Shaiva Siddhānta goal of becoming an ontologically distinct Shiva, through Shiva's grace was replaced by recognizing oneself as Shiva who, in Kashmir Shaivism's monism, is the entirety of the universe. Somānanda, the first theologian of monistic Shaivism, was the teacher of Utpaladeva, who was the grand teacher of Abhinavagupta, who in turn was the teacher of Kshemarāja.

Philosophical Overview

The point of view of Kashmir Shaivism can be summarised by the concepts of *chitti, mala, upāya* and *moksha*, as follows:

1.   ***Chitti***: Universal Consciousness. *Chitti* is the fundamental stuff of the universe. This Consciousness is one and includes the whole. It could also be called God or Shiva.

2.   ***Mala***: Consciousness contracts itself. The one becomes many. Shiva becomes the individual, *jīva*. This contraction is called *mala*, impurity. There are three malas, the mala of individuation *Ānava mala;* the mala of the limited mind, *māyiya mala*, and the mala of the body, *karma mala*.

3.   ***Upāya***: An individual caught in the suffering of embodied existence, afflicted by the three malas, eventually yearns to return to his or her primordial state of Universal Consciousness. To attain this, he or she undertakes *sādhanā* or spiritual practice. Kashmir Shaivism describes four methods, *upāya; ānavopāya*, the method of the body, *shaktopāya*, the method of the mind, *sāmbhavopāya*, the method of Consciousness, and *anupāya* the 'methodless' method.

4.   ***Moksha***: The fruit of the individual's sādhanā is the attainment of Self-realisation, Ātma Gyāna amd Salvation, *Moksha*. In Kashmir Shaivism, the state of liberation, *mukti* is called *sahaja samādhi* and is characterised by the attainment of unwavering bliss-consciousness while living one's normal life.

Anuttara, the Supreme

Anuttara is the ultimate principle in Kashmir Shaivism. It is the fundamental reality underneath the entire Universe. Among the multiple interpretations of *anuttara* are: "supreme", "above all" and "unsurpassed reality". In the Sanskrit alphabet *anuttara* is associated to the first letter — "A". As the ultimate principle, *anuttara* is identified with Shiva, Shakti as *Shakti* is identical to *Shiva*, the supreme consciousness, *chitta*, uncreated light, *prakāsha*, supreme subject, *aham* and a temporal vibration, *spanda*. The practitioner who realizes *anuttara* through any means, whether by her own efforts or by direct transmission by the Grace of Shiva and Shakti, is liberated and perceives absolutely no difference between herself and the body of the universe. Being and beings become one and the same by virtue of the "erotic friction," whereby subject perceives object and in that act of perception is filled with non-dual being/consciousness/bliss. *Anuttara* is different from the notion of transcendence. Though, it is above all, it does not imply a state of separation from the Universe.

Aham, the Heart of Shiva

Aham is the concept of supreme reality as heart. It is considered to be a non-dual interior space of Shiva, support for the entire manifestation, supreme mantra and identical to Shakti.

Pratyabhigya

Pratyabhigya is the philosophical articulation of Kashmir Shaivism. Pratyabhigya literally means "spontaneous recognition", as it does not have any *upāya* or means. There is nothing to practice; the only thing to do is recognize who one is. Kshemarāja, the student of Abhinavagupta, uses a mirror analogy to explain Pratyabhigya.

Kaula

Although domesticated into a householder tradition, Kashmir Shaivism recommended a *secret* performance of Kaula practices in keeping with its heritage. This was to be done in seclusion from public eyes, therefore, allowing one to maintain the appearance of a typical householder.

Svatantrya, self-created free will

The concept of free will plays a central role in Kashmir Shaivism. Known under the technical name of *svātantrya,* it is the cause of the creation of the universe: a primordial force that stirs up the absolute and manifests the world inside the supreme consciousness of Shiva.

Svātantrya is the sole property of God, all the rest of conscious subjects being co-participants in various degrees to the divine sovereignty. Humans have a limited degree of free will based on their level of consciousness. Ultimately, Kashmir Shaivism as a monistic idealist philosophical system views all subjects to be identical: all are one; and that one is Shiva, the supreme consciousness. Thus, all subjects have free will but they can be ignorant of this power. Ignorance too is a force projected by *svātantrya* itself upon the creation and can be removed by only *svātantrya*.

A function of *svātantrya* is that of granting divine grace; *Shaktipāt*. In this philosophical system spiritual liberation is not accessible by mere effort, but dependent only on the will of God. Thus the disciple can only surrender himself and wait for the divine grace to come down and eliminate the limitations that imprison his consciousness.

Causality in Kashmir Shaivism is considered to be created by *Svātantrya* along with the universe. Thus there can be no contradiction, limitation or rule to force *Shiva* to act one way or the other. *Svātantrya* always exists beyond the limiting shield of cosmic illusion, *māyā*.

The Shiva Sutras

The first great initiate recorded in history of this spiritual path was Vasugupta. Vasugupta formulated for the first time in writing the principles and main doctrines of the Shiva Sutra.

Traditionally, these *sutras* are considered to have been revealed to Vasugupta by Shiva. According to myth, Vasugupta had a dream in which Shiva told him to go to the Mahādeva mountain in Kashmir. On this mountain, he found verses of the Shiva Sutras inscribed on a rock. It outlines the teachings of Shaiva monism. This text is one of the key sources for Kashmir Shaivism. The work is a collection of aphorisms. The *sutras* expound a purely non-dual, *advaita* metaphysics. These *sutras*, which are classified as *āgamas*, are also known as the *Shiva Upanishad Samgraha;* Shivopanishada Sangraha or Shivarahasyāgama Sangraha.

✸ ✸ ✸

25

Kulārnava Tantra

Pratham Ullāsa

Once upon a time, Shri Devi Pārvati enquired from all blissful, God of gods, Devādhideva, father of the world Shiva when he was sitting on the peak of Mount Kailash:

Kailas-shikhar-āsinam deva-devam jagad-gurum;
Prapachchhesham parānandam pārvati parmeshwaram.

कैलासशिखरीसीनं देवदेवं जगद्गुरुम्।
प्रपच्छेषं परानन्दं पार्वती परमेश्वरम्॥

Pārvati addressed him as God, God of Gods; founder of the sacred practices; attainable with devotion; deliverer of those who take refuge; Kilesh; ocean of the nectar of passion. Then they talked, starting from the suffering of all creatures to their redemption; and the ways and means of final Moksha. Shiva answered Her enquiries regarding:

1. Characteristics of creatures and their conditions
2. Four kinds of creatures
3. Superiority of the human body
4. Causes of the decrease in life span
5. Fruits of action of one life reaped in another
6. Suffering due to own sins
7. Non-attachment is liberation
8. No liberation without knowledge
9. Truth is inherent in the self
10. Guru's supremacy
11. No spiritual knowledge without control of senses

Dvitiya Ullāsa

1. Superiority of Kula Dharma
2. Kaula enjoys both Bhoga and Yoga
3. Purification by Mantra and Japa
4. Worship of Shakti Devi
5. Six philosophies are limbs of Shiva
6. Knowledge is not for sinners
7. Drinking denounced
8. Eight kinds of animal killers
9. The Pancha-makārs must be followed in their true spirit

Tritiya Ullāsa

1. Urdhvāmnāya is Purna Brahma.

   No one else knows the Urdhvāmnāya other than the guru of pure conduct, devout, asectic, performer of religious rituals, worshipper, Kaulika, Yogi, satisfied man, pious, emancipated and himself a Shiva. 3:33-36

2. Details of Āmnāya

   The central truth of Purvāmnāya is Shristi, creation; of the Dakshina stithi, maintenance; of Pashchim is samhār, destruction; and that of Uttara is anugrah, compassion. 3:41

   The path of Purvāmnāya is Mantra Yoga; of Dakshina is Bhakti Yoga; of Pashchim is Karma Yoga and of Uttara is Gyān Yoga. 3:42

   The principles of Purva-āmnāya are twenty four; of Dakshina āmnāya are twenty five; of Pashchim are thirty two; and of Uttara are thirty six. 3:43

3. Shri Prasāda Mantra, Hans Mantra

   There is yet another Āmnāya called Urdhva-āmnāya. Its presiding Mantra is Shri Prasād Mantra which is also called Hansah Mantra. It possesses both Shiva and Shakti in the form of *ha* breath and *sah* breath. He who comes to know of it is Shiva himself. 3:49

In Hans Mantra *Ha* stands for Shiva, the Purush or the principle of Male; *Sa* stands for Shakti, Prakriti or the principle of Female. Thus, both together create all and pervade all, reside in each living being as incoming and outgoing breath; and hence, they are inseparable. The outgoing breath, the expiration makes the sound of *Ha*; and the incoming, the inspirations makes the sound *Sa*. The automatic repetition of *Ha* and *Sa* caused by the incessant and continuous breathing is also called *Ajapā Japa*; the effortless *Japa*; repetition without effort. A normal human being within twenty four hours of a day and night draws breath and make this sound 21,600 times. It is mentioned at many places. The following is from Dhyān-Bindu-Upanishad 61:64:

> *Hankāren bahiryāti sahāren vishet punah;*
> *Hanseti paramam mantram jivo japati sarvadā.*

हंकारेण बहिर्याति सहारेण विशेत पुनः।
हंसेति परमं मन्त्रं जीवो जपति सर्वदा॥

i. All else are the forms of Shakti
ii. Details of Parā Prasāda Mantra
iii. Enjoyment and emancipation through this Mantra

Chaturtha Ullāsa

i. Extrication of Shri Parā Prasāda Mantra
ii. Different Nyāsa related to it
iii. Exhibition of Mudrās

Pancham Ullāsa

i. Basic vessels
ii. Kula Dravya

iii.   Kinds of wine
iv.   Kinds of flesh
v.   Symptoms of emancipation
vi.   Prohibition of impure (Panch) Makārs
vii. Reality of Mānsa, Madya and Maithun

Shashtam Ullāsa

i.   Five purifications
ii.   Different Kailās
iii. Mantra for invocation of Devi
iv.   Ten places of worship for Devi
v.   Unity of Devatā Mantra and Yantra
vi.   Method of worship of Yantra
vii. Etymology of the word Yantra
viii. Meditation on the linage of the guru

Shaptam Ullāsa

i.   Mantras for oblation of Batuka
ii.   Mantras for oblation of Sarva-bhuta-pati; Kshetrapāla;
      Rāja-Rājeshwar;
iii. Kulāstak
iv.   Akulāstak
v.   Mantras for Devi; Sheshikā;
vi.   Tattva traya
vii. Method of drinking

Ashtam Ullāsa

i.   Seven exhilarations and their characteristics
ii.   Methods of offering libations
iii. Fruits of showing respect
iv.   Eight Pratayayas
v.   The world as the form of Shiva and Shakti
vi.   Samādhi forms the union with Shiva and Shakti

Navam Ullāsa

i.   Brahma Gyān
ii. No difference between Jivātmā and Parmātmā
iii. Knowledge of Supreme reality
iv. Four states of Sādhak
v.   Kula Yogi
vi. Kaulika
vii. Brahma Gyāni is free from Karma

Dasham Ullāsa

i.   Three kinds of worship
ii. Worship of Yoginis
iii. Shri Chakra
iv. Worship in different months
v.   Worship of Dākinis
vi. Eulogy of Kula poojā

Gyārah Ullāsa

i.   Drinking of Kula dravya
ii. Duties of Sādhak
iii. Prohibited actions
iv. Kula Vriksha
v.   Importance of good conduct
vi. Liability of guru for sins of disciple

Bārah Ullāsa

i.   Glory of Pādukā
ii. Devotion to guru
iii. Salutations to guru

Terah Ullāsa

i.   Unacceptable Shishya
ii. Guru
iii. Kinds of gurus

Chaudah Ullāsa

i. Initiations
ii. Method of testing disciples
iii. Kinds of shishyas
iv. Six conditions of bedha
v. Kinds and methods of initiations

Pandrah Ullāsa

i. Japa
ii. Purashcharan
iii. Prānāyāma
iv. Mantras
v. Food
vi. Success in Japa

Solah Ullāsa

i. Fruits of Japa and homa
ii. Sex of Mantras
iii. Triguna Dhyān
iv. Havan

Satrah Ullāsa

1. **Prayer of Gurudeva**

   Namaste nāth bhagawan shivāya guru-rupine;
   Vidyā-avatār-sansiddhaye parmātma-swarupine.
   Nārāyan swarupāya paramātma swarupine;
   Sarva-agyān-tamo-bhed-bhānave siddha nāth cha.
   Sarvagyāya dayā-klipt-vigrahāya shivātmane;
   Par-treha cha bhaktānām bhavyānām bhāva-āyine.
   Purastāt pārswayoh prishthe namah kuryā-bhuparyadhah;
   Sadā sachidā-rupena vidhehi tava dāstām. 17:3-6

2. **Definition of Guru**

   The syllable *Gu* signifies darkness, *ru* means to restrain. He is the guru who restrains darkness.

Gu-shabdahtva-andhakārah syāt ru-shabdah tannirodhakah;
Andhakār nirodhatvāt guru-iti-abhidhiyate. Ibid 17.7

Gu signifies giver of fulfillment; *r* stands for server of sin; *u* is Vishnu. He who contains all these three is the supreme Guru.

Gakārah siddhadah prokto rephah pāpasya dāhakah;
Ukāro Vishnuh-yuktāh-yatratayā-ātmā guruh parah. Ibid 17:8

गकार: सिद्ध: प्रोक्तो रेफ: पापस्य दाहक:।
उकारो विष्णु:युक्त: यत्रत्या-आत्मा गुरु: पर:॥

Ga signifies wealth of knowledge; *r* stands for illuminator; *u* symbolizes Shiva. He who contains all the three is the supreme Guru.

Gakāro gyān sampatti rephah tatra prakāshakah;
Ukārah shiva tādātamyam guru iti abhidhiyate. Ibid 17:9

गकारो ज्ञान सम्पत्ति रेफ: तन्त्र प्रकाशक:।
उकार: शिव तादात्मयं गुरु इत्यभिधीयते॥

Because he gives understanding to those who are blind to the truth of self and of the āgamas that is guhya, secret and because he is the form of gods like Rudra; he is called the guru.

Guhya-āgamātma-tattvān-dhanad-dhānām bodhanād api;
Rudra-ādideva-rupatyāt guruh iti abhidhiyate. Ibid 17:10

गुह्य आगमात्म-तत्वान् धनाद्दानं बोधनादपि।
रुद्रादिदेवारूपत्यात् गुरु: इत्यभिधीयते॥

3.   **Classifications and Definitions**

Āchārya: He conducts according to the norms of truth, and establishes his disciples in it. He assembles various connotations from the *Shāstras*. So, he is an *āchārya*.

Ārādhya: Because he gives consciousness to self, *ātmabhāva* and rejects attachment and averson, *rāga-dvesha,* and because his mind is centred solely in meditation or *Dhyāna,* he is *ārādhya*.

Desika: Because the guru wears the form of a deity; bestows grace on the disciples and is the embodiment of compassion, he is called *desika*.

Swāmi: Because a guru exudes his inner peace; deliberates on the supreme truth and is devoid of false knowing, *mithyāgyān*, he is called *swāmi*.

Shrināth: Because a guru imparts the knowledge for prosperity, Shri, and liberation; instructs on *Nādi Brahma* and *ātmā*; and is the emblem of blocking ignorance, so he is called *Shrināth*.

Deva: Because the guru crosses the limits of space and time; has acquired control over the world and worldly, he is called Deva.

Bhattārak: Because the guru removes the bonds of the world; and protects from charm and charming, he is called *Bhattārak*.

Yogi: Because the guru throbs with the glory of Mantras; and is adorable by the gods, he is called Yogi.

Sanyami: Because the guru rejects attachment; is indifferent to the stages of life; and fastens with the self in privacy, he is called *Sanyami*.

Mantra: By meditation, manan, on the luminous deity who is the form of Truth, it saves— trāyate— from all fear, therefore, it is called Mantra.

> *Mananā-tattva-rupasya devasya-amit-tejasah;*
> *Trāyate sarva-bhaya tastasmān-mantra iti-riti.*

मननातत्वरूपस्य देवस्यामित-तेजसः।
त्रायते सर्वभय तस्तस्मान्मंत्र इति ऋति॥

Various other things that have been defined and explained. They are:

Tapasvi	Avadhuta	Vira	Kaulika
Kula	Sādhak	Bhakta	Shishya

Yogini	Shakti	Pādukā	Japa
Stotra	Dhyān	Charan	Veda
Purāna	Shāstra	Smriti	Itihās
Āgama	Shākta	Pāramparya	Kaula
Sampradāya	Āmnāya	Shrout	Āchāra
Dikshā	Abhishek	Upadesha	Devatā
Nyāsa	Mudrā	Akshamālikā	Mandala
Kalasa	Yantra	Āsana	Madya
Surā	Amrit	Pātra	Ādhār
Mānsa	Poojā	Archan	Tarpan
Gandha	Āmod	Akshat	Pishp
Dhupa	Deep	Moksha-deep	Naivedya
Bali	Tattva-tray	Chaluka	Prasād
Pāna	Upasti	Purashcharan	Upahār
Udvāsan	Āvāhan	Sthāpan	Sannidhāpan
Sakal-kirti	Swāgat	Pādya	Arghya
Madhupark	Snān	Kshetra	Kshetrapāl

1.   Guru names

2.   Worship of book

3.   Reading and hearing of Urdhvāmnāya

★ ★ ★

Summary of Famous Tantra Shāstras

There are a lot of ancient *Tāntrik* texts which give details of various principles and practices of tantra. The Yogini Hridaya, Shri Tripura Rahasya, The Todala Tantra (which gives the Dasa MahaVidyās of Kāli, Tārā, Sodashi or Tripurasundari, Bhuvaneshvari, Chhinnamastā, Bhairavi, Dhumāvati, Baglāmukhi, Matāngi and Kamala, Mātrikabheda Tantra, Devi Rahasya Tantra, Vāmakeswari Tantra, Gandharva Tantra, Mahānirvāna Tantra, Mantra Mahodadhi, Mantra Yoga Samhitā, Mantra Mahārnava, Mantra Muktāvali, Mantra Kaumudi, Tattvānanda Tarangini, Yogini Tantra, Gupta Sādhanā Tantra, Devirahasyam are just some of the important works in Tantra. The Soundarya Lāhari by Ādi Shankara also has a special place in Tantra.

Kula Chudāmani Tantra

Kula Chudāmani Tantra is different for instead of Devi asking questions answered by Shiva; Shiva asks questions which have been answered by Devi, the Goddess. In this Tantra, the cult goddess is Mahishamardini, a Devi with some similarities to Durgā.

In seven short chapters, Devi expounds the essence of Her worship, sometimes in beautiful and nearly always in colourful language. But the uncanny side of Kaula and Kāli worship is death on in great detail, with references to siddhi, including a mysterious process where the adept *Tāntrik* leaves his body at night, apparently with the sole purpose of physical pleasure.

These uncanny elements may well have code meanings and be intended to throw the unwary off the scent. An example can be cited of the Gyāna Karika, which gives an entirely different slant to crossroads, Kula trees, Kula wine and the like.

Animal sacrifice also appears to have a place in this Tantra, as well as gruesome magical matters, including using the bones of a dead black cat to make a magical powder.

These practices were vehemently opposed and rejected as Indrajāla. The fact is that one who succeeds in getting his Kundalini awakened and also in piercing through one or two chakras, he also gets some siddhis. But since he has not gone higher and yet has some power, he loses his moral toughness and turns towards Aghore cult. He wastes his achievement, though, he should have saved it for the next life which begins from the Chakra attained in this life.

The siddhis are not the magical powers but real powers of various degrees based on the amount and context of duccess of the Sādhak. It is the main topic in Kula Chudāmani Tantra. The main *Tāntrik* rites are called the six acts, *shatkarma* of pacifying, subjugating, paralysing, obstructing, driving away, and death-dealing. But the Kula Chudāmani includes others such as Par-apura-praveshana, which is the power of reviving a corpse; Anjana, which lets a sādhaka to see through solid walls; Khadga which imports invulnerability to swords; Khechari, which gives the power of flying and Pādukā siddhi, magical sandals which take one to great distances.

Certainly, the importance of having a suitable Shakti forms the essence of the instructions Devi gives to Shiva. We see this emphasis over and over again, throughout the Tantra.

Devi takes the form of Mahishamardini, more popularly known as Durgā, who destroyed the two arch-demons Sumbha and Nishumbha in the epic battle between the Goddess and the horde of demons, described in detail in the Durgā Saptshati. It was at this time, according to legend, that Durgā created Kāli, by emanating her out of her third eye.

We learn more of Durga's legends and myths from the Kālikāpurāna, an influential source in Kaula Tantra. The Devi, Maha Māyā, appeared as Bhadra Kāli, identical with Mahishasurmardini in order to slay the demon Mahisha. He had fallen into a deep sleep on a mountain and had a terrible dream in which Bhadra Kāli cut asunder his head with her sword and drank his blood.

The demon started to worship Bhadra Kāli and when Maha Māyā appeared to him again in a later age to slaughter him again, he asked a boon. Devi replied that he could have his boon, and he asked her for the favour that he would never leave the service of her feet again. Devi replied that his boon was granted. "When I kill you in the battle, O demon Mahisha, you shall never leave my feet, there is no doubt about it. At every place where I'm worshipped, you'll be there. As regards your body, O Dānava, it is to be worshipped and meditated upon at the same time."

It is needless to state that all the texts of Tantra have a lot of similarities and yet there are many differences. It is because of the different cults and different Siddha Yogis.

Dakshināmurti Samhitā/Vāmkeshwar Tantra

Tripura is the ultimate, primordial Shakti, the light of manifestation. She is the pile of letters of the alphabet and created the three worlds. At dissolution, she is not dissolved and remains in the abode of all tattvas.

The Dakshināmurti Samhitā or Vāmkeshwar Tantra is a comprehensive digest on the subject of Shri Vidyā, from the Kaula point of view. It skips the philosophical implications of the cult and concentrates on the ritualistic aspects. Yet the work is of interest because it seems to represent a different branch of the tradition. For example, the mantras or Vidyās of the Devi's 15

Nityas or eternities differ from those encountered in, other texts including Tantra, Rāja Tantra, Kalpa Sutras, etc.

The different Patalas, chapters are of widely varying lengths, some consisting of only a few shlokas or verses while others go into considerable detail.

Chapter one begins with praise of Tripura in her five lion seat form. Shri Devi questions Ishvara about the different Amnāyas, identified with the four directions and the upper face. Shiva describes the different forms of Shri Vidyā and prefers Vidyā and dhyān, meditation of Lakshmi in her one syllable form. Chapter two describes Mahālakshmi *pujā*, together with Vidyā, dhyān, and purashcharana, preparatory acts of the Goddess. In the third chapter, Shiva describes the worship of the three Shakti form of Mahālakshmi.

Samrājya Lakshmi is the subject of the fourth chapter. After describing her form, Shiva gives her Vidyā and the different āvarana or attendants in her yantra.

In chapter five, Ishvara speaks of Shri Kosha Vidyā. A Sādhak who masters this Vidyā is never reborn. She is the supreme light, without any attributes whatsoever, the very self of creation, maintenance and dissolution.

Chapter six extends the subject of the Paranishkāla Devatā, the supreme goddess with no parts. She is the supreme form of Parabrahmna, wears white garments, white gems and is smeared with white paste. She shows the Mudrā of knowledge and is served by hosts of yogis.

The seventh chapter deals with the Ajapā or unpronounced mantra. According to the Kaulas, a human being breathes 21,600 times during the day. Half are Sun breaths and half are Moon breaths. This is called the Ajapā because it is pronounced spontaneously, as a person breathes, and is called the Hansa mantra. A Sādhak can meditate on different chakras in the human body, assigning sections of these breaths there.

Chapter eight speaks of Mātrikā, the goddess as the letters of the alphabet, starting with 'A' first and 'Ksha' last. Ishvara gives the mandala to create for her worship and gives a dhyān mantra of the goddess.

The next patala, chapter nine, begins to describe Bāla Tripurasundari in her form as a young woman. She sits on a beautiful jewelled lion seat in the midst of the Kadamba forest. The text gives details of her yantra, and other ritualistic accessories. This is a much longer chapter than the previous eight. Chapters 10 and 11 deal with the lion seat, in the four quarters.

In Chapter 12, Shiva describes the Kāma Bija, personified by Kāmeshvari. She is as effulgent as a rose, holds a bow and arrows, and is adorned with various beautiful jewels which delude the three worlds.

Chapter 13 describes Rakta Netra worship. She has the form of Lalitā, with rounded high buttocks, nitambini, a slender waist, a peaceful face and beautiful eyes. She is young and beautiful with swelling, high firm breasts.

In Chapter 15 the devatas associated with the southern amnāya are briefly described. Then Shiva, in the next chapter, describes those of the western Amnāya.

Chapter 16 describes the Mritasanjivini Devi, a female form of Mrityunjaya. The next, Patala 17, describes Vajreshi.

In Chapter 18, Shiva speaks of the Tripureshi Bhairavi Vidyā. This is Lalitā as a woman in whom menstruation has ceased.

Chapter 19 gives more details about the western Amnāya, while chapter 20 continues the topic by dealing with the northern, uttar Amnāya. Bhairavi resides here.

Chaitanya Bhairavi is the subject of Chapter 21, while Kuta Bhairavi forms the subject matter in Chapter 22. The form of the goddess known as Nitya Bhairavi is the topic of Chapter 23, while another fierce aspect of Tripurasundari, Aghora Bhairavi, Damareshi, forms the subject matter of Chapter 24. Devi Sampat Bhairavi is the subject of Chapter 25.

In chapter 26 Shiva tells Devi about Panchasundari. This is Lalitā in her form as the five elements of space, fire, air, earth and water. Chapter 27 deals with Parijāteshvari, while Chapter 28 covers Pancha Baneshi, or the goddess in her form as the five arrows. Pancha Kameshvari is the topic of Chapter 29, while Kalpalatā Vidyā is described in Chapter 30. Chapter 31 deals with Annapurnā or the Devi who fills one with everything desired. She is described as a Siddha Vidyā, giving endless articles to her devotees.

In Chapter 32, Matāngi Ratna Devi is described. Details of her *pujā*, her dhyān, her āvarana devatas and her Vidyā are described. Chapter 33 covers Bhuvaneshvari, and the same subject is continued in 34 and in Chapter 35 at some length. Chapter 36 speaks of the Ghatargala Yantra.

Varāhi, also known as Panchami, is the subject of Chapter 37. Her yantra can be inscribed on silver, gold or copper. Alternatively, it may be drawn on birch bark, bhoja patra, using substances including kumkum, aguru, sandal, rochana, or turmeric and water. She is as bright as a blue lotus, wears a garland of skulls, and is adorned with nine jewels.

In the 38th chapter, tarpana, oblation is described at some length, together with some prayogas, the nature of the pot to be used in the worship and other details. This chapter deals with the six magical acts, shatkarma.

The 39th, a brief chapter, speaks of the Pancharātra *Āgama*, known as the Vishnu *Āgama*. It gives a dhyān of the Lakshmi.

In Chapter 40, Ishvara starts to speak of Kameshvari Nitya. The other chapters up to and including Chapter 53, speak of the other Nityas. As noted elsewhere, these have different mantras and Vidyās to those spoken of in the Rāja Tantra.

Chapter 54 gives an explanation of the 15 Nityas or 16, if Lalitā is included. There follows an interesting correlation between the states of waking, dream and deep sleep with the three gunas. The fourth state, Turya Avasthā, is described as the ultimate Kalā, free from existence and non-existence, beyond the three gunas. There are 16 Kalās but beyond this there is a 17th Kalā which is the Absolute in itself. The text correlates the letters of the Shri Vidyā mantra with the Nityas and with that which is beyond them. It relates the three sections of Shri Vidyā with the three worlds and with the Mahapitha formed from the Sanskrit letters A-Ka-Tha. At the centre of the universe or prapancha is Tripura, who is of the nature of the Absolute.

In Chapter 55, Devi asks how one should perform the daily *pujā* of the goddess. Shiva gives details here which are similar to those in other Shri Vidyā Tantras and in Subhagodaya. In Chapter 56, Shiva says that the supreme Goddess is in the form of compassion, bears the universe — Jagadhātri — and is in the form of sound as Nada and Bindu. She is also beyond these various mantras. Shri Vidyā exists, including those first pronounced by Kubera and Lopāmudrā. She enumerates the other Vidyās of Shri Vidyā pronounced by other Rishis.

Towards the end of this chapter, Ishvara Shiva sings of the greatness of Lalitā and describes the Turya or fourth technique, by remembering which, an individual becomes one with the Brahmna or Mahapāda. He says: "One's self, svayam is Brahmna, one's self is Vishnu, one's self is Rudra, there is no doubt about it." One who pronounces the Vidyā even once surpasses thousands of millions of Ashvamedha Yagyas, winning the world by letting loose a horse, acts of homa, sacrifices, pilgrimages to holy places like Kāshi, bathing in sacred rivers and the rest. He adds that even if he had millions of tongues, it would be impossible to speak of the greatness of Shri Vidyā. After obtaining it from the guru, it washes away the most heinous of sins.

In Chapter 57, he continues the subject of the worship of Shri Vidyā and describes a great Nyāsa in which she is identified with the letters of the alphabet, Shri Ganesha, the planets, the sidereal constellations, nakshatras, the solar constellations, rāshis, the yoginis and the sacred sites.

Chapter 58 discusses the important subject of Kāmakalā. The three bindus are to be meditated on in Tripura's forehead and two breasts, while the Ha-Ardha kalā is in her yoni, below. One should meditate on being one with the Devi. Then follows a lengthy meditation on Lalitā, which is similar to the one in Vamakeshvara Tantra.

In Chapter 59, Shiva speaks of the famous Shri Yantra and describes the Shaktis or attendants worshipped in the different nine mandalas, together with how they should be visualised. The chapter concludes the nine different forms of Lalitā in each of these mandalas.

The 60th chapter speaks of how the sādhikā or Sādhak should end her or his *pujā*, with worship of Shoshika and the rest. In Chapter 61, he speaks of the different fruits of reciting or chanting mantras, japa and of homa, fire worship in a number of differently shaped kundas or fire pits. These produce different results according to the wish of she or he who does *pujā*, and demand different types of fruit, flowers, and scents, depending on the object of the homa.

In Chapter 62, Ishvara speaks of the Suvāsini, of her characteristics, and of the Sādhanā to attract her. A circle is to be drawn and everything therein should be red. She should be given flowers, fruit, scented water, food, clothes and jewels. The appropriate Mudrās should be displayed to her. Other rites are given which result in the acquisition of marvellous siddhis or powers. At the end of the chapter, the five Kāmas are described. By worshipping the Kāmas, an individual may "delude the world" and attract 64 kotis of yoginis to the chakra.

In Chapter 63, the subject of the sexual worship of Shaktis is discussed. Shiva describes the virya Sādhanā and says that once semen is emitted using this rite, it should be offered to the Shakti. Sacred substances include semen, menstrual blood and urine, the text says. If a person worships in this manner without being properly initiated, the text warns, it is the equivalent of slaying a Brāhmin, and he or she ends up in the different hells described in the Hindu tradition.

In Chapter 64, the subject of creating a pavitra is alluded to, together with the ritual method for consecrating it. The last, 65th chapter speaks in some detail, of a rite of subjugation.

Devirahasyam Tantra

There are many compilations or *Tāntrik* digests, discussing a variety of topics a Sādhak or Sādhvi needs to know. This summary of the contents of the Devirahasya will give an idea of the scope of this type of work. There is little philosophy here; practically the entire contents of the work, deals with mantra, yantra, *pujā* and Sādhanā of the different gods and goddesses.

Rahasya means secret and the work does cover most of the topics a practitioner would need to know. These include purashcharana, which is the preparatory work before proper *pujā* can start. This is very arduous, involving the recitation of mantra and a ritual which spans many hours. The Devirahasya, however, introduces some short-cuts for the Kaula initiate.

The panchāngas, five limbs, in this work give essential *pujā* information for a Sādhak or Sādhvi and give intriguing insights into various aspects of devatā worshipped by *Tāntrikas*.

Chapter 1

This deals with the characteristics of guru and pupil, with the planetary positions and times of initiation, and with the attendant disqualifications on both pupils and gurus. It also deals with the sequence of initiation, the purification of the disciple, and the initiation of shaktis.

Chapter 2

The different mantras of the Devis are given. The Devis mentioned are Bala (an aspect of Tripurasundari as a young girl), Panchadashi and Shodashi (Tripurasundari), Tripura, Vidyāranjani (Queen of Vidyā), Bhadra Kāli, Matāngi, Bhuvaneshvari, Ugra Tārā, Chinnamastā, (headless), Sumukhi (pretty face), Sarasvati, Annapurnā (full of grain), Mahālaksmi, Sarikā (Small Bodied), Shārada (autumnal), Indrākshi (Indra's eye), Baglāmukhi, Mahāturi (the transcendent forth), Mahārajni (great night), Jvālāmukhi (fire-mouth), Bhida, (crowdy), Kālaratri (night of time), Bhavāni, Vajrayogini, Dhumravarahi (smoky Varahi Devi), Siddhalakshmi, Kulavagisvari, Padmāvati, Kubjikā (crooked one), Gauri (Fair One), Khechari, Nilasarasvati, Parāshakti.

Chapter 3

This chapter deals with different Shiva mantras such as: Mrityunjaya (Shiva as Conqueror of Death), Amriteshvara, Vatukabhairava (Shiva in his aspect as a terrifying boy), Maheshvara, Shiva, Sadā Shiva, Rudra, Mahādeva, Karāla (Formidable), Vikarāla, Nilakantha, Sarva, Pasupati, (Master of all living beings), Mrida, Pināki, Girisha, Bhima, Mahāganapati, Kumāra, Krodhanesa, Isha, Kapālisa, Krurabhairava (Cruel Bhairava), Samhārabhairava (Dissolution Bhairava), Ishvara, Bharga, Rurubhairava, Kālagnibhairava, Sadyojāta (instantly arising), Aghora, Mahākāla and Kāmesvara.

Chapter 4

The different mantras for Vishnu are given in this chapter. These are the Laksmi-Nārāyana mantra, and the mantras of Radhākrishna, Vishnu, Laksmi-Nrisimha, Lakshmi-Vāraha, Bhārgava, Sitā-Rāma, Janārdana, Vishvaksena and Lakshmi-Vāsudeva.

Chapter 5

The different Utkelana, laying open of the mantras given above are given. These are mantras which themselves open the mantras up to use.

Chapter 6

Gives the vitalising mantras of the Devatas described in Chapters 2, 3 and 4.

Chapter 7

In this chapter the mantras used for reminding any curses that may have become attached to the mantras in chapters 2, 3 and 4; are given.

Chapter 8

The method of reciting mantras is described here. The guru *pujā* mantra is given.

Chapter 9

This chapter deals with the method of putting together the mantras already described in Chapters 2, 3 and 4.

Chapter 10

Purascharana, or the performance of acts by which a given mantra may be made efficacious, is described in this chapter. Purascharana should be done under auspicious astrological configurations after having worshipped one's own guru. A yantra is described which should be used in its application. The Sādhak has to fill four pots at the cardinal points. At the end of the chapter, alternative methods of doing this necessary act are described.

Chapter 11

This chapter continues the topic of the previous chapter, and describes the homa which should be done.

Chapter 12

Describes in code form the unfolding of the different yantras of the Devatas described in Chapters 2, 3 and 4.

Chapter 13

This chapter describes how an amulet kavacha may be made of the yantra of one's own Ishtadevatā, bound into a ball, and carried upon the person. This amulet is said to give miraculous results.

Chapter 14

This chapter presents the details of Rishis of various mantras.

Chapter 15

The Sādhanā of the cremation ground is described. This chapter contains only 13 verses but there is an extensive commentary provided on each of them.

Chapter 16

The Sādhanā continues. The different Bhairavas of the elements have to be worshipped. Mahākāla-bhairava is the seer of the mantra, Ushnik is the metre, Shri Smashāna is the Devatā, Hrim is the bija, Hum is the shakti and Krim is the kilaka. The application of the mantra is in the attainment of the four aims of mankind.

Chapter 17

The purification of the rosary formed from human skulls is discussed here.

Chapter 18

This chapter deals with rosary and yantra purification. The nature of the five products of the cow and the Yantreshvari mantra are also discussed.

Chapter 19

The origin of wine is the subject of this chapter. Nine vessels which form the receptacles in which wine is kept are discussed. The presiding Devatās of these are Sadā Shiva, Ishvara, Rudra, Vishnu, Parameshti, Indra, Guru, (Jupiter), Shukra (Venus) and the Sun and the Moon taken together.

Gupta Sādhanā Tantra

Chapter One

Set on the pleasant peak of Kailās mountain, Devi first says that she has heard of the greatness of the path of the Kulas, but now wants to hear more. Shiva says that as he is her slave, and out of love, he will tell her what she requests. Kulāchāra, he says, is great knowledge and should be concealed, particularly from those of the pashu herd like disposition, in the same way that Devi would hide her sexual organs from others. Kulāchāra, he says, is the essence of the vedas, the Purānas and other shāstras, and is very difficult to obtain. Even if he had tens upon tens of millions of mouths, he would not be unable to describe the magnificence of the path of Kula. Shakti, he says, is the root of the entire universe, pervading all, and she is the cause of knowledge arising in Sādhak. Knowing Shakti brings happiness in this world and causes the Sādhak to dissolve in the body of Shakti in the next. Kulashakti should be worshipped with the five makāras, and describes suitable shaktis for this worship as a dancer, a Kapālini, a whore, a washing girl, a girl who cuts hair, a Brahmani, a Shudrāni, a Bhopālā maiden and a flower-girl. These are the nine *Tāntrik* Kulashaktis.

Chapter Two

Pārvati wants to know about Sādhanā, and breaks into eulogy of the guru. The guru is Brahma, Vishnu and Rudra and is the refuge. Guru is sacred worshipping places, teertha, guru is tapas, guru is fire, guru is the sun and consists of the whole universe. She asks by which mantra and in which ways the guru should be served and worshipped. She asks what his meditation image is. Shiva says that women, because of their emotional nature, should not have secrets revealed to them. Nevertheless, out of love for her, he will tell her of the meditation image and the nature of the guru. It should not be revealed to pashus, he warns. He says that just as Kula represents Shakti, so Akula represents Shiva. A person who is dissolved in Shakti is called a Kulina. This is a reference to the idea that Shiva is the witness, inert, a corpse, and it is Shakti, Kula, who creates, maintains and destroys the universe. The guru is the Kula circle, and one should bow to the guru seated in the centre of a great lotus which has the colour of an autumnal moon. He has a face like the full moon, wears celestial clothes, and is scented with heavenly perfumes. He is united with the greatly alluring Suradevi, on his left, and his hands show the Mudrās giving boons and dispelling fear. He is marked with every auspicious sign, and is situated in the great 1,000 petal lotus on the head. Pārvati wanted to know about the meditation image of the guru's shakti. Shiva replies that she is like the red lotus, wearing beautiful red clothes. She has a slender waist, and is adorned with red jewels and a red diadem. She resembles the brightness of the autumn moon, wears beautiful shining earrings, and sits on the left of her nātha. She shows the signs giving boons and dispelling fear and holds a lotus in one of her hands.

Chapter Three

Pārvati asks Ishvara, whom she addresses as the giver of liberation, the God of breath and Mahādeva, about preparatory acts, purashcharana, Sādhaks must undertake. Shiva says that the way to accomplish Sādhanā of the great mantra is through one's own will, here described as Svechchhāchāra rather than Svekshāchārya. The usual defects and rules applying to whether worship is during the day or night do not apply. At morning and at midday, the Sādhak should recite the mantra and having performed *pujā* should once more recite the mantra at the evening twilight. In the evening, the Sādhak is to offer food and other offerings according to his will. After doing so, the best of Sādhaks should also recite the mantra at the dead of night. Together with his own Shakti, he should recite the mantra. Joined with his Shakti, the mantra gives siddhi, and not otherwise. There is no siddhi without a Kulashakti, even in thousands of millions of years. After worshipping the Kumāri, a Sādhak should give her offerings of food and recite the mantra 108 times. After doing so, one should give dakshinā to the guru, such as gold and clothes. Unless the guru is satisfied, success in the mantra cannot be obtained. Success means that one becomes like Bhairava or Shiva himself.

Chapter Four

This chapter deals with the Shakti and her characteristics. Shankara says that she may be one's own Shakti or another's. She should be youthful and intelligent, and should be free of shame, lajjā and disgust, ghrinā. After using the five elements according to the rule, the Sādhak should recite the mantra placing it 100 times on the head, 100 times on the forehead, 100 times where the hair is parted in the centre, sinduramandala or simanta, 100 times on the mouth, 100 times on the throat, 100 times in the region of the heart, 100 times for each of her breasts, 100 times for the navel, and 100 times at the yoni. After doing so, the Sādhak should think of himself as one with Shiva, and using the Shiva mantra should worship his own lingam. Chewing tāmbulā, pān, and with bliss or excitement in his heart, he should place his lingam in the yoni of Shakti. He should offer his ātma, together with dharma and adharma, and everything else in his nature as a sacrificer offers to fire in the susumnā nādi using a mantra ending with Svāhā. Then, while still joined with his Shakti, he should utter the mantra 100 or 1,000 times. The full sacrifice, which here implies orgasm, he should then offer using the prakāshak mantra, again ending with Svāhā. The semen which flows from this orgasm should then be offered to the Devi. It may be noted here that this whole process, though couched in explicitly sexual terms, can also refer to the bliss when Kundalini rises through the sushumnā nādi and the chakras. Whoever worships according to the previous method, says Shiva, becomes free from illness, wealthy, and equal to the god of love Kama himself. All his enemies are destroyed, and he becomes successful on earth, gaining all dominion, and equal to Shiva himself.

Chapter Five

Pārvati wants to know about preparatory acts, and how many times the mantra given to the disciple by the guru should be recited in the months after initiation. Shiva says that during:

i. the first month, the mantra should be recited 600,000 times.

ii. 1,200,000 times in month two.

iii. 1,600,000 times in the third month.

iv. In months four and five, the number is 3,000,000 times for each.

v. in month six, the mantra has to be recited 3,600,000 times.

vi. 4,200,000 times in the seventh month.

vii. japa is 4,400,000 times in the eighth month.

viii. in month nine 4,500,000 or could be 5,400,000 times.

ix. in tenth month, it should be recited 6,000,000 times.

x. in month 11 the number creeps up to 6,500,000 times.

xi. in the last month of the year, the mantra has to be recited 10,000,000 times.

The last figure can be the total mantra chanting during a year.

Chapter Six

The goddess says she wants to know about the Dakshina form of Kālikā, who is the giver of siddhi, and very hard to get knowledge of in the three worlds. Shiva says Dakshinā Kāli is also spoken of in the Kāli Tantra and in Yamala. Knowing the essence of Dakshina Kāli liberates an individual from the ocean of being. Bhairava is the Rishi who reveals the mantra, it should be pronounced in the Ushnik metre. He gives the linchpin, kilaka, Shakti and other details.

The application of the mantra is in achieving the four ends or aims of all human beings, dharma, artha, kāma and moksha. Devi asks about different elements in *puja* including meditation, the place of worship, the different āsanas, posture, sitting positions, seats, called Alidha and Pratyalidha. The cremation ground is the place, and she should be worshipped during the night.

That Sādhak is an adhikāri who is competent. He is entitled to worship Kālikā, and should do the daily *puja* dedicated to his or her guru, or the guru's son or the guru's Shakti. Without this, the fruit of Sādhak's *puja* is taken by the rākshas and the yakshas. The guru and his or her family are to be offered the fruit of the *puja* and satisfied in every way.

The Alidha and Pratyalidha postures are the form of Kāli as the destroyer and deluder of the universe. The form of Kāli is fire itself, and so is situated in the cremation ground. Those of the divine and heroic dispositions or bhāvas, should worship using the five tattvas at midnight, to achieve the highest results and become free from chakra.

☆☆☆

SECTION IV

YANTRA

Yantra: Physical, Scientific and Celestial Mechanism

- ➤ Yantra in Tantra
- ➤ Shri Yantra: Shri Chakra
- ➤ All the Yantras

27

Yantra in Tantra

In Sādhanā and Upāsanā, Yantras and Mantras are vehemently used. Yantra is called the body, mostly the body of Gods and Goddesses or the physical representation of something spiritual, sublime and divine or something really very important.

In the creation of Yantras, the symbols like Bindu; Rekhā; Trikon and Vritta (dots; lines; triangles and squares) and other geometrical shapes are used. It is definitely a pleasure to note that geometry was well developed during the primitive ages.

It is believed that when one worships and meditates concentrating on a particular Yantra before the eyes, he is able to see that form in the space or elsewhere in the Brahmānd. When one is able to know the hidden meaning and worth, everything becomes crystal clear. That clarity in vision and knowing the truth is the real reason behind the worshipping.

It is a very tough task to know exactly what they had in mind simply because neither do we possess the things mentioned nor feel what shape or form of those things should be used. One must be reminded again that we have drifted a vast distance away from the things that our forefathers knew and had perfected. We claim only this much that these Yantras are helping instruments for attaining concentration and for communicating with the deity whom one is worshipping. One must ask some simple questions and try to answer them. When there are many other ways of getting deep concentration why are only these methodically prepared ones? In their available shape, how can the shapes be used in communicating to desired deity? Would they create something so meaningless who knew mechanics; geometry, applied math, physics, astrology and the Universe so well?

The Rishis claimed that *yat pinde tat brahmānde*; whatever is there in the universe is in our body which is definitely true. They further claimed that the Universe as well as the human body is a replica of the God. The Yantras too are the Gods physical forms: *Devo bhutvā devān yajet.* देवो भूत्वा देवान्यजेत्। So, through the Yantra the communication becomes easier.

Some people claimed that the Yantras are the plans of laboratories; others claimed that they show the inner construction of electronic equipments but the truth eludes.

Yantra, the Mechanism of Mantra

Yantra is amply praised in Tantra Shāstras. Kulārnava Tantra gives the details of its etymology and the method of worshipping Yantra. Yantra are said to be Mantramaya, full of Mantras or of the form of Mantras. The deity is in the form of Mantra. So, when she is worshipped in the Yantra, she pleases instantly:

Yantram mantra-mayam proktam devatā mantra-rupini;
Yantre sā pujitā devi sah-shaiva prasidati. 6:85

यन्त्रं मन्त्रमयं प्रोक्तं देवता मन्त्ररूपिणी।
यन्त्रे सा पूजिता देवी सः शैव प्रसीदति॥

Yantras are the controller of all pains arising from out of desire, anger and other failings. That is why, it is called Yantra. The deity pleases when worshipped in the Yantras:

Kāma-krodha-ādi-doshāt sarva-dukha-niyantranāt;
Yantram-itya-āhuret-asmin devah preenāti poojitah. 6:86

कामक्रोधादि दोषात् सर्वदुःख नियन्त्रणात्।
यन्त्रं इत्याहुरेत अस्मिन् देवः प्रीणाति पूजितः॥

As the body is for the Jiva; and as oil or ghrita or clarified butter is for a lamp, so, the concerned Yantra is a seat for all the deities:

Shariaram-iva jivasya feepasyā snehavat priye;
Sarvesām-api devānām tathā-yantra pratishthitam. 6:87

शरीरमिव जीवस्य फीप्सया स्नेहवत् प्रिये।
सर्वेषामपि देवानां तथा यन्त्र प्रतिष्ठितम्॥

Therefore, drawing the Yantra and meditating in Shiva in his proper form after knowing everything from the Guru, one should properly perform the worship.

Tasmāt yantram likhitvā-wā dhyāyatvā sāvritikam shivam;
Gyātvā guru-mukhāt saram poojayet-vidhinā priye. 6:88

तस्माद्यन्त्रं लिखित्वा-वा ध्यायत्वा सावृत्तिकंशिवम् ।
ज्ञात्वा गुरुमुखात् सारं पूजयेत् विधिना प्रिय ॥

The proper method of the worship of Yantra lies in the fact that each Deity must be worshipped on separate Yantras. If one performs worship of different Devatās in the same pitha without their respective Yantra then due to the fault of embodiment and the embodied, that Sādhak entails the curse of the Deities.

Ek pithe prithak-poojā binā yantra karoti yah;
Anga-angitvam parityajya devatā-shāpam-apyunuyā. 6:89

एक पीठे पृथक्-पूजा बिना यन्त्र करोति यः ।
अंगंगित्वं परित्यज्य देवता शापमाप्नुया ॥

Hence, in the same pitha, worship of different deities should be performed separately in their respective Yantras in accordance with their respective procedures and coverings.

Ekpithe kuleshāni swe swe yantre prithak prithak;
Yajed-āvaranopetā devatāh tad-adhimānatah. 6:90

एक पीठे कुलेशानि स्वे स्वे यन्त्रे पृथक् पृथक ।
यजेदावरणोपेता देवताः तद्भिमानतः ॥

If one worships another deity then, invoking a particular different deity the Sādhak of such instable mind gets the curse of both the deities.

Āvāhya devatām-yekām poojyed-anya devatām;
Ubhābhyām labhate pangah mantra chanchal mānasah. 6:91

आवाह देवतामेकं पूज्येदन्य देवतां ।
उभाभ्यां लभते पंगः मन्त्र चन्चल-मानसः ॥

Kulārnava Tantra Defines Yantra:

Because of from all beings like Yama etc, and even from all fear, it always saves, trāyate, so, it is called a Yantra:

Yama-bhuta-ādi-sarvebhyo bhaye-bhayo-api kuleshwari;
Trāyate satat-shrava tasmāt yantra-iti-ritim. 17.61

यम भूतादि सर्वेभ्यो भये भयो-अपि कुलेश्वरी ।
त्रायते सतत्-श्रव तस्मात् यन्त्र इति ऋतिम् ॥

Three Dimensions of Yantras

Many people have seen only the pictures of Yantras but most of the people have not seen even the pictures. Only a few may have seen the actual Yantra. As yantras are now being prepared on a commercial basis and are sold at a premium price after a lot of ads in the electronic media, so it has become easy to see them. The householders can keep Yantras even the Shri Yantra and worship it as a part of daily prayer. It will be simple worshipping, but neither anushthān nor sādhanā.

Incidentally, only the pictures are given here. Pictures have only the length and width, rather reduced length and shortened width and no height at all. Pictures never give a true insight into the Yantras and don't present all its dimensions. All the Yantras are three dimensional. One can get a lot if one seriously reads the details of Shri Yantra given in the next chapter but won't get all. The dimensions are missing.

In most of the scriptures, the ways of constructing the Yantras are given. One can get it constructed by some expert goldsmith for own satisfaction or buy one from the market. Only then one can realize the real worth of the Yantras.

Worshipping Procedure

After cleaning the body by taking bath in a river, one should perform many things before actual poojan of the Yantra:

1. **Dvār Poojā**: The worshipping of the entrance of the living place or worshipping place.

2. **Prānāyāma**: Salute first Shri Ganesh, then the Guru and then the Ishta Devatā, the selected deity by Purak with thirty two Pranava; Kumbhak with sixty four Pranava and Rechak with sixteen Pranava.

3. **Bhuta Suddhi**: The next step is Bhuta Suddhi. The details are given elsewhere in the book. As a conclusion to the previous steps, the next step is to concentrate on: five karmendriya; five vishayas; five gyān-indriyas and to feel the presence of five Devatās; five kalās and five prānas in them.

4. **Prāna Pratishthā**: Life element is again instigated in with the following viniyoga:

    Aum asya prāna pratishthā mantrasya ajesh padmajā rishayahrig-yajuh sāmāni chhandāsi prāna Shaktih devatā pāsh āng hring Shakti krong keelakam prāna pratishthāpane viniyogah.

5. **Rishi-ādi-nyāsa**: Nyāsas should be performed with the following Mantras:

    Aum angang kang khang gang ghang nabho-vāyavya-agnih-wā-bhumi-ātmane hridyāya namah!

    Aum trang chang chhang jhang jang shabd-sparsh-roopa-rasa-gandha-ātmane sirase swāhā!

    Aum nang tang thang dhang dang shrotra-tvang-jihvā-prāna-ātmane shikhāya vashat!

    Aum nang tang thang dhang dang vāk-pāni-pād-pāyu-upastha-ātmane kawachāya hum!

    Aum mang pang bang bhang vang vaktavyāda-anāgaman-visarg-ānand-ātmane netra-trayāya aushat!

    Aum shang yang rang vang lang hang shang kshang lang buddhi-mama-ahankār-chitta-ātmane astrāya phat!

    Rest of the nyāsas should also be performed including the nyāsa of peetha Devatā and mātrikā nyāsa; kar-nyāsa and ang-nyāsa. The nyāsa vidhi is to be learnt meticulously for which a guru is definitely needed.

6. **Mantra Uddhār**: It differs from devatā to devatā and mantra to mantra. It must be learnt about the selected mantra with the help of the guru.

7. **Saraswati Dhyān**: Concentrate on the Goddess of Learning Sarswati and chant the Mantra or the Mantra selected and taught by the guru:

8. **Āvaran Poojan**: In āvarana poojan nine peetha Shakties: Medhā; Pragyā; Prabhā; Vidyā; Shri; Dhriti; Smriti; Buddhi; and Vidyeshwari; and Varga Shakties: Vyāpini; Pālani; Pāvani; Kledani; Dhārini; Mālini; Hansini and Shankhini are worshipped, then the poojan of Saraswati is performed.

9. **Pavitri and Teerth Mantra**: Pavitri of kusha is prepared and wore in the ring finger and the following teerth mantra is recited to purify the water:

Gange cha yamune chaiva godāvari saraswati;
Narmade sindhu kāveri jale-asmin sannidhim kuru.

गंगे च यमुने चैव गोदावरी सरस्वती।
नर्मदे सिन्धु कावेरि जलेऽस्मिन सन्निधिं कुरु॥

10. Only then a seeker should start chanting the Mantra for his Ishata Devatā. During that Anushthān the seeker must take only once any or many of the Havishyānna, the things allowed to be eaten which include: Oat; Moonga; Rice; Cow-milk; Curd; Ghee; Sugar; Butter; Tila; Khoyā; Coconut; Banana; Fruits; Mevā; āmalā and sendhā salt.

❀❀❀

28

Shri Yantra: Shri Chakra

Shri Yantra, the Yantra Rāja, the best among the Yantras, is supposed to be the Yantra for Shri Tripura Sundari Bhagawati but be sure it is much more than that or more than what our limited imagination can imagine. That is one reason that all the Yantras are being given in short and in one article but Shri Yantra is being presented in detail and analyzed well and in different ways in order to extract most out of it.

Shri Yantra is worshipped by all but most vociferously by the followers of Samaya Matta which was re-explained by Ādi Shankarāchārya. Householders worship it for their own reasons, the saints keep it and worship it in their hermitage, and the Tāntriks have their own reasons and purpose behind worshipping the Shri Yantra. The followers of Samhār Matta reverse the five and four triangles. The female triangles become the male and vice versa.

In its totality, Shri Chakra presents Brahmānd and its formation and layers. In the same way, it shows the inner organs and upper parts of human body. There are many Granthas on Shri Chakra but they are hardly available. It must be read as it will guide the scientists in creating equipments and instruments for the common good of all.

The **Shri Yantra** is a yantra formed by nine interlocking triangles that surround and radiate out from the central *bindu*, point, the junction point between the physical universe and its un-manifest source. It represents the goddess in her form of Shri Lalitā or Shri Tripura Sundari, the beauty of the three worlds, shown as Bindu. Four of the triangles point upwards, representing Shiva or the Masculinity, and are called Shri Kantha. Five of these triangles point downwards, representing Shakti or the Feminine power, and are called Shiva Yuvati. Thus, the Shri Yantra also represents the union of masculine and feminine divinity. In another Shri Chakra, the reverse is the order: five upwards and four downwards. The five energy triangles represent the five gross elements; five *tannamātrās*; five sense organs; five action organs and five Prānās. As it is composed of nine triangles, it is known as the *Navayoni Chakra*. The four Shri Kantha tringles, the male counterpart; show Chitta; Buddhi; Ahankār and Mana or in organs they represent marrow; Semen; Prāna and Jiva, living beings.

चित्र 1: श्रीयंत्र

The nine triangles are interlaced together in such a way as to form 43 smaller triangles in a web symbolic of the entire cosmos or a womb symbolic of creation. Together, they express Advaita or non-duality. This is surrounded by a lotus of eight petals, a lotus of sixteen petals, and an earth square resembling a temple with four doors.

The Shri Chakra is also known as the *nava chakra* because it can also be seen as having nine levels. "Nava" means "nine" in Sanskrit. Each level corresponds to a mudrā, a yogini, and a specific form of the deity Tripura Sundari along with her mantra. These levels starting from the outside or bottom layer are:

1. *Trailokya Mohana* or *Bhupara*, a square of three lines with four portals; green outer boundary.
2. *Sarva Āshā Paripuraka*, a sixteen-petal lotus of yellow colour.
3. *Sarva Sankshobahana*, an eight-petal lotus of rosy colour.
4. *Sarva Saubhāgyadāyaka*, composed of fourteen small triangles of blue colour.
5. *Sarva Arthasādhaka*, composed of ten small red triangles.
6. *Sarva Rogahar*, composed of ten small black triangles.
7. *Sarva Rakshāka*, composed of eight small green triangles.
8. *Sarva Siddhi Pradā*, composed of one small yellow triangle.
9. *Sarva Ānanda Mayi*, composed of a red point or *bindu* at the centre.

These nine triangles form forty five triangles. In the inner square there is an eight-petal lotus and outside there is a sixteen petal lotus and almost out of them all, there is Bhupur. Ādi Shankrāchārya has written about them in Ānand Lahari:

Chaturbhih shri kanthaih shiva-yuvatibhih panchabhih-api
Praminnābhih shambho-navabhih-api moola-prakritibhih;
Trayah-chatvārin-shadva-sudala-kalābjanni-valaya
Tri-rekhā-bhih sārdhamtava bhawan-konāh parinatāh.

चतुर्भिः श्रीकण्ठैः शिवयुवतिभिः पन्चभिः अपि।
प्रमिण्णाभिः शम्भोनवभिः अपि मूल-प्रकृतिभिः॥
त्रयः चत्वरिन् षड्व सुदल कलाब्जन्नि वलय।
त्रि रेखाभिः सारधमत्व भवनकोणाः परिणतः॥

The nine chakras are in the following sequence:

i. Bindu
ii. Trikon, tringles
iii. A group of eight triangles
iv. A group of ten triangles
v. Another group of ten triangles
vi. A group of fourteen triangles
vii. Eight petal lotus
viii. Sixteen petal lotus
ix. Bhupur

Shri Yantra: Its Significance

The Shri Chakra, called the Shri Yantra, is the symbol of Hindu Tantra. Though, it is very primitive yet it is deemed to be based on the Hindu philosophy of Kashmir Shivism, may be because the Kashmiri Shivas revived it in the Middle Ages. The Shri Yantra is the object of devotion of Shri Vidyā.

Shri Chakra as popularly known to be a symbol of Lakshmi, is actually a representation of Lalitā, Mahātripurasundari, another symbolic representation of Pārvati Devi. Shri does not mean only the wealth in this context but has different connotations and denotations. The term 'Shri' is used to denote the reverence to be given to this holy Yantra. The prefix 'Shri' denotes that the Yantra is auspicious, beneficent, salutary, benign and conducive to prosperity. Shri Chakra is often referred as the **Chakra Rāja** which means **King of all Chakras**. This makes it a supreme instrument in the path of spiritual advancement and of material gain as well. So, non-Tāntriks also worship it for overall prosperity. Whenever the material wealth is mentioned it points directly to its mechanical significance.

Creation of Shri Chakra

The Triple Goddess, from Her own will to manifest, extends Herself in a nine fold way, as modifications of moon, sun and fire. The attributes of various *mandalas* shows the type of energy represented. The meditation in Bhavana Upanishad is a figurative way of describing this celestial city or mountain, which is a human being. The island of jewels is the gross human body with its nine alchemical bases or *dhātus*. Each is figuratively described as a gem: diamond, emerald, sapphire, ruby, etc. The sea of nectar is the base for the human body. The diagram sums up the meditation. We can see that this island of gems is a very pleasant place to be. It is full of gardens, with a beautiful, be-gemmed palace, wafted with a gentle breeze upon which is carried great fragrance; cool and alluring. This indicates the Kaula view that one gains liberation by a very pleasant way, enjoying as one goes. This paradise island is very, very close. Each of the elements of the island in meditation a subtle meaning associated with the mystic physiology of Shri Vidyā.

Lalitā, united with Shiva, is subtlety of subtlety, hidden behind the curtain hanging from the canopy. Her forms may appear to become progressively less subtle, but she still remains herself.

The central dot formed with *nāda* and *bindu*, stands for Shri Tripur Sundari, also known as Lalitā. She is Shivā herself.

The following is her *dhyān* Mantra:

> *Bālārk-mandalā-bhāsām chatur-bāhām trilocha-nām;*
> *Pāshānkusha-dhanuh-vānān dhāryanti shivā bhaje.*

बालार्क मण्डलाभासं चतुर्बाहां त्रिलोचनाम् ।
पाशांकुश धनुर्वाणान् धारयन्ति शिवा भजे ॥

The weapons mentioned here symbolize attachment; jealousy; mana and pancha tanna-mātras. With the help of these weapons the deity controls Sadāshiva and presents Herself in physical form.

This central be-gemmed palace, the abode of the deity has been referred to as Sudhā-sindhu; the ocean of nectar or sweetness or Manidvip; an island of jewels. In human being it is called Hrit-pundarik. Its Dhyān has been described in detail in Dhyān Bindu Upanishad.

Shri Lalitā or Shri Tripura Sundari is principal one among Shodas Nityās; or Shodas Mātrikās; or the leader of Ashta Vashini Devatās. These opening or widening of meaning is known as Meru; Kailāsh and Bhu-prastār.

Mantra for Shri Poojan Chakra

Kalash Poojan Mantra for Surya:

> *Aum hāng hing hung ramalcharyun hāng surya mandalāya*
> *vasu prada dvādash kalātmane kling kalashāya namah.*

ॐ हां हीं हुं रमलचर्युड् हां सूर्य मण्डलाय ।
वसुप्रदा द्वादश कलात्मने क्लीं कलशाय नमः ॥

The following dvādasha kalās of Surya are also worshipped:

Tapini; Tāpini; Dhumrā; Marichi; Jvalini; Ruchira; Sushumnā; Bhogadā; Vishwā; Bodhini; Dhārini; and Kshamā.

Kalash Poojan Mantra for Agni:

Aum rāng ring rung ramalchyung rang agni mandalāya dharma prada dasha kalātmane aing kalashā dhārāya namah!

ॐ रां रीं रुं रमलचर्युङ् रं अग्निमण्डलाय।
धर्मप्रद दश कलात्मने ऐं कलशाधाराय नमः ॥

The following ten kalās of agni are worshipped:

Dhumrārchi; Ushmā; Jvalini; Jvālini; Visphulingini; Sushri; Suroopā; Kapilā; Havyavahā; and Kavyavahā.

Mantra of Kalash Poojan for Chandra:

Aum sāng sing sung ramalcharyung sāng soma mandalāya kāma prada shodash kalātmane sauh kalasha amritāya namah!

ॐ सां सीं सुं रमलचर्युङ् सां सोम मण्डलाय।
कामप्रद षोडश कलात्मन सौः कलश अमृताय नमः॥

The following Shodash kalās of Chandramā should also be worshipped:

Amritā; Mānadā; Pooshā; Tushti; Pushti; Rati; Dhriti; Shashini; Chandrikā; Kānti; Jyotsanā; Shri; Preeti; Angadā; Purnā; and Purna Amritā.

The Moola Mantra of Shri Chakra or Chakra Rāja:

Aing parāyai aparāyai par-aparāyai hasauh sadā shiva mahā-preta padmāsanāya namah!

ऐं परायै अपरायै पर-अपरायै हसौः सदाशिव महाप्रेत पदमासनाय नमः।

The Mantra to offer Pushpa, flowers:

Hring shring prakat gupta guptatar sampradāya kulāni garbha rahasyāti rahasya par-apar rahasya sangyaka shri chakra gatah yogini pādukābhyo namah!

ह्रीं श्रीं प्रकट गुप्त गुप्तातर सम्प्रदाय कुलानि गर्भरहस्याति रहस्य पर अपर रहस्य संज्ञक श्री चक्रगतः योगिनि पादुकाभ्यो नमः ॥

Āwāhan Mantra for Devi

Mahā padma avanāntasthe karan ānand vigrahe;
Sarva bhuta hite mātah yehyehi parameshwari.
Devesi bhakti sulabhe sarva āvaran sanyute;
Yāva-tvām poojayi-shyāmi tāvatvam susthirā bhava.

महापद्मः अवनान्सथे कर्ण आनंद विगरायै
सर्वा भूतः हिते मातः येह्येहि परमेश्वरी
देवेसि भक्ति सुलभे सर्व आवरन सन्यूते।
यावात्वाम पूजयिष्यामि तावत्त्वम् सुस्थिरा भवः॥

Peethas; Deities and Shaktis in Shri Chakra

1. **The Triangle**

    i. Three **Peethas**: Each angle of the central triangle represents one peetha:

    | Kāmaroopa | Purnagiri | Jālandhar Peetha |

    ii. The **Devatā** of the Peethas:

    | Kāmeshwari | Brajeshwari | Bhaga-mālini |

    iii. The **forms** of Devatas:

    | Prakrit | Mahat | Ahankār |

2. **Eight Triangles**

    i. **Devatas:**

    | Vashini | Kāmeshwari | Mohini | Vimalā |
    | Arunā | Jayanti | Sarveshwari | Kaulini |

    ii. **Symbols**

    | Sheeta, cold | Ushna, hot | Sukha, pleasure |
    | Dukha, suffering | Ikshā, desire | Sattva, Purity; |
    | Rāja, royal | Tama, darkness | |

3. **Ten Triangles**

    i. **Devatas**

    | Sarvagyā | Sarva Shakti Pradā | Sarva Aishwarya Pradā |
    | Sarva Gyānmayi | Sarva Vyādhi Nāshini | Sarva Dhārā |
    | Sarva Pāpa Harā | Sarva Ānand Mayi | Sarva Rakshikā |
    | Sarva Phala Pradā | | |

4.   **Fourteen Trinagles**

i. **Nādis**: The triangles represent the fourteen following Nādis:

Alambusā	Kuhu	Vishwodari Varnā
Hasti Jihvā	Yashovati	Payaswini
Gāndhāri Pushā	Shankini	Saraswati Idā
Pingalā	Sushumnā	

ii. **Devatas**

Sarva Sankshobhini	Sarva Vidrāvini	Sarva Ākarshini
Sarva Ahlādani	Sarva Sammohini	Sarva Stambhani
Sarva Jambhini	Sarva Ranjini	Sarva Vashakari
Sarva Unmādini	Sarvārtha Sādhini	Sarva Sampati Purani
Sarva Mantra Mayi	Sarva Dvandva Kshayakari	

5.   **Eight Petalled Lotus**

i. **Petals**

Vachan	Ādān	Gaman	Visarga
Ānand	Hān	Upādān	Upekshā

ii. **Devatas**

Ananga Kusumā	Ananga Mekhalā
Ananag Madanā	Ananga Madanāturā
Ananga Rekhā	Ananga Vegini
Ananga Madanāng Kushā	Ananga Mālini

6.   **Sixteen Petalled Lotus**

i. **16 Petals**

Mana	Buddhi	Ahankār	Shabda
Sparsha	Roopa	Rasa	Gandha
Chitta	Dhairya	Smriti	Nāma
Ārdhakya	Sukshma-sharira	Jivan	Sthula Sharira

ii. **Devatas**

Kāma Ākarshini	Buddhi Ākarshini	Ahankār Ākarshini
Shabda Ākarshini	Sparsha Ākarshini	Roopa Ākarshini
Rasa Ākardhini	Gandha Ākarshini	Chitta Ākarshini
Dhairya Ākarshini	Smriti Ākarshini	Nāma Ākarshini

Beeja Ākarshini   Ātmā Ākarshini   Amrit Ākarshini
Sharira Ākarshini

Mantras on Shri Yantra

1. In Shri Yantra, there are 101 Yantras that are worshipped
    with the Beejākshar Mantras. In the Saundarya Lāhari by
    Shri Shankarāchārya all the **101 Beeja Akshar Mantras**
    have been given. For ready reference for the reader, it is
    being given below:

    hring shring aum shring tang ang tvang hang dhang kwang
    dung mang sung chang tvang nang kshung shang āng

    kang sang tang mung king tang bhang tvang jang trang ving
    jang sung kling swang kling

    chang shing smang shang mang tang ving sang tang tang
    tang gang dhang van gang soung

    lang bhrung ang ving kang shing gang ving pang ning tang
    dring ang phung sang la-ye-e-la-hring

    ang prang sming ang rang ving kang bhung gang ming nang
    sang ang vang tang hang ja-sa-ka-ha-la hring

    yang sthing ning kung gung kang pang shrung nang mring
    hing oang nang dang pang sa-ka-la gring

    hring shring aum gang ang sang pung kang ginga sang kang
    ging sang kang shring hring aum.

2. The following are the 101 Yantras on Shri Chakra:

    i.   43 Triangles, Trikon
    ii.   08 Ashta Dal Kamal; its Dals, petals
    iii. 16 Shodasha Dala Kamal
    iv.   15 Trivritta, Yantras like bow
    v.   19 square Yantras. The total is 101.

3. Shri Yantra is prepared in three ways:

    i.   Meru Prishtha; like mountains
    ii.   Kurma Prishta; like the back of turtle

    iii.   Bhu Prishta; plain like the earth
            Just like modern machines: flat, oval or conical.

4.   Starting from Bindu, there is Sodasha Nityā Vidhā:

Shri Mahātripur Sundari	Kāmeshwari	Bhaga Mālini
Nitya Kalannā	Bherundā	Vanhi Vāsini
Mahā Vidyeshwari	Shiva Duti	Tvaritā
Kula Sundari	Nityā	Neela Patākā
Vijayā	Sarva Mangalā	Jwālā Mālini
Chitta Kalā		

5.   Dvādasha Yogini on Shri Yantra:

Vidyā Yogini	Rechikā Yogini	Mochikā Yogini
Amritā Yogini	Deepikā Yogini	Gyāndā Yogini
Appyāyani Yogini	Vyāpini Yogini	Meghā Yogini
Vyo Māghā Yogini	Siddhadā	Laxmi Yogini.

6.   Fifteen Senses

Among the 15 senses on the Shri Yantra, 5 Gyān Indriyān; 5 Karma Indriyān and 5 Tan Mātrās are counted.

7.   The following are the Dasha Dikpāl on the Shri Yantra:

Mahendra	Mahāgni	Mahāyam
Mahā Varna Daivat	Mahānirit	
Shri Mahānant Shakti	Mahā Vāyu Daivat	Mahā Soma
Ishāna/Madan Bhairava	Shri Dhumrā Shakti	

Fruits of Shri Chakra Darshanam

What to say for worshipping Shri Yantra, only by looking at it, one obtains all the fruits. Shri Yantra is worshipped by both the Rightists and Leftists. Its ways and other details along with different results are described in the Tripur Tāpini Upanishad and Tripurā Upanishad. One Yāmal Granth describes the fruits that one gets only after looking at it. Whatever fruits one gets after completing the worship; after performing sixteen types of charity; and by visiting all the teerthas; one gets all these fruits only after looking at Shri Yantra; only by 'Shri-chakra-darshanam.' This was the reason to separately discuss this divine Yantra.

Samyak shata-kratum kritvā yat phalam samvāpnuyāt;
Tatphalam labhate bhaktyā kritvā shri-chakra-darshanam.
Magā-shodash dānāni kritvā yat labhate phalam;
Tatphalam sam-vāpnoti kritvā shri-chakra-darshanam.
Shradha-tri-koti-teertheshu snātvā yat-phalam-ashnute;
Labhate tatphalam bhaktyā kritvā shri-chakra-darshanam.

सम्यक सतकतुं कृत्वायत् फलं समवाप्नुयात।
तत्फलम् लभते भक्त्या कृत्वा श्रीचक्र-दर्शनं॥
मगाषोडश दानानिकृत्वा यत लभते फलम्।
तत्फलं समवाप्नोति कृत्वा श्रीचक्र-दर्शनं।
श्रद्धात्रिकोटि तीर्थेसु स्नत्वा यत-फलं अस्नूते।
लभते तत्फलं भक्त्याकृत्वा श्रीचक्र-दर्शनं॥

It is advisable not to worship Shri Yantra or any other Yantra because it is limited to mostly worldly gains, and has the least to do with Moksha, salvation; but if one insists on performing Shri Yantra or any other Yantra, he should first learn and memorize and even make and keep a chart of all that has to be done, and **perform the poojan following all the rules and norms dictated by the Shāstras.** This is essential. If the norms are not followed then it can reverse the end result. Be careful and remain conscious if you do this.

❄ ❄ ❄

29

All the Yantras

Like all other poojans, Yantra poojan is also a tough task. It should be performed under the guidance of a Siddha Guru, accomplished preceptor or a gyāni pandit; or expert priest. One should not try to do it on one's own after reading books. There are many limitations in preparing a book in which many things are not repeated and many other things are completely omitted. Many things are given in short form with the Yantras. So, it is better to consult the Poojana Vidhi given elsewhere and at many places. One can get the systematic and standard procedure of worshipping but there are many substitutes and many things are changed according to Kula and Gotra. Popular or accepted ways are always followed, which may be different to what is given here. **Precautions must be taken at every step**.

It is needless to state that a new Yantra should be constructed on the Vedikā, worshipping place or place on it. Worship should be started when everything is ready and nearby or there is an assistant to hand over the articles. It will help a lot, if assistance is not availed of and the things are kept close by.

1. **Agni Poojan Yantram:** Agni Poojan Yantra should be placed or erected on the Vedi and agni should be started with Mantras. Peetha poojan is completed with the Mantra: *Aum hring vāgishi-vāgushwaryoh peethātmane namah!* ॐ ह्रीं वागिशि वागुश्वरयो: पीठात्मने नमः। If homa is to be offered to Vishnu Bhagawān then the Mantra will be: *Aum hring lakshmi nārāyanābhyām namah!* ॐ ह्रीं लक्ष्मी नारायणाभ्यां नमः। Agni should be established, sthāpit,

with the Mantra: *Vaishwānar-jat-veda ihā-vah lohitāksha sarva-karmāni sādhaya swāhā!* वैश्वानर जतवेद इहावह लोहिताक्ष सर्वकर्माणि साध्य स्वाहा। Then other things are performed called: *Sansthāpan; Tāpan; Abhidyotan; Sechan; Utapavan* and *Sampalvan.* After chanting the Ganesh Mantra, *Shri vakratundāya hum!* havan is offered. Tarpan is completed with the Mantra: *Aum hasti pishāchi likhe swāhā uchchhista-ganapati tarpayāmi.* ॐ हस्ती पिशाचि लिखे स्वाहा उच्छिष्ट गणपति तर्पयामि। Devatās moola mantra is to be chanted and at last Abhishek is completed with the Mantra designed for that.

चित्र 2: अग्नि (वहिनी) पूजन-यन्त्र

2. **Shri Ganesh Poojan Yantram:** Take for example, that the selected Mantra is sarva-abhista pradāyak; the mantra that fulfills all the desires: *vakratundāya hum*; the viniyoga; purashacharan; nyāsas; dhyān should be complete and in peetha pooja these nine Shaktis should be worshipped: Teevrā; Chālini; Nandā; Bhogadā; Kāma-rupini; Ugrā;

Tejovati; Satyā and Vighna-nāshini. Then pancha-āvaran poojā and ashta mātrikā poojā is completed.

The following Lakshmi Vināyak Mantra is very popular and it should also be worshipped and chanted on the above given pattern: *Aum shring gang saumyāya ganapataye var varad sarva-janam mey vasham-ānaya swāhā!* ॐ श्रीं गं सौम्याय गणपतये वरवराद सर्वजन्म मे वशं-आनय स्वाहा।

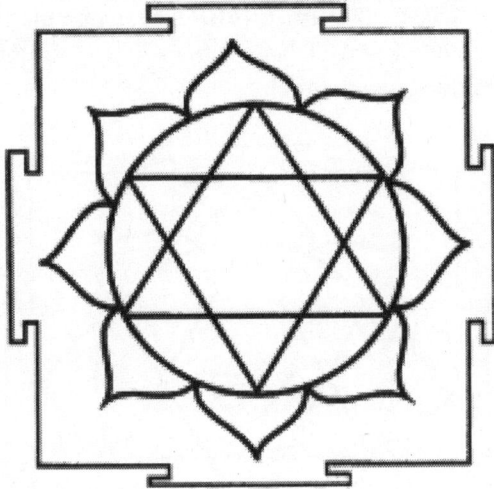

चित्र 3: गणेश पूजन-यन्त्र

3. **Kāli Poojan Yantram:** In the poojan of Kāli Yantram the following are the nine Shaktis: Jayā; Vijayā; Ajitā; Aparājitā; Nityā; Vilāsini; Dogadhri; Aghorā; and Mangalā. They are worshipped with Peetha Mantra: *Aum hring kālikā-yogātmane namah!* ॐ ह्रीं कलिका योगात्मने नमः। Then Pancha Varnācharan are completed. Kāli is worshipped with the following Mantra but a seeker can select a mantra of his choice: *Aum hring hring hung hung kring kring dakshine kālike kring kring hung hung hring hring!* ॐ ह्रीं हुं हुं क्रीं क्रीं दक्षिणे कालिके हुं हुं ह्रीं ह्रीं। Nyāsa and other related

poojan are performed. Two types of Kāli Poojan Yantras are being given below.

चित्र 4: काली पूजन-यन्त्र

चित्र 5: काली पूजन-यन्त्र

4. Sumukhi Poojan Yantra

Sumukhi Dhyān Mantra:

Gunjā-nirmit-hār bhusit kunchām sadya-yavana-ullāsini
Hastābhyām nrik-pāla-khadga-latike tamie mudā vibgratim;
Rakta-alankrit-vastra-lepan-lasad-deha-prabhām dhyāyatām
Nrinām shri sumukhim shavāsan-gatām syuh sarvadā sampadah.

गुंजानिर्मित हार भूषित कूंचां सदयावन उल्लासिनि।
हस्ताभ्यां नृकपाल खड्गलेतिके तमि मूडा विबग्रतिम्।
रक्तालंकृत वस्त्रलेपन लसडदेहा प्रभां ध्यायताम्।
नृनाम श्री सुमुखीं शवासनगतम् स्युः सर्वदा सम्पदः॥

One must complete one lakh chanting of the following Sumukhi Mantra: *Uchchhista chandālini sumukhi devi mahā-pishāchini hring thah thah thah!* उच्छिष्ट चन्डालिनि सुमुखी देवी महापिशाचिनि हीं ठः ठः ठः।

One tenth of havan should be performed with Kinshuk Pushpa and its branches as *samidhā*. Its mantra should be chanted after taking food and without washing the hands and mouth.

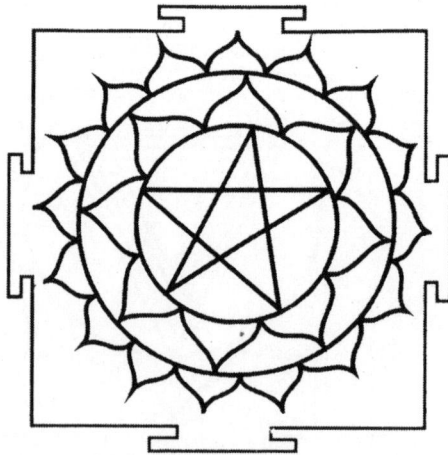

चित्र 6: सुमुखी पूजन-यन्त्र

5. **Tārā Poojan Yantram:** Perform Shri Ganesh Poojan; Batuka Bhairava; Kshetrpāla; Yoginis with their Mantras and Akshobhya Rishi with '*Akshobhya vajra-pushpam prateechchha swāhā!*' अक्षोभ्य वज्र-पुष्पं प्रतीच्छ स्वहा Mantra; and then Ashta Dal poojan. After that one should seek the permission of Devi with '*āvarana te poojayāmi devi agyāpaya*; and perform āvarana poojan. Then chant the Mantra: *Shrimad-ekajate neela-saraswati mahā-ugra-tāre de.* श्रीमद्एकजते नील सरस्वती महाउग्रतारे दे।

The following are some other Tārā Mantras:

i.   Brahma Upāsit, worshipped by Brahma:
Aum tring hring hung hring phat! ॐ ट्रीं ह्रीं हुं ह्रीं फट।

ii. Vishnu Upāsit, worshipped by Vishnu:
Aing hring shring kling saunha hung ugra-tāre hung phat!
ऐं ह्रीं श्रीं क्लीं सौनः हुं उग्रतारे हुं फट।

iii. Ek Jatā Mantra:
Aum hring hung hring hung phat! ॐ ह्रीं हुं ह्रीं हुं फट।

iv. Nārāyan Upāsit, worshipped by Nārāyan:
Tring hung phat kling aing! ट्रीं हुं फट क्लीं ऐं।

चित्र 7: तारा पूजन-यन्त्र

6. **Tārā Dhāran Yantra**: Tārā Dhāran Yantra should be folded in new yellow cloth and tied with yellow thread. It should be anointed with one thousand Tārā Mantra.

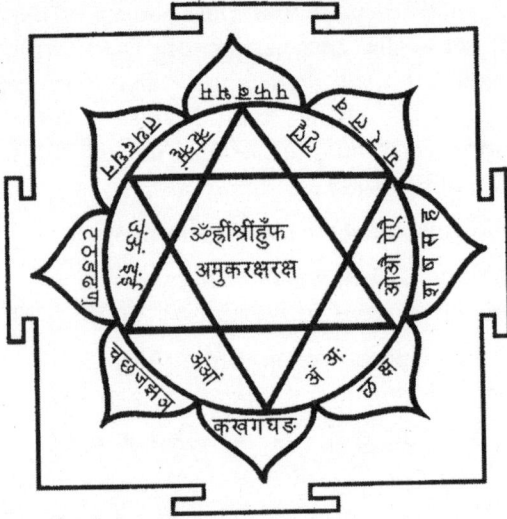

चित्र 8: तारा धारण यन्त्र

7. **Vidyā Rāgyi Poojan Yantram:** First, construct a triangle then double it to make six triangles; then eight petalled lotus; on its outer part another lotus with sixteen petals, then one with thirty two petals; yet another one with sixty four petals; then construct the bhupur of three lines. This is the Vidyā Rāgyi Poojan Yantram.

Worship it first with vakshya-māna mantra; then perform the poojan of Neela Saraswati with Shodash Upachār, sixteen articles. Worship sixty four Shaktis on the outer lotus, then thirty two Shaktis on the next lotus, sixteen on the next lotus. Perform the Poojan of eight petals with different Sarswati Mantras. The following are the Mantras along with the name of Saraswati:

i.   Vāgishwari Saraswati Mantra:

Aum namah padmāsane shabda-rupe aing hring kling vad vad vāg-vādini swāhā!

ॐ नमः पद्मासने शब्दरूपे ऐं ह्रीं क्लीं वद्-वद् वाग्वादिनि स्वाहा।

ii. Chitreshwari Saraswati Mantra:

Ha sa ka la hing vad chitreshwari aing swāhā!

हसकल हीं वद् चित्तेश्वरी ऐं स्वाहा।

iii. Kulajā Saraswati Mantra:

Aing kulaje aing saraswati swāhā!

ऐं कुलजे ऐं सरस्वती स्वाहा।

iv. Kirtishwari Saraswati Mantra:

Aing hring shring vad vad kirtishwari swāhā!

ऐं ह्रीं श्रीं वद् वद् कृतेश्वरी स्वहा।

v.   Antariksha Saraswati Mantra:

Aing hring antariksha saraswati swāhā!

ऐं ह्रीं अंतरिक्ष सरस्वती स्वाहा।

vi. Ghat Saraswati Mantra:

Hasa-shaphram hasnong asafrom aing hring shring drāng dring kling blung sah ghing ghata saraswati ghate vad vad tar tar rudra-āgyā mam-abhilāsham kuru kuru swāhā!

हस्फ्रं हस्त्रों इसफ्रों ऐं ह्रीं श्रीं द्रां द्रीं क्लीं बलुं सः घ्री घट सरस्वती घटे वद्-वद् तर तर रूद्राज्ञया ममाभिलाषं कुरु कुरु स्वाहा।

vii. Neela Saraswati Mantra:

Blung veng vad vad tring hung phat!

ब्लुं वें वद्-वद् ट्रीं हुं फट।

viii. Kini Saraswati Mantra:

Aing hang hing kini kini vichche!

ऐं हं हीं किणि किणि विच्चे।

Worship i. Dākini ii. Rākini iii. Lākini iv. Kākini v. Shākini and vi. Hākini Shaktis in Shashta-āvaran, six tringles.

Worship Parā, Bālā and Bhairavi in the first triangle. Worship eight Siddhis in the first Bhupur; eight Bhairavas in the 2nd Bhupur and ashta mātrikās, eight mothers in the 3rd Bhupur. This way all the seven āvaranas, coverings are worshipped.

चित्र 9: विद्याराज्ञी पूजन-यन्त्र

8.　Chhinna-mastā Poojan Yantram

Dhyān Mantra of Chhinna-mastā:

Bhāswan-mandal-madhya-gām nija-shir chhinnam vikirna-alakam;
Spharāsyam prapibad galāt swa-rudhiram vāme karebibhrateem.
Yābhā-sakta-rati-smar-uparogatām sakhyau nije dākini;
Varninyau paridrishya moda kalitām shri chhinnamastā bhaje.

भास्वन मंडलमध्यगां निज सिर छिनं विकीर्ण अलकं
स्फ्रेस्यं प्रपीबद गलातस्वरूधिरं वामे करेबिभ्रेतीम
याभासक्त रतिस्मर उपरोगतां साख्यौ निजे डाकिनि
वरनिन्यौ परिदृष्य मोद कलितां श्री छिन्नमस्ता भजे ॥

One in the centre and eight on the petals, the following nine Shaktis should be worshipped on Chhinna-mastā Yantra with the mantra given below: Jayā; Vijayā; Ajitā; Aparājitā; Nityā; Vilāsini; Doghril Aghorā and Mangalā.

> *Aum sarva buddhi prade dākiniye*
> *Aum vajra vairochaniye yehyohi namah!*

ॐ सर्वबुद्धिप्रदे डाकिनिए।
ॐ वज्र वैरोचनीय येह्योहि नमः॥

In the āvaran poojan, on the outer circle of the bhupur, Indra ādi dash dikpāla and four dwārpāls on the four gates of the Bhupur named: Karāla; Vikarāla; Atikāla and Mahākāla should be worshipped.

In the eight petals eight Shaktis called: Eklingā; Yogini; Dākini; Bhairavi; Mahābhairavi; Kendrākshi; Asitāngi and Sanhārini should be worshipped. At the centre, Chhinmastā with Vāgbeeja and two friends, Dākini and Varnini should be worshipped. If done properly and correctly, all the wishes get fulfilled.

चित्र 10: छिन्नमस्ता पूजन-यन्त्र

9. **Swamvar Kalā Vidyā Yantra:** Pitāmah Brahmā is the Rishi; Ati-jagati is the Chhanda; and Giriputri Swayamvarā is the Devatā of the following Swayamvar Kalā Vidyā Mantra:

Aum hring yogini yogini yogeshwari yogeshwari yaga bhayankari sakal sthāvar jangamasya mukham gridham mam vasham ākarshaya swāhā!

ॐ ह्रीं योगिनि योगिनि योगेश्वरी योगेश्वरी यग भयंकरी सकल स्थावरजंगमस्य मुखं गृद्धं मम वशं आकर्षय स्वाहा।

चित्र 11: स्वयंवर कला पूजन-यन्त्र

10. Madhumati Poojan Yantram

Madhumati Mantra:

Aum hring kong kling hung Aum swāhā!

ॐ ह्रीं कौं क्लीं हं ॐ स्वाहा।

In the karnikā shat-anga poojan and on the lotus petals following eight Shaktis should be worshipped: Nidrā; Chhāyā; Kshamā; Trishnā; Kānti; Āryā; Shruti; and Smriti.

चित्र 12: मधुमती पूजन-यन्त्र

11. Bandhan Mokshakaram Yantram

Mantra: Aing hring shring bandi amushya bandha moksham kuru kuru swāhā!

ऐं ह्रीं श्रीं बन्दी अमुष्य बन्ध मोक्षं कुरु कुरु स्वाहा।

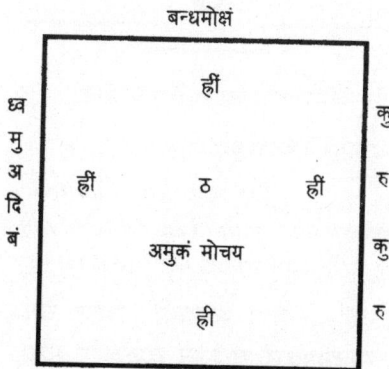

चित्र 13: बन्धन (बन्दी) पूजन-यन्त्र

12. Vat Yakshini Poojan Yantram

Mantra: Ahyehi yakshi yakshi mahā yakshi vat briksha nivāsini sheeghram mey darva daukhyam kuru kuru swāhā!

अयेहि यक्षि यक्षि महायक्षि वटवृक्ष निवासिनि
शीघ्रं मे दर्वदौख्यं कुरु कुरु स्वाहा।

In the petals the following eight Shaktis are worshipped: Sunandā; Chandrikā; Hāsā; Sulāpā; Madvihwalā; Āmodā; Pramodā; and Vasudā

चित्र 14: वटयक्षिणी पूजन-यन्त्र

13. Mātangi Poojan Yantram

Mātangi Pāth Mantra

Aum hring aing shring namo bhagawati uchhishta chandāli shri mātangeshwari sarva jan vasham kari swāhā!

ॐ ह्रीं ऐं श्रीं नमो भगवती उछिष्ट चण्डाली
श्री मातंगेश्वरी सर्वजन वशंकरि स्वाहा।

The following nine Shaktis are worshipped which fulfill the desires:

Bibhuti; Unnati; Kānti; Srishti; Kirti; Sannati; Vyushti; Utakrishti Riddhi and Mātangi.

चित्र 15: मातंगी पूजन-यन्त्र

14. Bāneshi Poojan Yantram

Bāneshi Mantra: *Drāng dring kling blung sah*!

द्रां द्रीं क्लीं ब्लं स:।

Rishi: Sammohan; Chhanda: Gāyatri; Devatā: Bāneshi

चित्र 16: बाणेशी पूजन-यन्त्र

15. Kāmeshi Poojan Yantram

Kāmeshi Devi Mantra: *Aum hring kling aing blung string*!
ॐ ह्रीं क्लीं ऐं ब्लं स्त्रीं।

In the four diections worship: Manobhava; Makardhvaja;
Kandarpa; Manmath; and Kāmadeva

चित्र 17: कामेशी पूजन-यन्त्र

16. Bālā Poojan Yantram

Mantra: *Aing kling saung*! ऐं क्लीं सौं।

Ater three Nyāsas; Nava Yoni Sangyak Nyāsa; Nava Yoni
Nyāsa; Rati Nyāsa; Murti Nyāsa; Bāna Nyāsa; Shad-anga
Nyāsa are performed, the Dhyān is concentrated on Bālā:

> *Raktāmbarām Chandralā vatansām*
> *Samudyā dādityā nibhām trinetrām;*
> *Vidyāksha mālā bhaya dān hastām*
> *Dhyāyāmi bālām arun ambuja-asthām.*

रक्तांबरां चन्द्रलावतंसाम्।
समुदया दादित्यानिभाम त्रिनेत्राम्।
विद्याक्षमाला भयदान् हस्ताम्।
ध्यायामि बालां अरुण अंबुजास्थाम्।

The following nine Peetha Shaktis are worshipped: Ikshā; Gyān; Kriyā; Kāmini; Kāma Dāyani; Rati; Rati Priyā; Nandā and Mana Unmani.

The following eight Yoni Shaktis are also worshipped: Subhagā; Bhagā; Bhaga Sarpini; Bhaga Māli; Anangā; Ananga Kusumā; Ananga Mekhalā; and Ananga Madanā.

In all the ten directions of the Bhupur the following are worshipped: Hetuka; Tripurāntak; Vetāla; Agni Jihvā; Kā; āntak; Kapāli; Eka Pāda; Bhima Roopa; Malaya; Jātkeshwar.

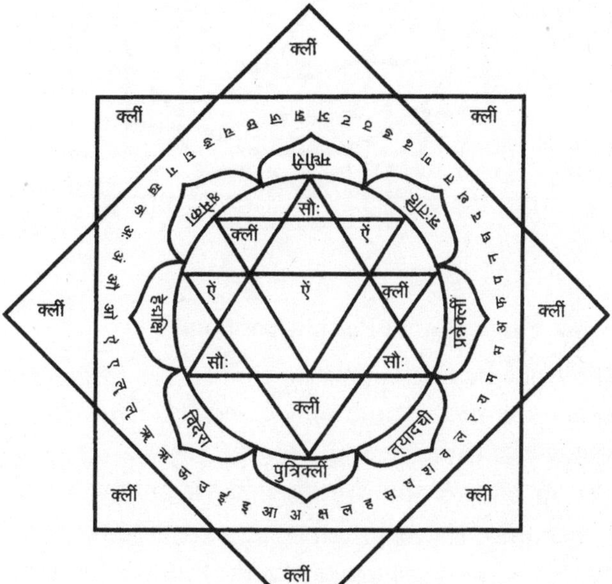

चित्र 18: बाला धारण-यन्त्र

17. **Laghu Shyāmā Poojan Yantram:** Laghu Shyāmā Devi is worshipped on the Mātangi Peetha with the following Mantra:

Aing namah uchhishtā chāndāli mātangi sarva vasham kari swāhā! ऐं नमः उच्छिष्टा चण्डाली मातंगी सर्ववशं करि स्वाहा।

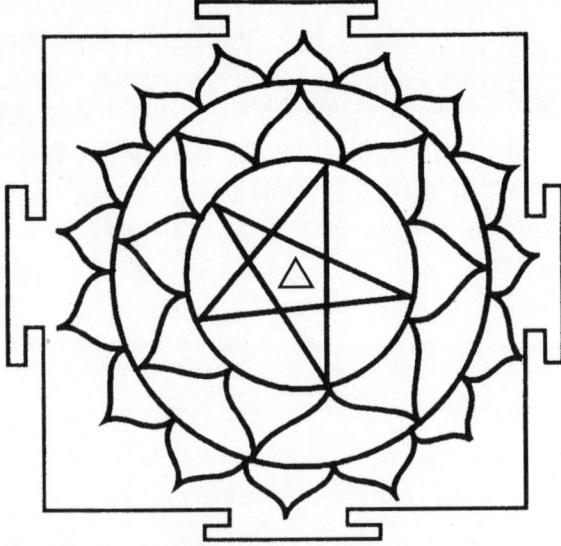

चित्र 19: लघुश्यामा पूजन-यन्त्र

18. Anna Purneshwari Poojan Yantram

Shri Anna Purnā Mantra:
Aum hring shring kling namah bhagawati māheshwari annapurne swāhā!

ॐ ह्रीं श्रीं क्लीं नमः भगवती माहेश्वरी अन्नपूर्णे स्वाहा।

In the three, starting from āgneya kone, Shiva; Vārāha and Nārāyana are worshipped with the following Mantras:

Shiva Mantra: *Aum haung namah shivāya!* ॐ हौं नमः शिवाय।

Vārāha Mantra: *Aum namo bhagawate vārāha-roopāya bhur bhuvah svah pataye bhu patitvam mey dehi dadāpaya swāhā!* ॐ नमो भगवते वाराहरूपाय भूर्भुवः स्वः पतये भूपतित्वं मे देहि ददापय स्वाहा।

NārāyanMantra: *Aum namo nārāyanāya!* ॐ नमो नारायणाय: ।
Another Annapurnā Mantra:

Aum shring hring namo bhagawati prasanna parijāteshwari annapurne swāhā! ॐ श्रीं ह्रीं नमो भगवती प्रसन्न परिजातेश्वरी अन्नपूर्णे स्वाहा।

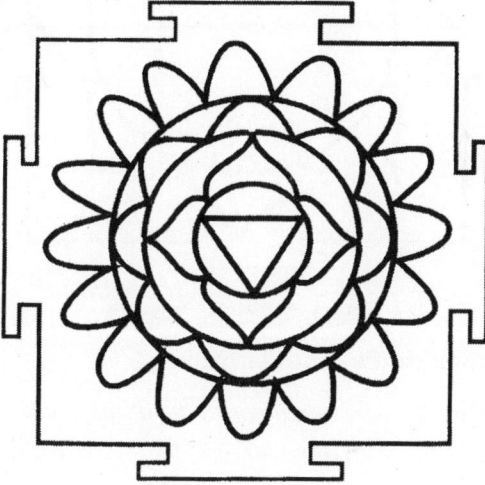

चित्र 20: अन्नपूर्णेश्वरी पूजन-यन्त्र

19. **Trailokya Mohan Poojan Yantram:** The Rishis of the following Trailokya Mohan Mantra is Aja; composed in Nichrut Gāyatri Chhanda and the Edvatā is Trailokya Mohini Gauri:

Hring namah brahmā shri rājipujite traya vijaye gauri gāndhāri tribhuvan vasham kari sarva loka vasham kari sarva stri purusha vasham kari su su du du ghe ghe vā vā hring swāhā!

ह्रीं नमः ब्रह्मा श्रीराजिपूजिते त्रयविजये गौरी गान्धारी त्रिभुवनवशंकरि सर्वलोक वशंकरि सर्व स्त्रीपुरुष वशंकरि सु सु दु दु घे घे वा वा ह्रीं स्वाहा।

20. Vāgalāmukhi Poojan Yantram

Aum hring vagalāmukhi sarva dushtānām vācham mukham pada stambhayam jihvā kilaya buddhi bināshaya hring Aum swāhā!

ॐ ह्रीं बगलामुखी सर्वदुष्टानां वाचं मुखं पदस्तभ्यं
जिह्वा किलय बुद्धि बिनाशय ह्रीं ॐ स्वाहा।

The Rishi of this Mantra is Nārada; chhanda is Brihati and Devatā is Vagalāmikhi. The shada-anga nyāsa should be performed with 2, 5, 5, 9, 5 and 10th letters of the Mantra.

Vāgalāmikhi should be worshipped in yellow garb; on a yellow seat; with yellow rosary basically of turmeric; with yellow anointed forehead; with yellow flowers by concentrating on yellow coloured Devi and chant ten thousand Mantras.

चित्र 22: बगलामुखी पूजन-यन्त्र

21. **Vāgalāmukhi Stambhan Yantram:** Mix the juice of Dhaturā with haritāl and haldi powder; prepare the shat-kone with that and write the second varna of the name of the person to be steadied or stilled and make bhupur around that.

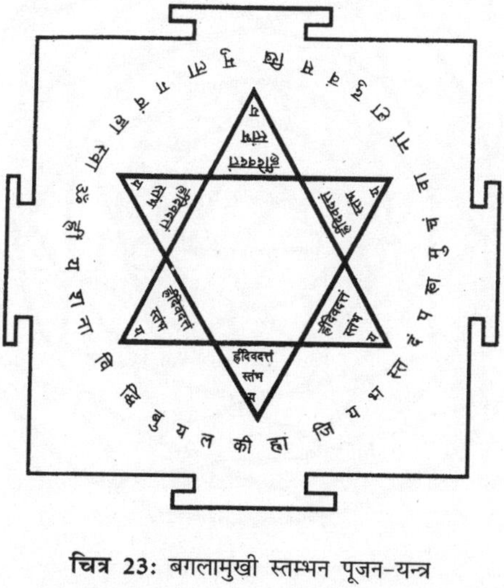

चित्र 23: बगलामुखी स्तम्भन पूजन-यन्त्र

After prāna pratishthā place yellow thread around it; take some soil from the moving wheel of a potter. Make an ox with the soil and place the Yantra inside its abdomen after anointing it with hartāl powder. Worship that ox everyday for wonderous results.

22. **Swapna Vārāhi Poojan Yantram:** Swapna Vārāhi Mantra whose Rishis is Ishwar; Chhanda is Jagati; Devatā is Swapna Vārāhi Pranava is the beeja and hring is the Shakti: *Aum hring namah vārāhi ghore swapnam thah thah swāhā!* ॐ ह्रीं नम: वाराहि घोरे स्वप्नं ठ: ठ: स्वाहा।

The following sixteen Shaktis are worshipped: Uchchātani; Uchchātanishwari; Shoshani; Shoshanishwari; Mārani; Māranishwari; Bhishani; Bhishanishwari; Trāshani; Trāshanishwari; Kampani; Kampanishwari; Āgyā Vivartani; Āgyā Vivartanishwari; Vasu Jāteshwari and Sarva Sampādani.

चित्र 24: स्पप्नवाराही पूजन-यन्त्र

23. **Swapna Vārāhi Stambhan Yantram:** Add the name of the targeted person in the beginning then chant the Mantra:

- - - - - uchchātaya uchchātaya shoshaya shoshaya māraya
māraya bhishaya bhishaya nāshaya nāshaya swāhā kampaya
kampaya mam āgyā vartinam kuru sarva abhimat
vastu jātam sampādaya sampādaya sarvam kuru kuru swāhā!

.....उच्चाटय उच्चाटय शोषय शोषय मारय मारय
भीषय भीषय नाशय नाशय स्वाहा कम्पय कम्पय
मम आज्ञा वर्तिनं कुरु सर्व-अभिमत
वस्तुजातं सम्पादय सर्व कुरु कुरु स्वाहा।

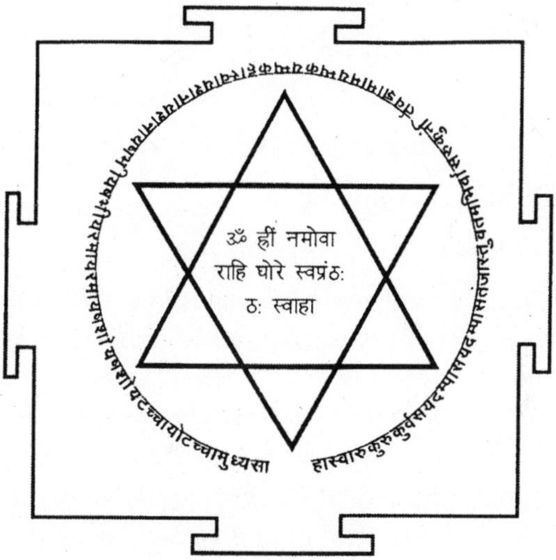

चित्र 25: स्पप्नवाराही वशीकरण यन्त्र

24. **Swapna Vārāhi Dhāran Yantram**

Mantra: Aing āng hring krong shring hung swāhā!

ऐं आं ह्रीं क्रौं श्रीं हं स्वाहा।

Chant this Mantra after writing the Mantra on Bhojapatra and then chant the original mantra given above in 22 and then tie it up on the right arm for name, fame and prosperity.

चित्र 26: स्पप्नवाराही धारण-यन्त्र

25. Vārtāli Poojan Yantram

Vārtāli Mantra

Aum aing glaung aing namo bhagawati vārtāli vārāhi vārāhi
vārāhi mukhi; aing glaung aing andhe andhini namo rundhe
rundhini namo jambhe jambhini namah; mohe mohini namah;
stambhane stambhani namah; aing glaung aing sarva dushta
pradushtānām sarveshām sarva vāk chitta chakshuh mukha gati
jihvām stambham kuru kuru sheeghra vashyam kuru kuru aing
glaung aing thah thah thah thah hung phat swāhā!

ॐ ऐं गनौं एं नमो भगवति वार्ताली वराहि वराहि
वराहिमुखी ऐं गनौं ऐं अंधे अंधिनि नमो रुन्धे
रुन्धिनि नमो जम्भे जम्भिनि नमः मोहे मोहिनि नमः
स्तम्भने स्तम्भनि नमः ऐं गलौं ऐं सर्वदुष्ट
प्रदुष्टानां सर्वेषां सर्ववाक् चित्त चक्षुः मुखगति
जिह्वं स्तम्भं कुरु कुरु शीघ्र वशयं कुरु कुरु ऐं
गलौं ऐं ठः ठः ठः ठः हं फट स्वाहा।

चित्र 27: वार्ताली पूजन यन्त्र

26. **Vārtāli Stambhan Yantram:** Write this Mantra as shown in the picture on a new tile, kharpar; worship with black flowers and drop in the house of the enemy to gain full control over him.

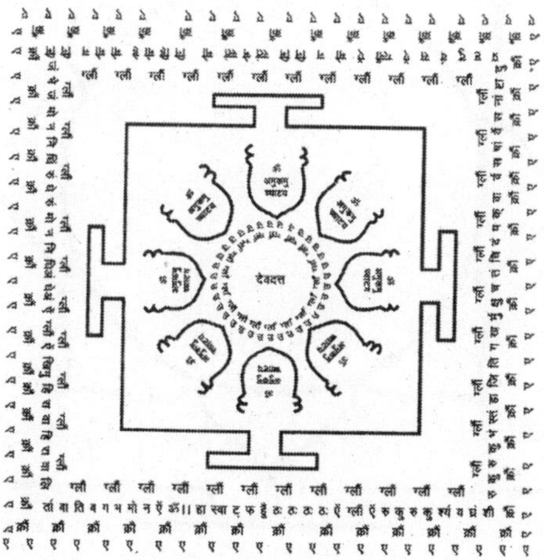

चित्र 28: वार्ताली स्तम्भन यन्त्र

27. Gopāl Sundari Poojan Yantram

Mantra: *Hring shring kling krishnāya govindāya gopiballabhāya swāhā!* ॐ श्रीं क्लीं कृष्णाय गोविन्दाय गोपीवल्लभाय स्वाहा।

After anga poojā, in the four directions, Vāsudeva; Sankarshana; Pradymna and Aniruddha are worshipped. In the āgneya, anles Rukmini; Satybhāmā; Kālindi; Jāmbawatil Mitra Bindā; Sunandā; Sulakshanā and Nāgnijiti, eight queens of Shri Krishna are worshipped. After that, the following Nava Nidhis are worshipped: Mahā Padma; Padma; Shankha; Makar; Kachcchap; Mukunda; Kunda; Neela and Kharva.

All the nine āvaranas are worshipped as it is worshipped for Tripur Subdari.

चित्र 29: गोपालसुन्दरी पूजन-यन्त्र

28.   Hanumat Poojan Yantram

Mantra: *Haung hasphren khaphren hasraung haskhaphren hasaung hanumate namah!* हौं हस्फ्रें ख्फ्रें हस्रौं हस्ख्फ्रें हसौं हनुमते नमः।

Rishi Ramchandra; Jagati Chhanda; Devatā Hanumān; hasaung beeja and hasphren is the Shakti.

चित्र 30: हनुमत्पूजन-यन्त्र

29.   Hanumat Dhārana Yantram

Mantra: *Aum aung shring hrāng hring hung hasphren khaphren hasraung haskhaphren hasaung!* ॐ ऐं श्रीं ह्रां ह्रीं हुं हस्फ्रें ख्फ्रें हस्रौं हस्ख्फ्रें हसौं।

Another Mantra: *Aum yo yo hanumantam phala phalita dhaga dhagitāyu-rāsha-parudāh!* ॐ यो यो हनुमन्तं फल फलित धग धगितायु रास परुदाः।

Prepare a Yantra as shown below and wear it for freedom from diseases and for strength and fearlessness.

चित्र 31: हनुमत् धारण यन्त्र

30. Hanumat Swaroopa Yantram

Mantra: *Namo bhagawate ānjaneyāya mahābalāya swāhā!*

नमो भगवते आंजनेयाय महबलाय स्वाहा।

There are various ways of making the figure of Hanumān as given below. One should tie around the head after Mantra anushthān. It also works as victorious flag.

चित्र 32: हनुमत् स्वरूप यन्त्र

31. **Hanumān Rakshā Kāraka Yantram:** One should get a replica of the Yantram shown below and put it in a gutkā, small box of gold or silver and tie it either on arm or forehead after performing a sampāt sādhit homa with either of the following Mantras or both. If it is for the safety of someone else who cannot wear it then write his/her name at the centre.

चित्र 33: हनुमान रक्षाकारक यन्त्र

Mantra 1: *Aum hrāng hring hroong   hraing hraung hrung Aum!* ॐ हं हीं हूं हौं हूं ॐ।

Mantra 2: *Aum vajrakāya vajra tunda kapil pingal urdhva keshah mahā varnā bala rakta mukha tadi jihvā mahā-raudra dranshta utakat hahakarāline mahā dridha prahārin lankeshwar vadhāya mahā setu bandha mahā shail pravāh gaganecher aihyehi bhagawan mahā bala parākram bhairava āgyāpaya ahyehi mahā raudra deergha puchchhena vestya vairinam bhanjaya bhanajaya hung phat!*

ॐ वज्रकाम वज्रतुण्ड कपिलपिंगल
ऊर्ध्वकेश: महावर्णा बलरक्तमुख तडिजिह्वा
महारौद्र द्रंष्टोत्कट हहकारलिने महादृढ़
प्रहारीण लंकेश्वरवधाय महासेतुबन्ध महाशैल
प्रवाह गगनेचर एहयेहि भगवन महाबल पराक्रम
भैरव आज्ञापय एहयेहि महारौद्र दीर्घपुच्छेन
वेष्ट्य वैरीणं भंजय भंजय हुं फट।

32. Nrisinha Poojan Yantram

One syllable Mantra: *Kshraung*! क्ष्रौं।

Three syllable Mantra: *Aum kshraung Aum*! ॐ क्ष्रौं ॐ।

Adter peetha poojan and āsan poojan, one should perform āvaran poojan. In the four directions, Khageshwar (Garuda); Shankar; Sheshnāga; and Shatānand (Brahmā) should be worshipped. In the four corners, Shri; Hring; Dhriti and Pushti should be worshipped. On the 32 lotus petals, Nrisingha should be worshipped with his following thirty two names:

Krishna	Rudra	Mahāghore	Bhima
Bhishan	Ujjwal	Karāla	Vikarāl
Daityāntak	Madhusudan	Raktāksha	Ānjan
Deepta-teja	Sughona	Hanoo	Vishwāksha
Rākshasāntak	Vishāl	Dhoomra	Keshava
Hayagriva	Ghanashwar	Meghanād	Meghavarna
Kumbhakarna	Kritāntak	Teebra-tejā	Agni Varna
Mahogra	Vishwabhushan	Vighna-kshama	Mahsena

Abhaya Prada Shri Nrisingh Mantra:

*Aum namo bhagwate nar-sinhāya; namah tejah tejase
ābir-ābirbhava vajra-nakha vajra-danshtra karma-āshayān
randhaya randhaya tamo grasa grasa swāhā abhaya ātmani
bhri-yishthā Aum ksharaung.*

ॐ नमो भगवते नरसिंहाय नमः तेजः तेजसे
अविराविर्भव वज्रनख वज्रदंष्ट्र कर्माशयान
रन्धय रन्धय तमो ग्रस ग्रस स्वाहा अभय आत्मनि
भृयिष्ठा ॐ क्षरैंग।

चित्र 34: नृसिंह पूजन-यन्त्र

33. Gopāl Poojan Yantram

Mantra: *Gopijana ballabhāya swāhā!*
गोपीजनः वल्लभाय स्वाहा।

Another Mantra: *Kling hrishikeshāya namah!*
क्लीं ऋषिकेशाय नमः।

Sammohan Nārada is the Rishi; Gāyatri is the Chhand; Trailokya Mohan is the Devatā.

Dvādasha Gopāl Mantra: *Shring hring kling krishnāya govindāya swāhā!* श्री ह्रीं क्लीं कृष्णाय गोविन्दाय स्वाहा।

Rukmini Ballabha Mantra: *Aum namo bhagawate rukmini ballabhāya swāhā!* ॐ नमो भगवते रुक्मिणि वल्लभाय स्वाहा।

Santā Dāyaka Gopāl Mantra: *Devaki suta govinda jagat-pate. Dehi mey tanayam Krishna tvam aham sharanam gatah!* देवकीसुत गोविन्द जगत्पते। देहि मे तनयं कृष्ण त्वमहं शरणं गत:।

Gopāl Dhyān Mantra:

Shankha chakra gade kar-airu-dadhijā sanshlishta deham garim; Nānā bhushanam rakt lep kusumam peetāmbaram sansmaret.

शंख, चक्र, गदे करेरूद्धिजा संसलिष्टा देहं गरिम।
नानाभूषणं रक्तलेप कुसमं पीताम्बरं संस्मरेत॥

चित्र 35: गोपाल पूजन-यन्त्र

34. **Surya Poojan Yantram:** After performing peetha poojan give āsan to Surya with the Mantra: *Brahma Vishnu shivātmak sayrāya yoga peeth ātmane namah!* ब्रह्मा विष्णु शिवात्मक सेराय योगपीठ आत्मने नमः।

Perform āvaran poojan etc. then perform poojan with *poonah tatraiva* Mantras:

i.   *Aum ung shodash kalātmane soma mandalāya namah!*
     ॐ यं षोडश कलात्मने सोममण्डलाय नमः।

ii. *Aum rang dasha kalātmane vanhi mandalāya namah!*
     ॐ रं दशकलात्मने वह्निमण्डलाय नमः।

iii. *Aum ang dvādash kalātmane surya mandalāya namah!*
     ॐ ऐं द्वादश कलात्मने सूर्य मण्डलाय नमः।

Then chant **Surya Dashākshar Mantra:** *Aum hring ghrinih poorva ādityah shring!* ॐ ह्रीं घृणिः पूर्वादित्यः श्रीं।

चित्र 36: सूर्य पूजन-यन्त्र

35. Bhauma Poojan Yantram

Mangal Mantra for son and wealth: *Aum hāng hansah khang khah!* ॐ हैं हंस: खं ख:।

Vedic Mangal Mantra: *Aum agni murdhā divah kukutpatih prithiviyām apām retānsi jinvati!* ॐ अग्नि मुर्धा दिव: कुकुट्पति: पृथिव्याम् अपां रेतांसि जिन्वति।

Mangal Gāyatri Mantra: *Aum angārkāya vidyehe Shakti hastāya dhee mahi. Tanno bhaumah prachodayāt!*

ॐ अंगारकाय विद्महे शक्तिहस्ताय धीमहि तन्नो भौम: प्रचोदयात्।

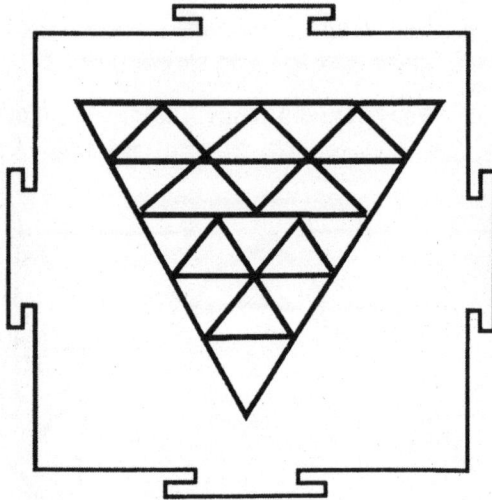

चित्र 37: भौम पूजन-यन्त्र

36. Vyāsa Poojan Yantram

Mantra: *vyām veda vyāsāya namah!* व्यां वेदव्यासाय नम:।

Mritunjaya Putot Vyāsa Mantra: *Aum jung sah vyām veda vyāsāya namah sah jung Aum!* ॐ जूं स: व्यां वेदव्यासाय नम: स: जूं ॐ।

Mritunjaya Mantra: *Aum jung sah!* ॐ जूं स:।

चित्र 38: व्यास पूजन-यन्त्र

37. Mahāmritunjaya Poojan Yantram

Mantra: *Aum haung Aum jung sah Aum bhur bhuvah swah Trayambakam yajāmahe sugandhim pushti-vardhanam; Urvā-rukamiva bandhanām mrityor-mukshiya māmritāt; Aum bhurbhuah swarong jung sah haung Aum!*

ॐ हौं ॐ जूं ॐ स: ॐ भूर्भुव: स्व:
त्र्यम्बकं यजामहे सुगन्धिं पुष्टिवर्द्धनम् ।
ऊर्वारुकमिव बन्धनान् मृत्योर्मुक्षीय-मामृतात्
ॐ भूर्भव: स्वरों जूं स: हौं ॐ ॥

In the first āvaran pooja, worship: Tatpurusha; Aghore; Vāmadeva; and Sadyojāt.

In the second āvaran poojan worship: Nibriti; Pratishthā; Vidyā; Shānti; and Shāntyateetā.

In the third āvaran poojan worship: Saurya; Chandra; Prithivi; Jala; Agni; Pavan; Ākāsha and Vāyu.

In the fourth āvaran poojan worship: Ramā; Rākā; Prabhā; Jyotsanā; Purnā; Ushā; Purani; and Sudhā.

In the fifth āvaran poojan worship: Vishwā; Vandyā; Sitā; Prahvā; Sārā; Sandhyā; Shivā and Nishā; all dark colored Shaktis.

In the sixth āvaran poojan worship: Āryā; Pragyā; Prabhā; Medhā; Shānti; Kānti; Dhriti and Mati; all Shaktis with reddish glow.

In the seventh āvaran poojan worship: Dharā; Umā; Pāvani; Padmā; Shāntā; Amoghā; Jayāand Amalā; all golden coloued Shaktis.

In the eighth āvaran poojan worship: Anant; Sukshma; Shivottam; Ek-netra; Ek-rudra; Trimurti; Shri Kantha; and Shikhandi.

In the nineth āvaran poojan worshp: in the four directions starting with North worship: Umā and Chandeshwar; Nandi and Mahākāla; Ganesh and Vrishabha; and Bhringi-riti and Skanda.

In the tenth āvaran poojan worship Ashta Mātrikās.

चित्र 39: महामृत्युन्जय पूजन-यन्त्र

38. Rudra Poojan Yantram

Mantra: *Aum namo bhagawate rudrāya!* ॐ नमो भगवते रूद्राय।

Outside the Bhupur one must worship the following eight Nāgas: Shesh Nāga; Takshak; Annat Nāga; Nāga Vāsuki; Shankhpāla; Mahāyagya; Kambal and Kakortak.

चित्र 40: रुद्र पूजन-यन्त्र

39. Gangā Poojan Yantram

Mantra: *Aum namah shivāyai nārāyanyai dashaharāyai gangāyai swāhā!* ॐ नमः शिवाय नारायणी दशहरायै गंगायै स्वाहा।

Rishi: Veda Vyāsa; Chhand: Kriti; Devatā: Gangā.

Another Mantra: *Aum namo bhagawati aing hili hili mili mili gange mām pāvaya pāvaya swāhā!* ॐ नमो भगवति ऐं हिलि हिलि मिलि मिलि गंगे माम पावय पावय स्वाहा।

Another Mantra: *Aum hili hili mili mili gange devi namah!*
ॐ हिलि हिलि मिलि मिलि गंगे देवि नमः।

Another Mantra: *Aum hring shring namo bhagawati gang dayite namo hung phat!* ॐ ह्रीं श्रीं नमो भगवति गंगदयिते नमो हं फट।

चित्र 41: गंगा पूजन-यन्त्र

40. Kārta Veerya Poojan Yantram

Mantra: *Aum phrong vring kling bhrung oung hring phrong shring hung phat kārta Veerya Arjunāya namah!*

ॐ फ्रौं वृं क्लीं भ्रूं ओं ह्रीं फ्रौं श्रीं हुं फट कार्तवीर्य अर्जुनाय नमः।

All types of Nyāsas; dhyān; Shakti Poojan; Āyudha Poojan; are performed then abhishek is completed.

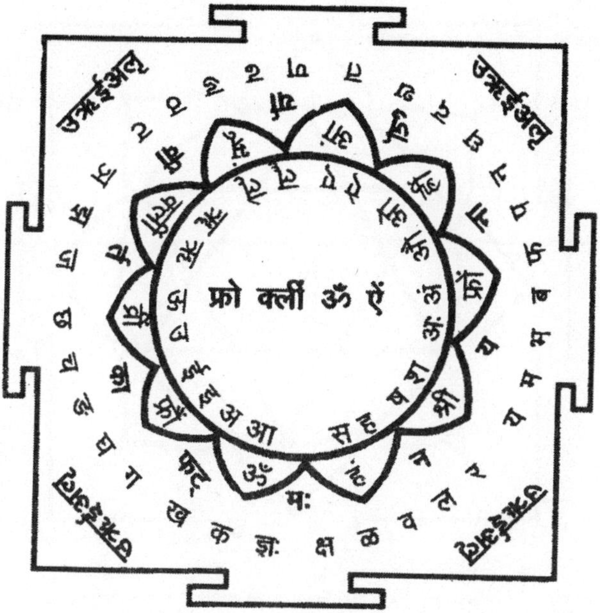

चित्र 42: कार्तवीर्य पूजन-यन्त्र

41. Kārta Veerya Arjunasya Kāmya Proyog Yantram

After initial poojan, perform āvāhan. Then proceed ahead.

Ten different Mantras are:

i.   Phrong kārtveerya arjunāya namah!
ii. Phrong vring kārtveerya arjunāya namah!
iii. Phrong kling kārtveerya arjunāya namah!
iv. Phrong bhrung kārtveerya arjunāya namah!
v.   Phrong ānga kārtveerya arjunāya namah!
vi. Phrong hring kārtveerya arjunāya namah!
vii. Phrong krong kārtveerya arjunāya namah!
viii. Phrong shring kārtveerya arjunāya namah!
ix. Phrong aing kārtveerya arjunāya namah!
x.   Hung kārtveerya arjunāya namah phat !

चित्र 43: कार्तवीर्यार्जुनस्य काम्यप्रयोगार्थ पूजन-यन्त्र

42. Kārt Veerya Deepa Sthāpan Yantram

Deepa Dāna is performed to please Kārt Veerya. It can be done in Vaishākha; Shrāvan; Māgha Sheersha; Kārtika; Āshwin; Pausha and Māgh; and in Hasta; Uttarā; Ashwini; Ādrā; Pushya; Shravan; Swāti; Vishākhā; and Rohini Nakshatras; on any *tithi* and day except the blank 4th; 9th and 14th day; and Tuesday and Saturday.

Samkalpa Mantra: *Aum āng hring vashat kārtveerya arjunāya māhishmati nāthāya sahasra bāhave; sahasra kratu deekshit hastāya dattātreya priyāya ātrey anusuyā garbha ratnāya hung āng emam deepam grihān ------ (name of the person to be protected) raksha raksha dushta nāshaya nāshaya pātaya pātaya ghātaya ghātaya shatrun jahi jahi hring Aum phrong kling swāhā; anena deepa varyena pashchim abhimukhena ------- (name of the person to be protected) raksha-var-pradānāya hring hring hring*

Aum kling vring swāhā; tang thang dang dhang nang pang phang bang bhang mang Aum swāhā!

ॐ ऐं ह्रीं वषट्कार्तवीर्यअर्जुनाय महीस्मति नाथाय सहस्रबाहवे सहस्रक्रतु दीक्षित हस्ताय दत्तात्रेय प्रियाय आत्रेय अनसुइया गर्भ रत्नाय हुं ऐं एमाम दीपं गृहान्... रक्ष रक्ष दुष्टनाशय नाशय पातय पातय घातय घातय शत्रुण जहि जहि ह्रीं ॐ फ्रौं क्लीं स्वाहा, अनेनदीप वर्येन पश्चिम अभिमुखेन.... रक्षवर प्रदानाय ह्रीं ह्रीं ह्रीं ॐ क्लीं वृं स्वाहा, टं थं वं धं नं पं फं बं भं मं ॐ स्वाहा।

Navākshar Mantra: *Aum āng hring phring vring swāhā krong Aum!* ॐ आं ह्रीं फ्रीं वृं स्वाहा क्रौं ॐ।

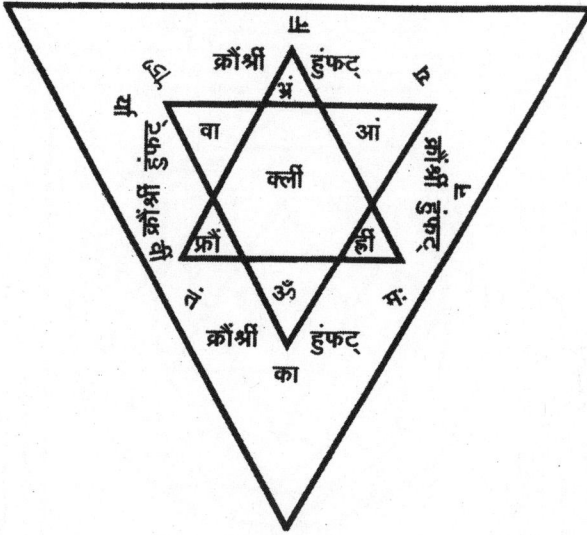

चित्र 44: कार्तवीर्य दीप स्थापन यन्त्र

43. Kāla Rātri Poojan Yantram

Kāla Rātri Mantra whose Rishi is Daksha; Chhand is Ati Jagati and Devatā is Alarka Nivāsini Kāla Rātri:

Aum aing hring kling shring kānheshwari sarva jana manohari sarva mukha stambhani sarva rāja vasham kari sarva dushta nirdalini sarva stri purush karshini bandi

shrikhalā trotaya trotaya sarva shatrun bhanjaya bhanjaya
dveshtrin nirdalaya nirdalaya sarva stambhaya mohan
sterna dveshijan uchchātaya uchchātaya sarva vasham kuru
kuru swāhā; dehi dehi sarva kāla rātri kāmini ganeshwari
namah!

ॐ ऐं ह्रीं क्लीं श्री कान्हेश्वरी सर्वजन मनोहरी सर्वमुख स्तम्भनी सर्वराजवशं करि सर्वदुष्ट निर्दलिनि सर्वस्त्रीपुरुष कर्षिणी बंदी श्रीखला त्रोतय सर्वशत्रुन भंजय भंजय द्वेषित्रण निर्दलय निर्दलय सर्वस्तम्भय मोहन स्त्रेण द्वेषिजन उच्चाटय उच्चाटय सर्ववशं कुरु कुरु स्वाहा, देहि देहि सर्वकालरात्रि कामिनि गणेशवरी नमः।

चित्र 45: कालरात्रि पूजन-यन्त्र

44. Kāla Rātri Deepa Sthāpanam Yantram

Sarovar Poojan Mantra: *Aum namo jaloukāyai jaloukāyai*
sarva-janam vasham kuru kuru hung! ॐ नमो जलौकायै जलौकायै
सर्वजनंवशं कुरु कुरु हुं।

Kājal Abhimantran Mantra: *Aum aing kling hring shring gloung blung hasauh namah kānheshwari sarvānna-mohaya mohaya krishne Krishna varne krishnāmbar samanvite sarvān-ākarshaya ākarshaya sheeghram vasham kuru kuru aing hring kling shring!*

ॐ ऐं क्लीं ह्रीं श्रीं गलौं ब्लुं हसौं नमः कान्हेश्वरी सर्वणा मोहया मोहया कृष्णे कृष्णः वर्णे कृष्णाम्बर समन्विते सर्वअकांक्षा अकाश सिंहरम् वशं कुरु कुरु ऐं ह्रीं क्लीं श्रीं।

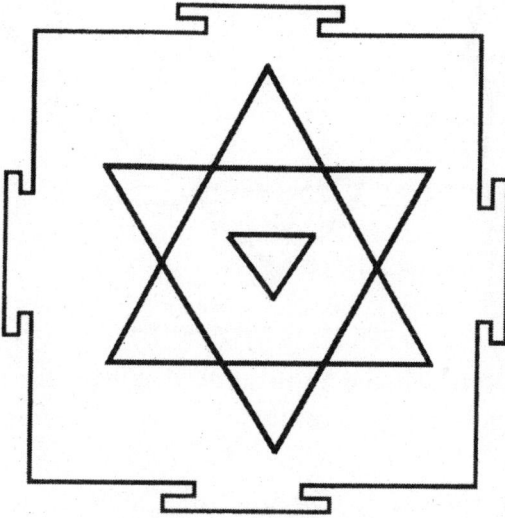

चित्र 46: कालरात्रि दीपस्थानम यन्त्र

45. Kāla Rātri Stambhan Yantram: Write the name of the person who is to be paralyzed.

Japa Mantra: *Aum hrāng hring hrung kāmākshi māyā rupini sarva manohārini stambhaya stambhaya rodhaya rodhaya mohaya mohaya klāng kling klung kāmākshe kāmeshwari hung hung hum!*

ॐ ह्रैं ह्रीं हूं कामाक्षी मायारूपिनि सर्वमनोहरिनि स्तम्भय स्तम्भय रोधय रोधय मोहय मोहय क्लां क्लीं क्लूं कामाक्षे कामेश्वरी हुं हुं हुम।

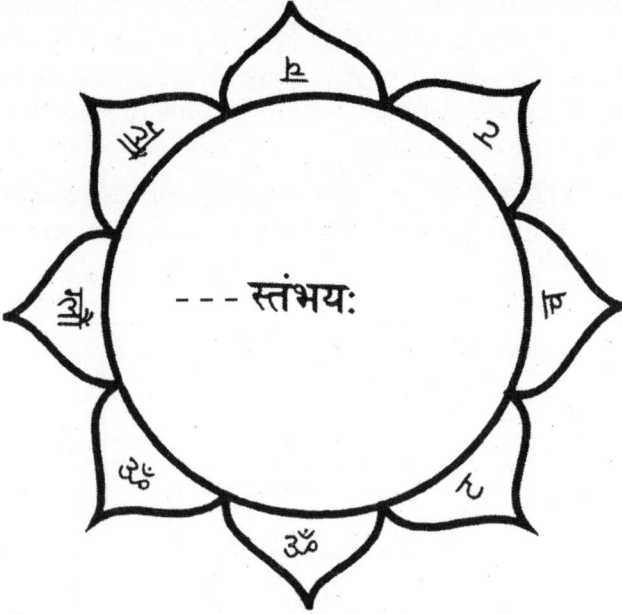

चित्र 47: कालरात्रि स्तम्भन यन्त्र

46. **Kāla Rātri Mohan Yantram:** Chant the Mantra given one
     thousand times for five nights in a row on the Yantram given
     below:

     Aum kāmāya kling kling kāminyai kling!

     ॐ कामाय क्लीं क्लीं कामिन्यै क्लीं।

     For enchanting someone, chant the following 44 lettered
     Mantra for 1100 while standing in waist deep water:

     *Aum namah kālikayai sarva ākarshayai ------- (two words
     from the name of the person) ākarshaya ākarshaya sheeghra
     mānaya sheeghra mānaya āng hring krong bhadra kālayai
     namah!*

     ॐ नमः कालिकायै सर्वआकर्षायै आकर्षय शीघ्र मानय शीघ्र मानय ऐं ह्रीं क्रौं
     भद्रकालयै नमः।

चित्र 48: कलरात्रि मोहन यन्त्र

47. Chandi Poojan Yantram

Mantra: *Aing hring kling chāmundāyai vichche!*

ॐ ह्रीं क्लीं चामुण्डायै विच्चे।

Dhyān of Mahā Chandil Mahā Lakshi and Mahā Saraswati is to be completed befor the Durgā Shapta Shati Pāth is started. Nyāsa and āvaran poojan must be performed befor chanting the Mantra and one hundred virgin girls are to be fed for greater and faster result.

चित्र 49: चण्डी पूजन-यन्त्र

48. **Charan Āyuddha Poojan Yantram:** Mantra whose Rishi is Mahā Rudra; Chhand is Ati Jagati; and Devatā is Charanāyuddha:

चित्र 50: चरणायुध पूजन-यन्त्र

Āng yung koli yung wā hi yung koli yung koli chu wā krong!

ऐं यूं कोलि यूं वा हि यूं कोलि यूं कोलि चू वा क्रौं ।

49. **Vashya Karam Yantram**

Prepare a Yantra on the pattern given below and worship it for seven days.

चित्र 51: वश्यकरं यन्त्र

50. **Beeja Samput Vashikaran Yantram:** Write the Yantra with Gorochana; Chandan and Kesar on a Bhoja Patra and worship with Beejākshar for five days.

51. **Swāmi Vashikaran Yantram:** Write the following Yantra on Bhoja Patra with a pen of Chameli and worship with Pranava.

चित्र 52: वश्यकरं (द्वितीय) यन्त्र

चित्र 53: स्वामीवश्यकरं यन्त्र

52. **Divya Stambhan Yantram:** Write the following Yantra on Bhoja Patra with Gorochana and Kumkum and with a pen of Chameli. Replace the word 'Devadutta' with the name to be hypnotized.

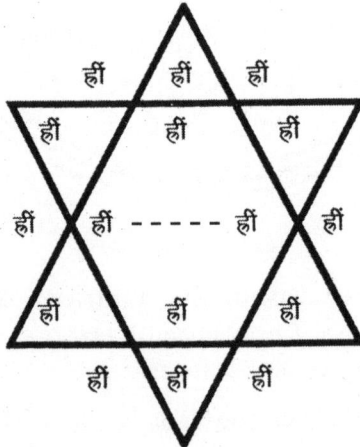

चित्र 54: दिव्य स्तम्भन यन्त्र

53. **Rājā Mohanāya Panchamākhya Yantram:** Write the following Yantra on Bhoja Patra with Gorochana and Kumkum and with a pen of Chameli. Worship it for seven nights with Māyā Beeja Mantra Hring.

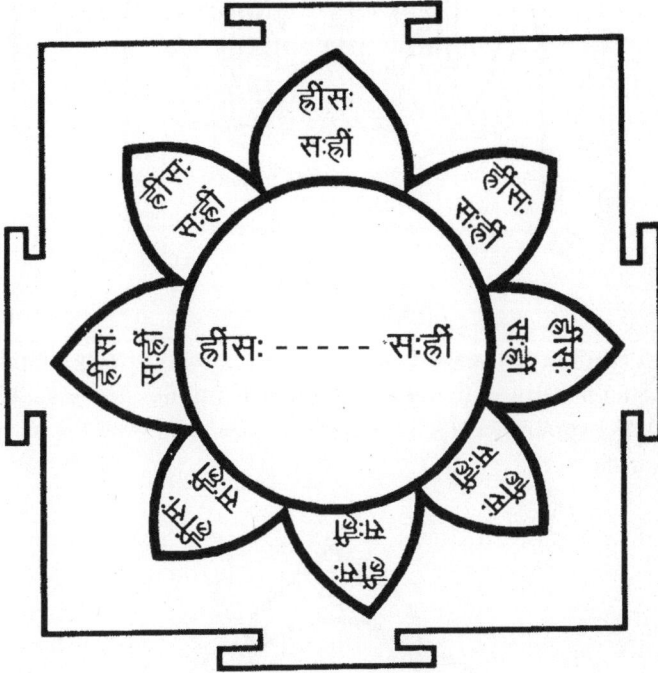

चित्र 55: राजामोहनाय पन्चमाख्य यन्त्र

54. **Mritunjaya Yantram:** Prepare the Yantra for the death of some. But it is better to avoid this and be far away from any immoral act as some day it will prove harmful, as all misdeeds are punished.

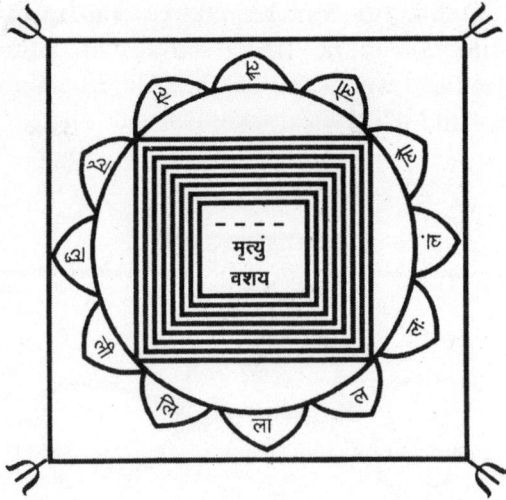

चित्र 56: मृत्युन्जय यन्त्र

55. **Vivād Jayakaram Yantram:** Write the following Yantra on Bhoja Patra with Gorochana and Kumkum and with a pen of Chameli. Replace the word 'Devadutta' with the name to won.

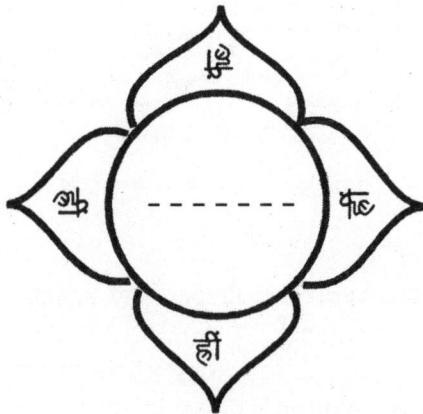

चित्र 57: विवादजयकरं यन्त्र

56. **Dhani Vashya Karam Yantram:** Write the following Yantra on Bhoja Patra with Gorochana and Kumkum and with a pen of Chameli. Replace the word 'Devadutta' with the name to be hypnotized and controlled.

चित्र 58: धनिकवश्यकरं यन्त्र

57. **Dushta Mohnākhym Mohan Yantram:** Write the following Yantra on Bhoja Patra with Gorochana and Kumkum and with a pen of Chameli. Replace the word 'Devadutta' with the name to be hypnotized and controlled.

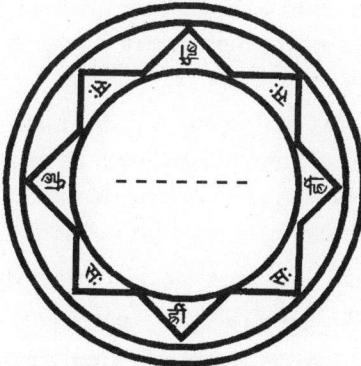

चित्र 59: दुष्टमोहनाख्यं मोहन यन्त्र

58. **Sarvartra Jayadam Yantram:** Write the Yantra on Bhoja patra with Gorochan. Replace 'Sādhya Nāma' with the name of the person to be won over.

    This Yantra should be worshipped with Trailokya Mahan Mantra.

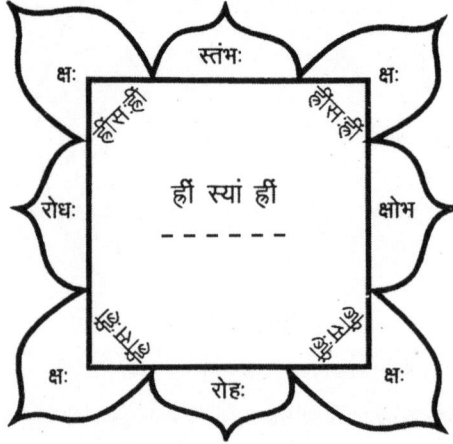

चित्र 60: सर्वत्रजयदं यन्त्र

59. **Yāvajjiva Vashyakar Yantram:** Write and place the Yantra in the abdomen of Shri Ganesh made of black soil and in panchopachār chant the Mantra: *Gang ganpataye namah*! गंग गणपतये नमः।

    Then chant the following Vakshyamān Mantra. Replace the word Deva Dutta, everywhere, on each Mantra with the name of the person to be controlled and hypnotized because this name is imaginary used for completing it.

    Deva deva ganādhyaksha sura asura namaskrit;
    Deva dutta mamāyattam yājjivam kuru prabho.

    देवः देवः गणध्यक्षा सुर असुर नमस्कृत।
    देवदत्त ममायत्तं याजीवं कुरु प्रभो॥

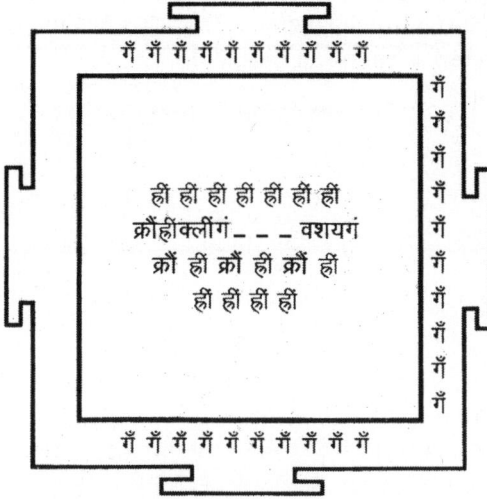

चित्र 61: यावज्जीवनवश्यकरं यन्त्र

60. **Nripa Vashya Karan Yantram:** This Mantra is written on four petalled lotus shape and worshipped with Ajitā Mantra for three days as Ajitā is its Devatā. Tie it on the arm in golden locket.

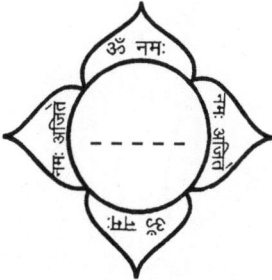

चित्र 62: नृपवश्यकरं यन्त्र   चित्र 63: भृत्यवश्यकरं यन्त्र

61. **Bhritya Vashya karan Yantram:** Prepare the Yantra, write the name of the servant in place of Deva Dutta and put it into curs. The servant is sure to obey you.

62. **Dushta Vashyakaran Yantram:** Prepare the Yantra as shown and write the name of the cruel person; make his idol and place the Yantra in that idol.

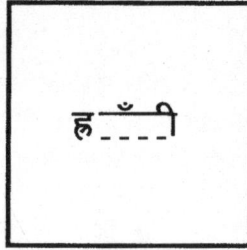

चित्र 64: दुष्टवश्यकरं यन्त्र

63. **Lalitākhyam Pati Vashyakaran Yantram:** Prepare the Yantra on the Trayodashi of the Shukla Paksha and worship it for seven days with Lalitā Mantra and after providing feast to seven ladies who have sons, tie it in a locket of gold, silver or bronze.

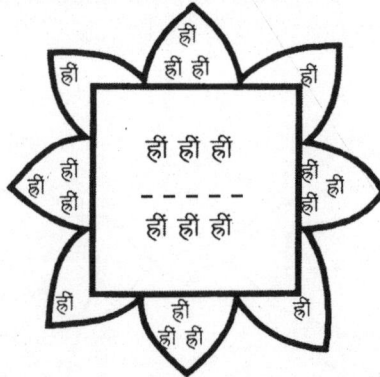

चित्र 65: ललिताख्यंपतिवश्यकरं यन्त्र

64. **Pati Vashyakaran Yantram:** This is another Yantra to keep the husband under control. With these two yantras durbhāgya, misfortune runs away and saubhāgya, good fortune resides. It is also written with gorochan and kumkum on a bhoja patra

with the pen prepared from chameli. Worship this Yantra
with the name of the husband samputit, written between sā
for two nights with Māyā beeja Mantra; feed three happy
ladies and wear it in a locket of gold, silver or bronze.

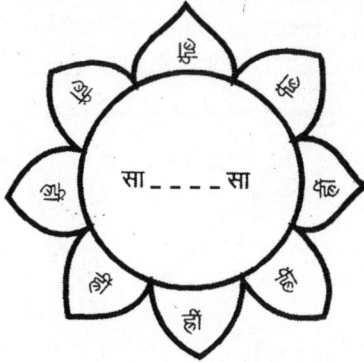

चित्र 66: पतिवश्यकरं यन्त्र

65. **Daurbhāgya Nāshan Beeja Yantram:** There is a separate
Yantra for getting rid of bad days and living happily in good
days. It should be prepared on a bhoja patra written with
gorochan and chandan and worshipped with Sundari Mantra
for three days, then wear it around the neck or tie on the arm.

चित्र 67: दौर्भाग्यनाशन बीजयन्त्र

66. **Ākarshan Yantram:** One should write this Yantra with chandan mixed with own blood; and the name of the person to be enchanted in the Karnikā. Worship it with Dashākshar Rudra Mantra and put the Yantra in ghee for expected result.

67. **Tripurākhya Ākarshan Yantram:** Prepare the Yantra as shown below, write the name of the person and worship it for three days with Tripurā Bhairavi Mantra for success.

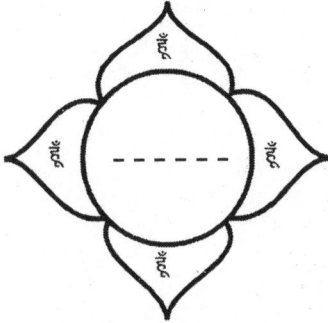

चित्र 68: आकर्षण यन्त्र

चित्र 69: त्रिपुराख्यमाकर्षण यन्त्र

68. **Mukha Mudranam Yantram:** Prepare the Yantra as shown below; write the name of the person whose mouth us to be kept should worship it with Bhu Beeja Mantra and after digging a small hole on earth, push the Yantra inside and covering it with soil.

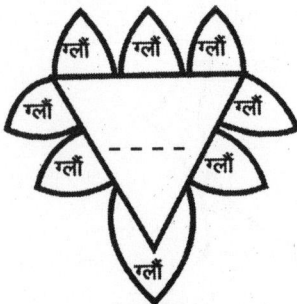

चित्र 70: मुखमुद्रणं यन्त्र

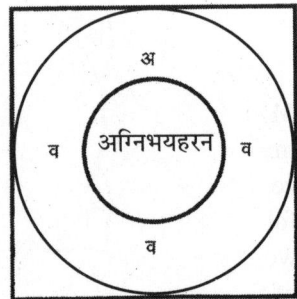

चित्र 71: अग्निभयहरन यन्त्र

69. **Agnibhaya Haran Yantram:** Prepare the Yantra as shown below and worship it with Mātrikā Mantra and tie around the arm for getting rid of fear from fire.

70. **Vidvesh Karam Yantram:** Prepare this Yantra and write the name of the two persons; worship it with Māyā Beeja Mantra; feed a lady and place it under the soil near a temple or nurning ghāt or graveyard. It is certain that within a week both the persons will be at dagger's end.

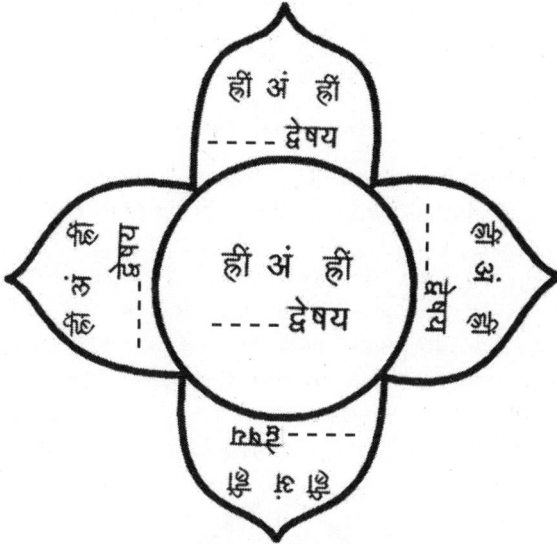

चित्र 72: विद्वेषकरं यन्त्र

71. **Māran Yantram:** Although, it is not to be used as it is immoral and inhuman yet it is being given to show the zenith and nadir of Mantra, Tantra and Yantra. Prepare the following Yantra with the pen of a crows feather and after worshipping burn a bit for twenty days to ensure the death of the person whose name has been inscribed in it.

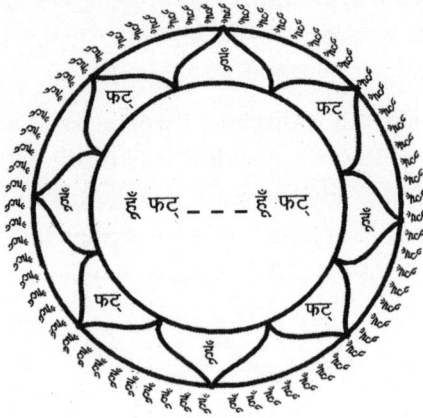

चित्र 73: मारणयन्त्र

72. **Uchchātan Yantram:** The seeker, after taking bath must
wear red clothes; red chandan; gardland of red flowers and
worship the Yantra with Vāyu beeja Mantra for twenty days
starting from the 14th day of Krishna Paksha a feed a dame
and pay her dakshinā everyday; and on the 20th day tear
the Yantra into pieces and mix with cooked rice and feed
crows. That person loses almost everything whose name is
inscribed on the Yantra.

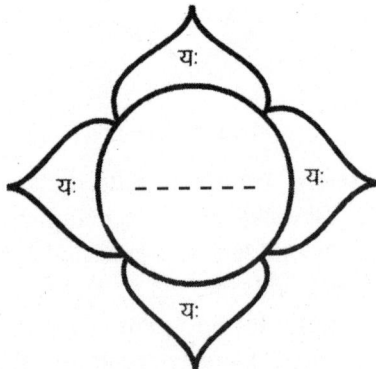

चित्र 74: उच्चाटनकरं यन्त्र

73. **Shāntikaram Yantram:** After preparing this Yantra, if one keeps on worshipping Mātrikā Devatā, feeding the Brāhmins and sleeps on land with the Yantra on arm, he is bound to get peace everwhere.

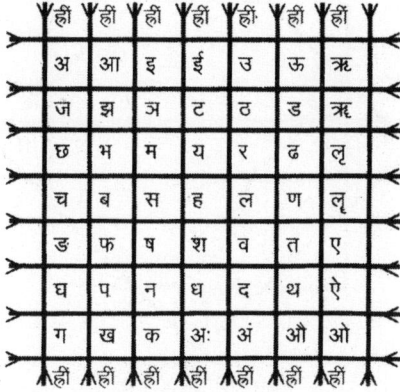

ह्रीं	ह्रीं	ह्रीं	ह्रीं	ह्रीं	ह्रीं	ह्रीं
अ	आ	इ	ई	उ	ऊ	ऋ
ज	झ	अ	ट	ठ	ड	ॠ
छ	भ	म	य	र	ढ	ऌ
च	ब	स	ह	ल	ण	ॡ
ङ	फ	ष	श	व	त	ए
घ	प	न	ध	द	थ	ऐ
ग	ख	क	अः	अं	औ	ओ
ह्रीं	ह्रीं	ह्रीं	ह्रीं	ह्रीं	ह्रीं	ह्रीं

चित्र 75: शान्तिकरं यन्त्र

74. **Shākini Nivartak Yantram:** It is the Yantra for pacifying the supernatural elements. Prepare the Yantra and wear on arm or tie it on affected person for his/her good health.

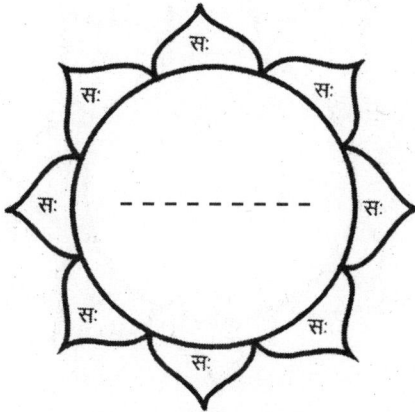

चित्र 76: शाकिनीनिवर्तक यन्त्र

75. **Jwar Haram Yantram:** Prepare this Yantra and worship it with Agni Mantra, then tie it on affected person.

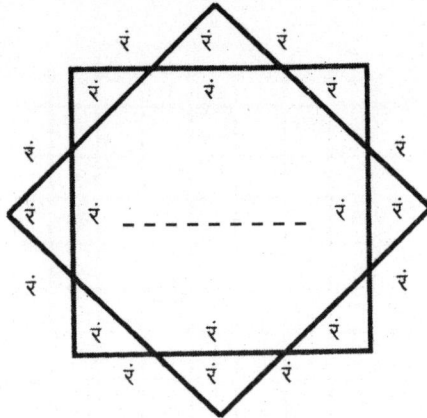

चित्र 77: ज्वरहरं यन्त्र

76. **Sarva Bhaya Haram:** The Yantra frees one from different sorts of fears if tied on the arm after worshipping it with the Hans Mantra.

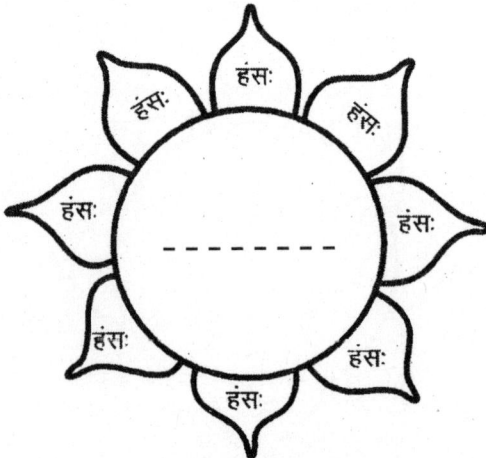

चित्र 78: सर्पभयहरं यन्त्र

77. **Bandha Moksha Karam Yantram:** It should be written on a dish of Kāndā and worshipped for seven days with Mātrikā Mantra. Many types of fetters are broken by it.

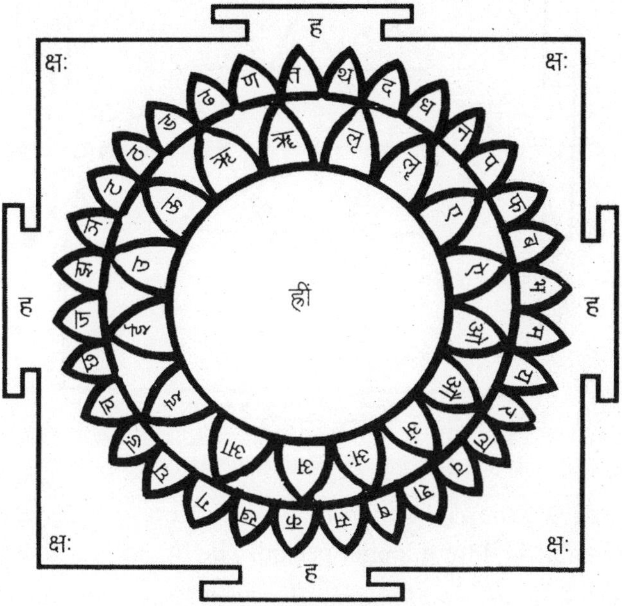

चित्र 79: बन्धमोक्षकरं यन्त्र

78. **Swarn Ākarshan Bhairava Poojan Yantram:** The mantra for this Yantra is: *Aum aing klāng kling grāng hring hrung sah vang āpad uddhāranāya ajāmal baddhāya lokeshwarāya swarna ākarshan bhairavāya mam dāridrāya vidveshanāya Aum shring mahā bhairavāya namah!*

ॐ ऐं क्लां क्लीं ग्रें ह्रीं हुं स: वं अपदउद्धरनन्या अजमय बाध्य लोकेश्वर्य स्वर्णाकर्षण भैरवाय मम दरिद्राय विदवेशनाय ॐ श्रीं महा भैरवाय नम:।

Brahmā is the Rishi; Pankti is the Chhand and Swarnākarshan Bhairava is the Devatā.

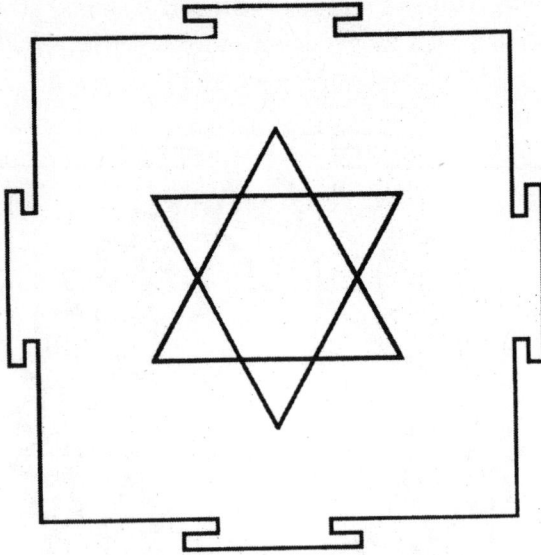

चित्र 80: स्वर्णाकर्षण भैरव पूजन-यन्त्र

79. **Pātra Sthāpan Yantram:** Ādhār Pātra or Arghya Pātra is established for a longer period. The Mantra for that is:

Aum mang vanhi mandalāya dash kalātmane deva arghya pātrāsnāya namah!

ॐ मं वन्हिमण्डलाय दशकलात्मने देव अर्ध्य पात्रास्नाय नमः।

A shankh conch is placed over it with the Mantra:

Aum ang surya mandalāya dvādasha kalātmane deva arghya pātrāya namah!

ॐ अं सूर्यमण्डलाय द्वादशकलात्मने देव अर्ध्य पात्राय नमः।

After putting the conch, wash it again, prakshālit, with the Mantra:

Aum kling mahā jala charāya hung phat swāhā pānchajanya namah!

ॐ क्लीं महाजलचराय हूं फट स्वाहा पंचजन्य नमः।

Worship dvādash Surya Kalā and Vilom Mātrikā; and ten Chandra Kalā on the conch. Keep vessel for āchaman and pādya in the north of the established pātra.

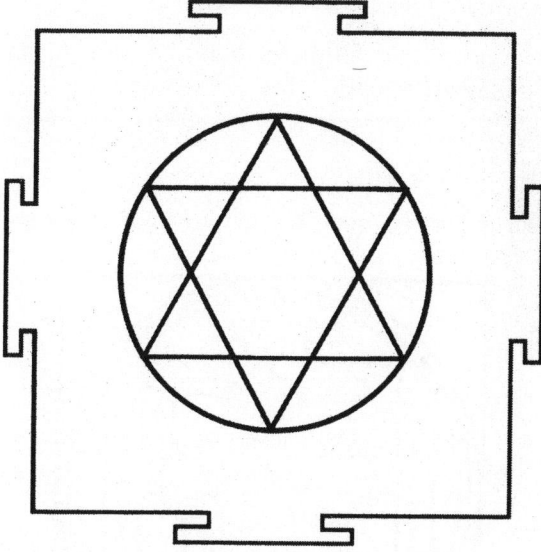

चित्र 81: पात्रस्थापन यन्त्र

80. **Damanak/Daman Poojan Yantram:** Damanak, Ashok tree, called Daman poojan is the poojan of both Vishnu and Kāmadeva. One should go to Ashok forest a day before the poojan, buy a sapling of Ashok tree for poojan nad worship it with the following Mantra:

Adhokāya namastubhyam kāma-stri-shok-nāshanam;
Shokārti har mey nityam ānandam janayaswa mey.

अधोक्य नमस्तुभ्यं कामस्त्रीशोक नाशनम्।
शोकृति हर मे नित्यं आनन्दं जनयस्व मे॥

After that it should be transplanted to a basket with fertile soil and bought home ceremoniously with songs and music. It should be planted at a place convenient for poojā, and worshipped with the following Kāma deva and Rati Mantra:

Kling kāma devāya namah! क्लीं काम देवाय नमः।

Hring ratyai namah! ह्रीं रत्यै नमः।

Then construct the following Yantra as shown and chant the Kāma Gāyatri Mantra:

Kāma devāya vidmahe pushp banāya dheemahi. Tanno anangah prachodayāt!

कामदेवाय विद्महे पुष्पबनाय धीमहि तन्नो अनंगः प्रचादयात्।

चित्र 82: दमन पूजन-यन्त्र

81. **Pavitra Yajane Yantram:** The seeker must prepare many Pavitrak/Nava Sutrikā with the cotton thread prepared by a sincere married lady: three threads multiplied thrice with 36/ 24/ 12 knots which should be abhimantrit with 108 Ishta Deva Mantra and 108 Gāyatri Mantra. A nava sutrikā with 108 knots is called Van-mālā.

Then prepare the Pavitra Yajan Yantra as shown below and fill them with different colours. Worship the Yantra with the following Mantra and flowers and offer kheer, a sweet dish prepared with milk and rice:

Āmantrito-asi devesha sārdham dvyā ganeshwaraih;
Mantres haih loka-pālah cha sahitah parivārakaih.
Āgachchha bhagawannisha vidhi sampurti kārakah;
Prātah tvām poojayiswāmi sānnidhyam kuru keshavah!

आमन्त्रितो असिदेवेसा सारधंदेव्या गणेश्वराय: ।
मंत्रेश है: लोकपाल: च साहित्य: परिवारकै: ॥
आगच्छ भगवनिशा विधि संपूर्ति कारक: ।
प्रात: त्वां पूजयैस्वामि सान्निध्यं कुरु केशव: ॥

चित्र 83: पवित्र यजने यन्त्र

82. **Janan Yantram:** Make a Yantra as shown below. Starting from the Ishān Kone and purify each Varna with Mātrikā Mantra. This is known as Janan Samskār, and the Yantra as Janan Yantram. This is essential as there are faults in numerous Mantras. There are exceptions, but they are different.

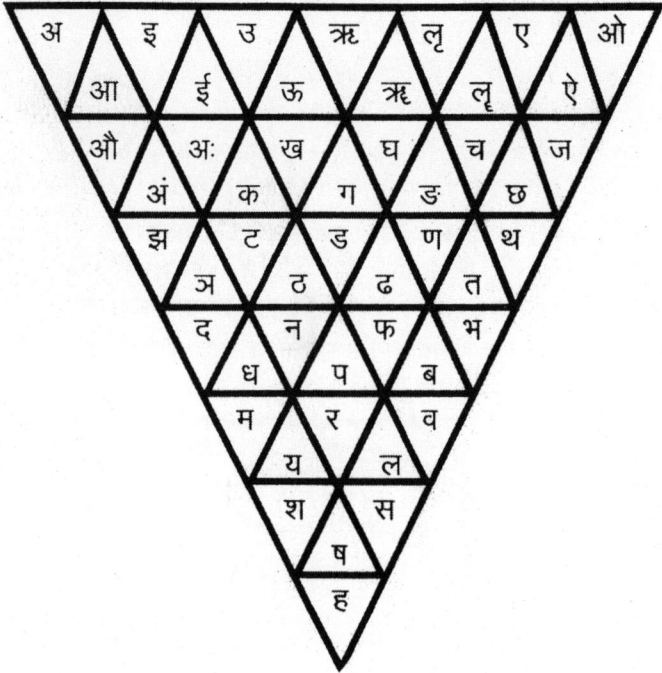

चित्र 84: जनन यन्त्र

✿ ✿ ✿

SECTION V

Attainment and Use

- ➢ **Mantra Varnas and their Meaning**
- ➢ **Mantra in Life**

30

Mantra Varnas and their Meaning

All the Varnas used in different Mantras have special meanings. They stand for something else. The following are some of them with their meanings as given in Mantra Mahodadhi as Varna-sanket-suchi; list of symbolic varnas. This will help in deciphering the mystery of Mantra and knowing their scientific use in **mass communication and space travel**. It can be easily understood with the fact that *Sphatik* associated with the Goddess of Knowledge and Wisdom, Saraswati, is nothing but **Quartz,** changed the whole scenario in Europe, and mass communication leapt up high and wide. In fact, many systems have been systematically and intrinsically woven in one system to create a complex one. That is the reason behind its secret and strange coding.

All the Yantras are three dimensional, and all the Varnas of Mantras are the names of materials used. The shapes and petals are connections to be given. Of course, they are given in symbols. A lot of research and concentrated thinking may help in the sincere effort to decypher the symbols to reveal the inner reality behind these unique, strange and powerful mantras and yantras. It can be done with higher spiritual power, divine, wisdom and sublime consciousness.

As a help, something very important is being given here. In the first long and doubled chart **shabd, varna** and **meaning** is given alongwith the equivalent in Roman Script. In the end chart the **symbols** and **meaning** of **numbers** given as the word and the number it stands for. (It will be essential to take each mantra separately to clarify it to light of the charts and other available hints.)

शब्द	वर्ण	Meaning	Letter	शब्द	वर्ण	Meaning	letter
अक्रूर	अं	Akrura	Ang	भगी	ए	Bhagi	Ye/A
अक्षि	इ	Akshi	E	भानु	म	Bhānu	Ma
अग्नि	र	Agni	R	भुवनेश्वरी	ह्रीं	Bhuvane shwari	Hring
अग्नि बीज	रं	Agnibeeja	Rang	भूबीज	ग्लौं/लं	Bhubeeja	Glaung/Lang
अर्घीश	ऊ	Arghish	U:	भृगु	स	Bgrigu	Sa
आतिथीश	ॢ	Atithish	Rii	भौतिक	ए	Bhautika	Ye/A
अमरेश	उ	Amaresh	U	मनु	औ	Manu	Au
अजपा	हंस:	Ajapā	Hansah	मनोजन्मा	क्लीं	Manojan-mā	Kling
अन्तिम	क्षं	Antim	Kshang	मन्मथ	क्लीं	Manmath	Kling
अत्रि	द	Atri	Da	मातृकाद्य	अ	Mātrikā-dya	A
अधार	ए	Adhar	Ye/ A	माधव	इ	Mādhava	E
अर्द्धनारीश	द्	Ardha-nārish	Dh	माया	ह्रीं	Māyā	Hring
अनन्त	अ:	Anant	Ah	मारूत	य	Māruta	Ya
अनल:	रं	Analah	Rang	मीनेश	ध	Meenesha	Dha
अनलान्तिम	ल	Analāntim	La	मुरारी	औ	Murāri	Au
अम्भ	ब	Ambha	Ba	मुसली	छ	Musali	Chha
अस्त्र	अस्त्रय न्ट्	Astra	Astrāya Phat	मेघ	घ	Megha	Gha
आकाश बीज	हं	Ākāsha Beeja	Hang	मेरू:	छ	Meruh	Chha
आत्मभू:	क्लीं	Ātmabhuh	Kling	मेश	न	Mesha	Na
आप्यायनी	ॐ	Āpyāuami	Aum	मृत्यु	श	Mrityuh	Sha
आशाढ़ी	त	Āshādhi	Ta	मांस	ल	Mānsa	La
अंकुश	क्रों	Ankush	Krong	युग्वसु	र	Yugavasu	Ra
औरस	औ	Aurasa	Au	रमा	श्रीं	Ramā	Shring

शब्द	वर्ण	Meaning	Letter	शब्द	वर्ण	Meaning	letter
इन्दु	अनुस्वार	Indu	Anuswār	रति	ण	Rati	Na
इन्धिका	ड	Indhikā	U	रात्रीश	अनुस्वार	Rātrish	Anus-wār
उमाकान्त	ण	Umākānt	N:	लकुली	ह	Lakuli	Ha
उष: बुध प्रिया	स्वाहा	Ushah Buddha Priyā	Swāhā	लक्ष्मी	च	Lakshmi	Cha
एकनेत्र	छ	Ek-netra	Chha	लक्ष्मी बीज	श्रीं	Lakshmi Beeja	Shring
कपोल	लृ	Kapole	Lri	लज्जा	ह्रीं	Lajjā	Hring
कमण्डलू	ठ	Kamandalu	Tha	लांगलीश	ठ	Langlish	Tha
कमला	श्रीं	Kamalā	Shring	लोहित	प	Lohita	Pa
कर्ण	उ	Karna	U	वक	श	Vak	Sha
कवच	हुं	Kawacha	Hung	वराह	ह	Varāh	H
काम बीज	क्लीं	Kāma beeja	Kling	वह्न्यासन	र	Bhu-nyāsan	Ra
कामिका	त	Kāmikā	Ta	वह्नि	र	Banhi	Ra
कूर्च	हूं	Kurcha	Hung	वह्नि कामिनी	स्वाहा	Vangi-kāmini	Swāhā
कूर्म	च	Kurma	Cha	वाक्	ऐं	Vāk	Aing
कृष्ण	थ	Krishna	Tha	वागीश	ऐं	Vāgish	Aing
क्लीब वर्ण	ऋ/ॠ / लृ/ॡ	Neuter Varna	Ri/ Rii/ Lri/ Lrii	वाणी	ऐं	Vānee	Aing
क्रोध बीज	हूं	Krodha beeja	Hung	वामकर्ण	ऊ	Vāma Karna	U:
क्रोधीश	क	Krodhish	Ka	वाम कूर्पर	छ	Vāma Kurpar	Chha
क्रिया	ल:	Kriyā	Lah	वाम नेत्र	ई	Vām netra	Ee
खड्गीश	ब	Kjadshisha	Ba	वाम-नासिका	ॠ	Vāma Nāsikā	Ri

शब्द	वर्ण	Meaning	Letter	शब्द	वर्ण	Meaning	letter
खम्	हं	Khama	Hung	वाम नेत्र	ई	Vāma Netra	Ee
गणपति बीज	गं	Ganapati beeja	Gang	वामाक्षि	ई	Vāmākshi	Ee
गणनायक बीज	गं	Gan-nāyaka	Gang	वाल	व	Vāla	Va
गोविन्द	ई	Govind	Ee	वायु	य	Vāyu	Ya
गदी	खः	Gadi	Khah	वायुबीज	यं	Vāyu beeja	Yang
गजमुख	गं	Gajamukha	Gang	विष	म	Vish	Ma
गगन	ह	Gagan	Ha	विधु	अनुस्वार	Vidhu	Anus-wār
गिरिसुता बीज	ह्रीं	Girisutā beeja	Hring	विमल	लं	Vimal	Lang
गिरिजा	ह्रीं	Girijā	Hring	वियत्	ह	Viyat	Ha
चक्री	कं	Chakri	Kang	विशालाक्ष	थ	Vishālāk-sha	Tha
चतुरानन	क	Chaturānan	Ka	वेदादि	ॐ	Vedādi	Aum
चन्द्र	अनुस्वार	Chandra	Anuswār	वैकुण्ठ	म	Vaikuntha	Ma
चन्द्रमा	अनुस्वार	Chandramā	Anuswār	व्याघ्रपाद	ड	Vyāghra pāda	Da
जर्नादन	फ	Janārdan	Pha	व्यापिनी	औ	Vyāpini	Au
जरासन	ट	Jarāsan	Ta	व्योम	ह	Vyoma	Ha
जल	व	Jala	Va	शक्ति	ह्रीं	Shakti	Hing
झीण्टीश	ए	Jhintisha	Ye/A	शक्ति बीज	ह्रीं	Shakti beeja	Hing
ठद्वयं	स्वाहा	Thadvyam	Swāhā	शशि शेखर	अनुस्वार	Shashi-shekhar	Anus-wār
णान्त	त	Nānta	Ta	शारंगी	ग	Shārangi	Ga
तन्द्री	म	Tandri	Ma	शान्तिः	ई	Shāntih	Ee
तरल	त	Taral	Ta	शिखी	?ः	Shikhi	Phah

शब्द	वर्ण	Meaning	Letter	शब्द	वर्ण	Meaning	letter
तर्जनी	न	Tarjani	Na	शिर:	क	Shirah	Ka
तार	ॐ	Tāra	Aum	शिव	ल	Shiva	La
तीव्र	त	Teevra	R	शिवा	ह्रीं	Shivā	Hring
तोयं	व:	Toyam	Vah	शिवोत्तमा	घ	Shivot-tamā	Gha
त्रपा	ह्रीं	Trapā	Hring	शुचिप्रिया	स्वाहा	Shuchi priyā	Swāhā
त्रिधुव	प्रणव	Tridhruva	Pranava	शूर	प	Shoor	Pa
त्रिपुरान्तक	ऋ॒	Tripurān taka	Rii	शीरी	थ	Shiri	Tha
त्रिमूर्ति	ईकारं	Trimurti	Ee-kāram	श्वेत्	श	Shweta	Sha
दक्षपाप अंगुलीमूल	ढ	Daksha-pāpa Angu-limula	Dha	सत्य:	द	Satyah	Da
दण्डी	तृ	Dandi	Tri	सदगति	य	Sadgati	Ya
दहनांगना	स्वाहा	D a h a n ā n-ganā	Swāhā	सदाशिव	ह	Sadāshiva	Ha
दारक	ड	Dāraka	Da	सदृक्	इ	Sadrik	E
दीर्घत्रय	आ,ई,ऊ	Dwwegha-traya	Ā, Ee, U:	सद्य	ओ	Sadya	O
दीर्घनन्दी	डा	D e e r g h a Nandi	Dā	समीरण:	य:	S a m i r a-nah	Yah
दीपिका	ऊ	Deepikā	U:	सर्ग	विसर्ग	Sarga	Visarga
द्युति	च्छि	Dyuti	Chachhi	सर्गिन्न्दज	ठ:	S a r g i n-andaj	Thah
ध्रुव	प्रणव	Dhruva	Pranava	सात्वत	ध	Sātvat	Dha
नकुल	ह	Nakula	Ha	सुधाबीज	वं	Sudhā beeja	Vang
नन्दी	ड	Nandi	Da	सूर्य:	म:	Sueyah	Mah
नभ	हं	Nabha	Hang	सृष्टि:	क:	Srishtih	Phah

शब्द	वर्ण	Meaning	Letter	शब्द	वर्ण	Meaning	letter
नभबीज	हं	Nabha-beeja	Hang	सृणि	क्रौं	Srini	Kraung
नील	त	Neela	Ta	संकर्षण	औ	Sankarshan	Au
नृसिंहाङ्ग	औ	Nrisinghādga	Au	संवर्तक	क्ष	Damvartak	Ksha
पंचान्तक	ग	Panchāntak	Ga	स्थिरा	ज	Sthirā	Ja
पद्नाभ	ए	Padmanābha	Ye/A	स्मृति	ग	Smriti	Ga
पद्मा	श्रीं	Padmā	Shring	स्वर्गवल्लभा	स्वाहा	Swargaballabhā	Swāhā
परा	हीं	Parā	Hing	हयानन	ह	Hayānan	Ha
पावक	र	Pāvaka	Ra	हरि:	त	Harih	Ta
पावक कामिनी	स्वाहा	Pāvak-kāmini	Swāhā	हाटकरेतस	वह्नि	Hātkaretas	Vanhi
पावक मोहिनी	स्वाहा	Pāvaka Mohini	Swāhā	हिमाद्रिजा	हीं	Himādvijā	Hring
पाश	आं	Pāsha	Ānga	हुतासन	र	Hutāsan	Ra
पाशबीज	आं	Pāsha beeja	Ānga	हंस:	स:	Hansah	Sah
पिनाकी	ल	Pināki	La	हृत	नम:	Hrit	Namah
पुरुषोत्तम	य	Purushottam	Ya	हृदय	नम:	Hridaya	Namah
प्राण	ह	Prāna	Ha	हृलेखा	हीं	Hrikekhā	Hring
प्रीति	ध	Preeti	Dha				
गन्त	ब	Phānta	Ba				
बलानुज	ब	Balānuja	Ba				
बिन्दु	अनुस्वार	Bindu	Anuswār				
ब्रह्मा	क:	Brahmā	Kah				
भग	ए	Bhaga	Ye/A				

Symbols for Numbers

अक्षि	दो	Akshi	Two	बाहु	दो	Bāhu	Two
अधार	एक	Adhar	One	भुजा	दो	Bhujā	Two
अद्रि	सात	Adri	Seven	भू	एक	Bhu	One
अर्क	बारह	Arja	Twelve	मनु	चौदह	Manu	Four-teen
आदित्य	बारह	Āditya	Twelve	मुनि	सात	Muni	Seven
इषु	पांच	Ishu	Five	रवि	बारह	Ravi	Twelve
क्षमा	एक	Kshamā	One	रस	छह	Rasa	Six
गुण	तीन	Guna	Teen	राम	तीन	Rāma	Three
चन्द्र	एक	Chandra	One	रूद्र	एकादश	Rudra	Eleven
तिथि	पन्द्रह	Tithi	Fifteen	वह्न्य:	तीन	Vahnya	Three
दिक्	दस	Dik	Ten	वसु	आठ	Vasu	Eight
धरा	एक	Dharā	One	वेद	चार	Veda	Four
नक्षत्र	सताइस	Nakshatra	Twenty Seven	शिव	एकादश	Shiva	Eleven
नन्द	नौ	Nand	Nine	सागर	चार	Sāgar	Four
नन्दा	नौ	Nandā	Nine	सायक	पांच	Sāyak	Five
नेत्र	दो	Netra	Two	सूर्य	बारह	Surya	Twelve

✿ ✿ ✿

31

Mantra in Life

The world of Mantra, Tantra and Yantra is not only mysterious but also very vast and deep. When a famous mantragya Shri Mahidhar started writing a book on this topic, particularly the Mantras, he named it as Mantra-Mahodadhi, i.e., Mantra Mahā-Udadhi which means the great ocean of Mantras. This world is very vast and deep and has a separate entity and recognition like a great ocean.

The biggest difficulty is that:

i.   Most of the things in the three ways are deeply related and inseparable.

ii.   All the things, limbs and parts of the three Tantra, Mantra and Tantra are so essential that nothing can be left out.

iii. If something is not mentioned then the whole process remains incomplete and will not yield the desired result.

iv.   The topics are vast and deep and the ways, means, meanings and other things given here are very short.

v.   It is almost impossible to get at the bottom and understand everything on the meagre information presented here.

Hence, it is very tough to maintain balance among the three and numerous things are needed to perfect them. None among them is easy to follow. Moreover, the danger always looms large because a single and simple mistake will reduce the whole effort to 'naught'. Instead of getting rewards, seekers can be punished. All those persons who became mad while performing some Tāntrik Sādhanā or while trying to awaken the Kundalini were those who were not pious and strong enough to pursue such a task and failed to follow the norms and purity. This resulted in their madness.

This is being stated so that the seekers will either not practice it or if one starts practicing then the seeker will follow the righteous and moral path and the norms given in scriptures; and definitely under the guidance of a pure and powerful preceptor. There are numerous Mantra Doshas. Anyone can commit one or the other mistake, which will ruin his efforts. So, be sincere and remain careful. Grow your consciousness and alertness; be mentally and physically prepared for the difficult task of Sādhanā ahead.

Mantras and Yantras are apparently the ways of worshipping of different gods. But they have some hidden meanings too. They are different configurations and techniques of something abstract or concrete; and definitely that of a machine, equipment.

It will definitely give insight into them but it will not make you competent to start Sādhanā. One can do what the *girhasthas* do or expected to do. They opt for *mānsika pāth* and perform it with sole intention to retain what they possess and to grow a bit and move towards Moksha.

Inner and Outer Form: Antar Yāga and Bahir Yāga

There are two types of poojan or worshipping: inner and outer. In inner worshipping everything is done silently and in the mind of the seeker while the outer worshipping is performed with articles. It is believed that without performing the outer worshipping it is very difficult to go for inner worshipping. It is also accepted that those who have been performing outer and inner worshipping in their previous life can easily do mentally worshipping without doing outer worshipping. Yet, preceptors order the disciples to go for both the ways of worshipping.

Outer Worshipping

There are five limbs of outer worshipping. When a seeker becomes expert in performing all the limbs of outer worshipping, only then he does acquire the right to perform inner or Mānsik Poojan.

1. **Japa**: To chant the Mantra dealing with any one manifest form of the Shakti according to the rules and rituals prescribed by the Scriptures and taught by the guru.

2. **Homa**: To offer sacred and prescribed articles to fire equivalent to 1/10th of the Japa.

3. **Tarpan**: To offer water, teel, sand and flower or with *pancha dravya* according to one's rights.

4. **Mārjan**: To refine worldly deeds and become cultured.

5. **Brahma bhoja**: To spend rightful, righteous and moral earning to feed the Brāhmins.

Inner Worshipping

There are five limbs of inner worshipping:

1. **Patal**: To make imaginary flowers with the Varnas of the Mantra of Shakti in the thickness of Nādis; and thus to empower one's mind, *chitta*, is called Patal.

2. **Paddhati**: To establish the Varnas of the Devi Mantra in the heart like different peethas with five or sixteen ways of worshiping is called the process or paddhati.

3. **Varna/Kawach**: After performing the first two, to anoint the whole body with the varnas of the selected Devi Mantra for the protection of both the Mantra and the self is called varma or kawach or shield.

4. **Stotra**: To repeat the stotras or thousand shlokas in order to keep the memory of the deity and the mantra in the conscious and functional mind is called stotra.

5.   **Nāma Sahasra**: To salute the Devi with her thousand names, which reflect and represent her different qualities, is called Nāma Sahasra. In the intermediary role, the seeker salutes the Deity, Devi or Shakti.

Pictures and Actual Yantras

Most of the people have seen only the pictures of Yantras. Incidentally, only the pictures are given here. Pictures have only the length and width; rather, a reduced length and shortened width and no height at all. Pictures never give the true insight into the Yantras and don't present all its dimensions. All the Yantras are three dimensional. One can get a lot if one seriously reads the details of Shri Yantra but won't get everything. The dimensions are missing.

Yantras are prepared by painstaking cutting the stones, quartz, *shāligrām, tāmra* or *suvarna patra*. The angles and triangles are formed equal or unequal on the basis of Bhu or Meru construction. They are different and the sketch diagram will not be a complete picture.

It is said that the best Shri Yantra at Bhairava Kunda is in Vindhyavāsini region near the temple of Ashta Bhujā Shakti.

Shri Tripur Sundari

Before concluding the descriptions, it is alluring to describe the Shakti, Shri Tripur Sundari. It has been taken from a famous Tāntrik Grantha 'Kāma Kalā Vilās' by Punyānand. It says: The triputi or trikuti, the centre between the brows is formed by gyātā, gyān and gyeya; (the seeker; the knowledge and the object to be known) or mātā, māna and meya (mother; respect and that which could be measured).

These are the three worlds and Tripurā Devi is its master, owner and creator. The three things mentioned in different ways twice above are actually one element. The seeker is to know this fact that all are one. He who realizes this fact becomes Shri Tripura Sundari because She pervades all; and the moment one comes to know her changes or is metamorphosed into that original energy:

Mātā mānam meyam bindu trya abhinna beeja rupāni;
Dhāma trya peetha trya Shakti trya bheda-bhāvitānya-api cha.
Teshu kramena ling-tri-tayam tadvacha mātrikā-tri-tayam;
Ityam tri-tayapuri yā turiya-peetha-ādi-bhedani vidyā.
Iti kāma kalā vidyā devi chakra-kramātmikā seyam;
Viditā yena sa mukto bhavati mahā-tripur-sundari roopah.

माता मानं मेयं बिन्दु त्रय अभिन्न बीज-रूपाणि।
धाम त्रय पीठ त्रय शक्ति त्रय भेद-भावितान्यऽपि च।
तेषु क्रमेण लिंग त्रितेयं तद्वच मात्रिका त्रितयम्।
इतं त्रीतयपुरी य तुरियपीठादि भेदनि विद्या।
इति कामकला विद्या देवि चक्र क्रमात्मिका सेयम्।
विदितायेन स मुक्तो भवति महा त्रिपुरसुन्दरी रूपः॥

Punya Phala

The Punya Phala of Kāmya Karma is very ambiguous, so the preceptors advise the disciples not to opt for Kāmya Karma. The reason is clear. It will not free one from the cyclical chain of birth-death and rebirth. What will it do? It will provide material support but will not enrich one with spiritual energy.

So, it is always advised, and is best to worship God without attachment and without expectation, which is known as Nishkāma Upāsanā.

If one insists on doing Kāmya Karma: *Shānti; Vashya; Stambhan; Vidveshan; Uchchātan* and *Māran*, one should first take all the protective steps with *nyāsa* and other *vidhānas* before going for such *anushthān*. If one is not well protected, then a simple slip will prove dangerous and a lot of damage will occur in no time at all, before one realizes that the loss has been caused by the *anushthān*. It is far better not to go for *Kāmya Karma* although it has been discussed in detail in this book. Its presence in the book is only for knowledge and not for practice.

Upāsanā and Sādhanā for Moksha

There are simple questions: Why Upāsanā? Why Sādhanā? Why chanting of Mantras? Although the answer is everywhere in the book, it must be concluded.

The whole creation, existence and sustenance of all living beings is based on Mantra, Tantra and Yantra: literally, philosophically and symbolically.

Everything is a Yantra; rather, many Yantras combined in one and synchronized well to function in one system as a single machine. The Universe is also like that. Umpteen numbers of machines in the Universe in the form of concrete celestial bodies, particles and meteors are there, but are functioning in one system as if one machine. The universe is a single machine that contains octillions of machines. What a grand arrangement!

All those machines, bodies, living entities chant some Mantra all the time, reproducing the initial power of Nāda, Nāda Brahma. So, the Universe never sleeps; or even if sleeping it still keeps on working. Neither the action, movement nor the sound or the music ceases ever. It is called Brahma and we are made by Him, like Him and must acquire His qualities through refinement and progress. In that lies our final freedom; otherwise, we are destined to remain tied inside a womb, take birth, enjoy and suffer and the chakra moves and goes on and on.

The most peculiar thing is that every human being is striving for independence; freedom without realizing that not a single thing is independent and free. Each Yantra, each part, each organ, each body is dependent on this or that; here or there; for this or that and this way or that way. For the existence of one the other must exist because energy is needed for everything, for sustenance too and it comes from the 'other'.

The energy producing system and Yantra depends on others for energy. The most classic thing is that if one entity can't eat or digest something then some other entity takes that as food. Hence everything is essential: from always dying nails and hair to always functioning heart and mind.

Mantra, Tantra and Yantra make it easier to obtain immense energy; help in survival; in getting better and better and in getting released from this chakra of birth, death and rebirth. That does not mean that one becomes free. No. One becomes a vital part of yet another system; Yantra, or body. So, for numerous things and gains Mantra, Tantra and Yantras are needed.

One must indulge in Upāsanā, worshipping and Sādhnā, devotional practice only for Moksha and never for worldly riches or for bringing some harm to someone. It should be performed without attachment, expectation or lust. It must be performed with *nishkāma bhāva* and complete surrender to God. Everything has come from God and everything belongs to God. All the living things also belong to and are for all the living beings. There should be no selfishness. All are like one self. Each individual should feel all others to be like his or her own self: *ātmavat sarva-bhuteshu yah pashyati sah panditā.* आत्मवत्सर्वभूतेषु यः पश्यति सः पण्डिता।

As we have seen Mantras strengthen us from inside and give confidence and fearlessness, so, whatever the mental condition or physical position may be, chant the Mantras any time and every time when they come to mind to remain healthy and happy.

Sarve Subhe!

✾✾✾